March of America Facsimile Series
Number 66

Travels through the Northwestern Regions of the United States

---

Henry Rowe Schoolcraft

Travels through the Northwestern Regions of the United States

Henry Rowe Schoolcraft

ANN ARBOR
UNIVERSITY MICROFILMS, INC.
A Subsidiary of Xerox Corporation

LIBRARY OF CONGRESS CATALOG CARD NO. 66-26336

MANUFACTURED IN THE UNITED STATES OF AMERICA

Foreword

The *Narrative Journal Of Travels From Detroit Northwest* by Henry R. Schoolcraft was published in 1821. Schoolcraft accompanied the Cass expedition of 1820 which explored the southern shore of Lake Superior and water communications to the Mississippi River. Information supplied by Schoolcraft's journal hastened the flow of settlers into this region. His journal showed that the United States government could establish order among the Indians and that the land could support a considerable population.

Lewis Cass, Governor of the Michigan Territory, had wished to visit the Lake Superior area in order to extend United States authority over the Indians in the confused aftermath of the War of 1812, and to halt the illegal activities of English trappers there. With War Department sponsorship, Cass prepared to leave from Detroit. Henry Schoolcraft, appointed to serve as geologist for the party, came from New York City to join the other members at Detroit. Schoolcraft began his journal with his departure from New York City. The journey westward through New York State impressed him greatly. What had only a few years before been wilderness "is now smiling under the hand of agriculture, and checquered with towns, and villages, roads and canals, the seats of learning, and the temples of religion."

Schoolcraft had evidently read a number of accounts about the territory he was to help explore, and he liked to make rather ostentatious comparisons of his impressions with those of his predecessors. He had high praise, however, for the "early enterprize and sound judgment of the French in seizing upon the points, commanding all the natural avenues and passes of the lakes." Their wisdom was proved each year, he explained, "by the re-occupation of posts and places long neglected."

Naturally Schoolcraft wrote at length about the geological formation of the land. While he found evidence of mineral wealth, his investigation convinced him of "what little reliance can be placed upon Indian information, with respect to mineralogy." The Indians themselves held an even greater interest for Schoolcraft, foreshadowing the time when he would accept an appointment as Superintendent of Indian Affairs for Michigan. The inferior position of women in Indian society evoked his shocked surprise. He noted that "if it is a woman that dies, a paddle and carrying strap are buried with her, that she may perform the same drudgery in a future state she is required to do in this." Yet how could the level of Indian society be raised, he asked? "The savage mind, habituated to sloth, is not easily roused into a state of moral activity." If Americans were to help them, "it is necessary that letters, arts, and religion should go hand in hand."

The present edition of Schoolcraft's journal includes his map of the Great Lakes region and illustrations showing the country. Mentor L. Williams provides additional information about Schoolcraft in his edition of Henry R. Schoolcraft, *Narrative Journal of Travels* (Michigan State College Press, 1953), pp. 1-24, as does Philip P. Mason in *Henry R. Schoolcraft, The Literary Voyager; or, Muzzeniegun* (Michigan State University Press, 1962), pp. xiii-xxvi.

Travels through the Northwestern Regions of the United States

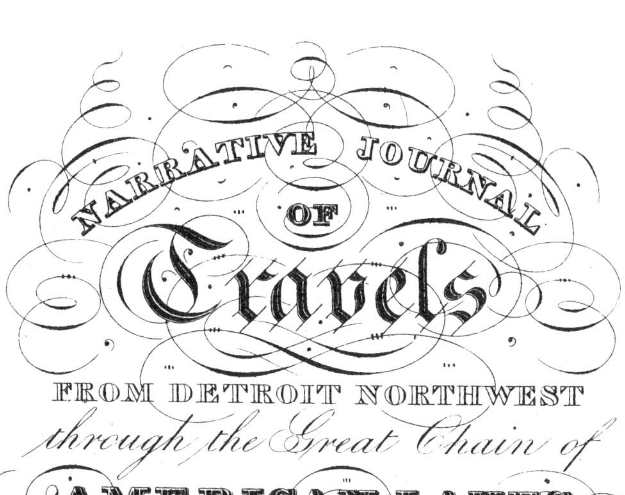

to the sources of the

Mississippi River

IN THE YEAR 1820

BY

HENRY R. SCHOOLCRAFT.

PAGE 153

DORIC ROCK, LAKE SUPERIOR

ALBANY, PUBLISHED BY E. & E. HOSFORD

1821.

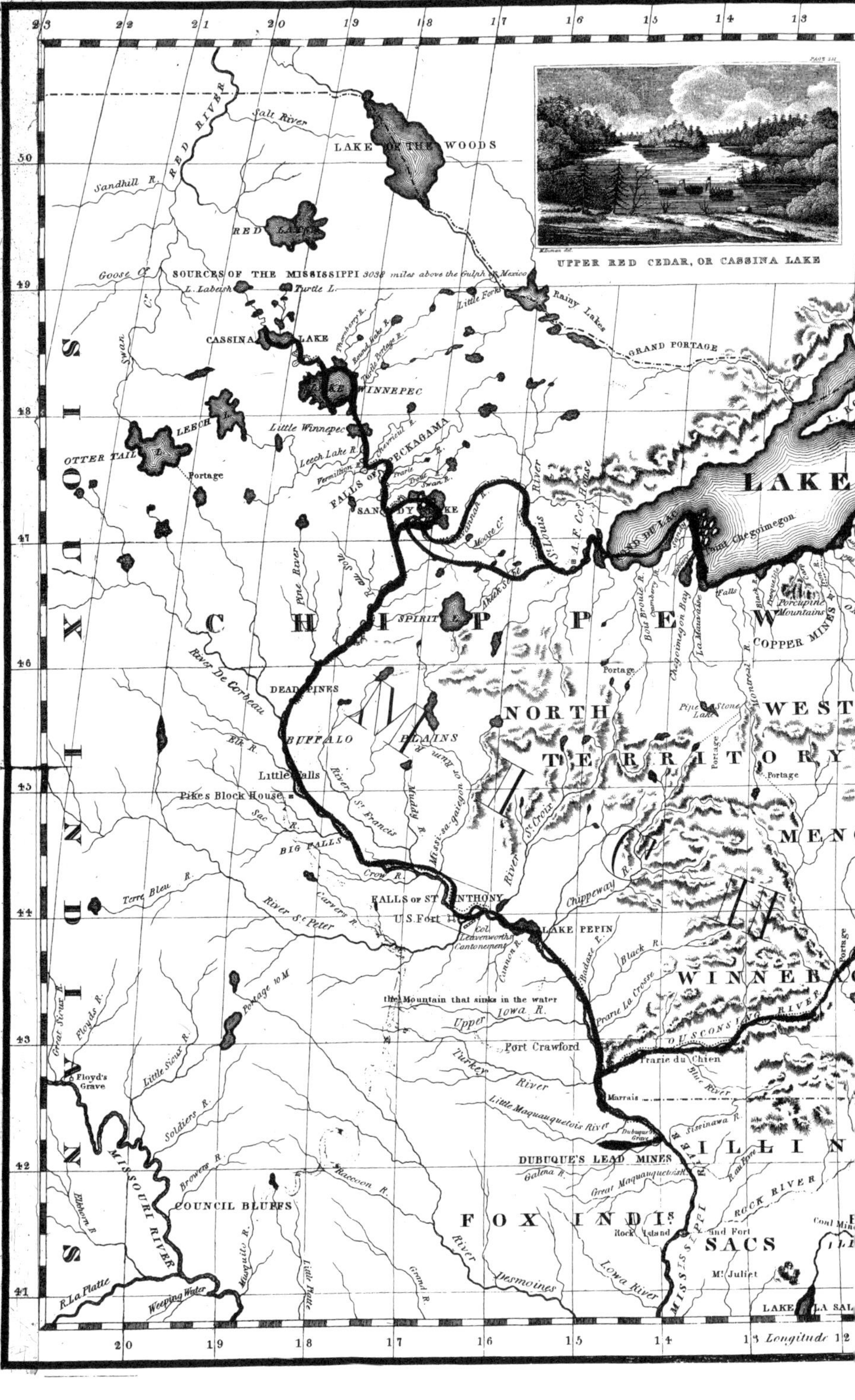

UPPER RED CEDAR, OR CASSINA LAKE

Map
OF THE
NORTHWESTERN TERRITORIES
OF THE
UNITED STATES
Shewing the Track pursued by
the Expedition under Gov. Cass
in 1820
BY HENRY R. SCHOOLCRAFT.
Scale of Miles. 60 to an inch
LAKE HURON
LAKE MICHIGAN
LAKE ERIE
LAKE ONTARIO
LAKE SIMCOE
LAKE NEPESSING
DETROIT
NEW YORK
PENNSYLVANIA
INDIANA
OHIO
IROQUOIS
NIAGARA FALLS
Fort Niagara
BUFFALO
CLEAVELAND
Ft. GRATIOT
Ft. Malden
Sandwich
FORT WAYNE
Ft. Defiance
North West Co. Establishment
Secondary Limestone Ceases
Sault de St. Marie
MICHILIMACINACK
Bois Blanc I.
Middle I.
Shallow Lakes
Rice Lake
Franklin
Warren
Waterford
ERIE
OLEAN
Chatauque
I. Maurepas
Caribou
PICTURED ROCKS
GRAND ISLE
Phillipeaux
Portage
Sleeping Bear
Fertile Land
New Settlement
R. Thames
Grand River
Black R.
Rapids
Mr. Askins
Gloucester Bay
R. Rawdon fc. Alby.

NARRATIVE JOURNAL

OF

TRAVELS

THROUGH THE NORTHWESTERN REGIONS OF THE UNITED STATES

EXTENDING

FROM DETROIT THROUGH THE GREAT CHAIN

OF

AMERICAN LAKES,

TO

THE SOURCES OF

THE MISSISSIPPI RIVER.

PERFORMED AS A MEMBER OF THE EXPEDITION UNDER GOVERNOR CASS.

IN THE YEAR 1820.

By HENRY R. SCHOOLCRAFT,

Member of the New-York Historical Society, of the Academy of Natural Sciences at Philadelphia, of the New-York Lyceum of Natural History, and of the Lyceum of Natural History of Troy.

EMBELLISHED WITH A MAP AND EIGHT COPPER PLATE ENGRAVINGS.

ALBANY:

PRINTED AND PUBLISHED BY E. & E. HOSFORD,

NO. 100, STATE-STREET.

TO THE

HON. JOHN C. CALHOUN,

SECRETARY AT WAR.

SIR,

Allow me to inscribe to you the following Journal, as an illustration of my several reports, on the mineralogy of the regions visited by the recent expedition, under Gov. Cass.

I beg you will consider it, not only as a proof of my anxiety to be serviceable in the station occupied, but also, as a tribute of individual regard, for those exertions which have been made, during your administration of the War Department, to develope the physical character and resources of all parts of our country,—to the patronage it has extended to the cause of science,—to the protection it has afforded to a very extensive line of frontier settlements, by stretching our cordon of military posts, through the territories of the most remote and hostile tribes of savages,—and particularly, to the notice it has bestowed upon one of the humblest cultivators of natural science.

HENRY R. SCHOOLCRAFT.

INTRODUCTORY REMARKS.

CHARLEVOIX informs us, that the discovery of the Mississippi river, is due to Father Joseph Marquette, a Jesuit missionary, who manifested the most unwearied enterprize in exploring the northwestern regions of New France; and after laying the foundation of Michilimackinac, proceeded, in company with the Sieur Joliet, up the Fox river of Green Bay, and crossing the portage into the Ousconsing, first entered the Mississippi, in 1673.

Mons. Robert de la Salle, to whom the merit of this discovery is generally attributed, embarked at Rochelle, on his first voyage of discovery, July 14, 1678—reached Quebec in September following, and proceeding up the St. Lawrence, laid the foundation of Fort Niagara, in the country of the Iroquois, late in the fall of that year. In the following year, he passes up the Niagara river—estimates the height of the falls, at six hundred feet—and proceeding through lakes Erie, St. Clair, and Huron, reaches Michilimackinac, in August. He then visits the Sault de St. Marie, and returning to Michilimackinac, continues his voyage to the south, with a view of striking the Mississippi river—passes into the lake of the Illinois—touches at Green Bay—and enters the river St. Joseph's, of Lake Michigan, where he builds a fort in the country of the Miamies. In December, of the same year, he crosses the portage between the St. Joseph's and the Illinois—descends the latter to the lake; and builds a fort in the midst of the tribes of the Illinois, which he calls *Crevecœur.* Here he makes a stand—sends persons out to explore the Mississippi—traffics with the Indians, among all of whom he finds abundance of Indian corn; and returns to Fort Frontenac, on Lake Ontario, in 1680. He revisits fort Crevecœur, late in the autumn of the following year; and finally descends the Illinois, to its junction with the Mississippi, and thence to the embouchure of the latter, in the Gulf of Mexico, where he arrives on the seventh of April, 1683, and calculates the latitude between 23° and 24° north. The Spaniards had previously sought in vain for the mouth of this stream, and bestowed upon it, in anticipation, the name of *Del Rio Ascondido.* La Salle now returns to Quebec, by the way of the lakes, and from thence to France, where he is well received by the king, who grants him an outfit of four ships and two hundred men, to enable him to continue his discoveries, and found a colony, in the newly discovered territories. He leaves Rochelle, in July, 1684—reaches the bay of St. Louis, which is fifty leagues south of the Mississippi, in the Gulf of Mexico, in February following, where he builds a fort—founds a settlement, and is finally assassinated by one of his own party. The exertions of this enterprising individual, and the account which was published of his discoveries by the Chevalier Tonti, who had accompanied him in all his perilous expeditions, had a greater effect, in the French capital, in producing a correct estimate of the extent, productions, and importance, of the Canadas, than all that had been done by preceding tourists; and this may be considered as the true era, when the eyes of politicians and divines, merchants and speculators, were first strongly turned towards the boundless forests,—the sublime rivers and lakes,—the populous Indian tribes, and the profitable commerce of New France.

Father Louis Hennepin, was a missionary of the Franciscan order of Catholics, who accompanied La Salle on his first voyage from France; and after the building of fort Crevecœur, on the Illinois, was despatched in company with three French voyageurs, to explore the Mississippi river. They departed from fort Crevecœur, on the twenty-ninth of February, 1780, and dropping down the Illinois, to its junction with the Mississippi, followed the latter to the Gulf, where they left some memorial of their visit, and immediately commenced their return. When they had proceeded up the Mississippi, a hundred and fifty leagues above the confluence of the Illinois, they were taken prisoners by some Indian tribes, and carried towards its sources, nineteen days' journey, into the territories of the Naudowessies and Issati; where they were detained in captivity three or four months, and then suffered to return. The account which Hennepin published of his travels and discoveries, served to throw some new light upon the topography, and the Indian tribes of the Canadas; and modern geography is indebted to him, for the names which he bestowed upon the falls of St. Anthony, and the river St. Francis.

In 1703, the Baron La Hontan published in London his voyages to North America, the result of a residence of six years in the Canadas. La Hontan served as an officer in the French army, and first went out to Quebec in 1683. During the succeeding four years he was chiefly stationed at Chambly, Fort Frontenac, Niagara, St. Joseph at the foot of Lake Huron, and the Sault de St. Marie. He arrives at Michilimackinac in 1688, and there first hears of the assassination of La Salle. In 1689, he visits Green Bay, and passes through the Fox and Ousconsing rivers into the Mississippi. So far, his work appears to be the result of actual observation, and is entitled to respect; but what he relates of Long River, appears wholly incredible, and can only be regarded as some flight of the imagination, intended to gratify the public taste for travels, during an age when it had been highly excited by the extravagant accounts which had been published respecting the wealth, population, and advantages of Peru, Mexico, the English and Dutch colonies, New France, the Illinois, and various other parts of the New World. To convey some idea of this part of the Baron's work, it will be sufficient to observe, that after travelling ten days above the mouth of the Ousconsing, he arrives at the mouth of a large stream which he calls *Long River*, and which he ascends *eighty-four days* successively, during which he meets with numerous tribes of savages, as the Eskoros, Essanapes, Pinnokas, Mozemleeks, &c. He is attended a part of the way by five or six hundred savages as an escort—sees at one time, two thousand savages upon the shore—and states the population of the Essanapes, at 20,000 souls; but this tribe is still inferior to the Mozemleeks in numbers, in arts, and in every other prerequisite for a great people. "The Mozemleek nation," he observes, "is numerous and puissant. The four slaves of that country informed me, that at the distance of 150 leagues from the place where I then was, their principal river empties itself into a salt lake of three hundred leagues in circumference—the mouth of which is about two leagues broad; that the lower part of that river is adorned with six noble cities, surrounded with stone, cemented with fat earth: that the houses of these cities have no roofs, but are open above like a platform; that besides the above mentioned cities, there are an hundred towns great and small round that sort of sea; that the people of that country make stuffs, copper axes, and several other manufactures, &c."

In 1721, P. De Charlevoix, the historian of New France, was commissioned by the French Government, to make a tour of observation through the Canadas; and in addition to his topographical and historical account of New France, published a journal of his voyage through the lakes. He was one of the most learned divines of his age, and although strongly tinctured with the doctrines of fatality, and disposed to view every thing relative to the Indian tribes with the over-zealous eye of a Catholic missionary, yet his works bear the impress of a strong and well cultivated mind, and abound in philosophical reflections, enlarged views, and accurate deductions; and notwithstanding the lapse of a century, he must still be regarded as the most polished and illustrious traveller of the region. He first landed at Quebec in the spring of 1721, and immediately proceeded up the St. Lawrence to Fort Frontenac and Niagara, where he corrects the error in which those who preceded him had fallen, with respect to the height of the cataract. He proceeds through lakes Erie, Huron, and Michigan, descends the Illinois and Mississippi to New Orleans, then recently settled, and embarks for France. The period of his visit, was that, when the Mississippi Scheme was in the height of experiment, and excited the liveliest interest in the French metropolis; people were then engaged in Louisiana in exploring every part of the country, under the delusive hope of finding rich mines of gold and silver; and the remarks he makes upon the probability of a failure, were shortly justified by the event.

In 1760, Alexander Henry, Esq. visited the upper lakes in the character of a trader, and devoted sixteen years in travelling over different parts of the northwestern region of the Canadas and the United States. The result of his observations upon the topography, Indian tribes, and natural history of the country, was first published in 1809, in a volume of travels and adventures, which is a valuable acquisition to our means of information. His work abounds in just and sensible reflections, upon scenes, situations, and objects of the most interesting kind; and is written in a style of the most charming perspicuity and simplicity. He was the first English traveller of the region.

The date of Carver's travels over those regions, is 1766. Carver was descended from an ancient and respectable English family in Connecticut, and had served as a captain in the provincial army which was disbanded after the treaty of peace of Versailles, of 1763; and united to great personal courage, a persevering and observing mind. By his bravery and admirable conduct among the powerful tribes of Sioux and Chippeways, he obtained a high standing among them; and after being constituted a chief by the former, received from them a large grant of land, which was not, however, ratified by the British government. The fate of this enterprising traveller, cannot but excite regret.—After having escaped the massacre of Fort William Henry, on the banks of Lake George, in 1757, and the perils of a long journey through the American wilderness, he was spared to endure miseries in the heart of the British metropolis, which he had never encountered in the huts of the American savages; and perished for want, in the city of London, the seat of literature and opulence.

Between the years 1769 and 1772, Samuel Hearne performed a journey from Prince of Wales's fort in Hudson's bay, to the copper mine river of the arctic ocean.

McKenzie's voyages to the Frozen and Pacific Oceans, were performed in 1789 and 1793.

Pike ascended the Mississippi in 1805, and 1806.

Such is a brief outline of the progress of discovery in the northwestern regions of the United States, by which our sources of information have been from time to time augmented, and additional light cast upon the interesting history of our Indian tribes, their numbers, manners, customs, trade, religion, condition with respect to comforts, and other particulars connected with the regions they inhabit. Still, it cannot be denied, that amidst much sound and useful information, there has been mingled no inconsiderable proportion, that is deceptive, hypothetical, or false; and upon the whole, that the progress of information has not kept pace with the increased importance which that section of the union has latterly assumed—with the great improvements of society—and with the spirit and the enterprize of the times. A new era has dawned in the moral history of our country, and no longer satisfied with mere geographical outlines and boundaries, its physical productions, its antiquities, and the numerous other traits which it presents for scientific research, already attract the attention of a great proportion of the reading community; and it is eagerly enquired of various sections of it, whose trade, whose agriculture, and whose population, have been long known, what are its indigenous plants, its zoology, its geology, its mineralogy, &c. Of no part of it, however, has the paucity of information upon these, and upon other and more familiar subjects, been so great, as of the extreme northwestern regions of the union—of the great chain of lakes—and of the sources of the Mississippi river, which have continued to be the subject of dispute between geographical writers.

Impressed with the importance of these facts, Governor Cass, of Michigan, projected, in the fall of 1819, an expedition for exploring the regions in question; and presented a memorial to the Secretary at War upon the subject, in which he proposed leaving Detroit in the ensuing spring, in two Indian canoes, as being best adapted to the navigation of the shallow waters of the upper country, and to the numerous portages which it is necessary to make from stream to stream.

The specific objects of this journey, were to obtain a more correct knowledge of the names, numbers, customs, history, condition, mode of subsistence, and dispositions of the Indian tribes—to survey the topography of the country, and collect the materials for an accurate map—to locate the site of a garrison at the foot of Lake Superior, and to purchase the ground—to investigate the subject of the northwestern copper mines, lead mines, and gypsum quarries, and to purchase from the Indian tribes such tracts as might be necessary to secure to the United States the ultimate advantages to be derived from them, &c. To accomplish these objects, it was proposed to attach to the expedition a topographical engineer, a physician, and a person acquainted with mineralogy.

Mr. Calhoun, not only approved of the proposed plan, but determined to enable the Governor to carry it into complete effect, by ordering an escort of soldiers, and enjoining it upon the commandants of the frontier garrisons, to furnish every aid that the exigencies of the party might require, either in men, boats, or supplies. It is only necessary to add, that I was honoured with the appointment of mineralogist to the expedition, in which capacity, I kept the following Journal.* In presenting it to the public, it will not be deemed improper if I acknowledge the obligations which I have incurred in transcribing it, by availing myself of a free access to the valuable Library of His Excellency De Witt Clinton; and of the taste and skill of Mr. Henry Inman, in drawing a number of the views which embellish the work.

HENRY R. SCHOOLCRAFT.

Albany, May 14th, 1821.

* I have received enquiries from several individuals, grounded on the supposition that my Journal would contain *all* the topographical information, collected on the expedition. It may be proper to observe, that it only embraces my individual observations upon that, and the other subjects brought into view; and that another work may be expected, containing Professor Douglass' Topographical Report and Map, together with the other Reports, and the scientific observations of the expedition generally.

CONTENTS.

THE PLATES.

NARRATIVE JOURNAL

OF

TRAVELS,

THROUGH THE NORTHWESTERN REGIONS OF THE UNITED STATES.

CHAPTER I.

PRELIMINARY TOUR, FROM THE CITY OF NEW-YORK TO DETROIT.

THE determination of limiting the operations of the expedition to the arctic regions of the United States, and thereby putting it in our power to accomplish the journey within the current year (1820); and the desire of visiting the most remote points on our northwestern frontier during the summer season, had rendered an early departure an object of the first moment. But the mode of our conveyance (in Indian canoes) naturally detained us until the breaking up of the ice in the lakes, and it was considered extremely hazardous to undertake the navigation until they were perfectly clear of floating ice. This point being determined, the members of the expedition, were left to exercise their own judgment and convenience, as to the time and mode of proceeding to the place of embarkation, Detroit. A time not capable of being designated with astronomical precision, but dependant wholly upon the natural distribution of atmospheric heat, shewed the necessity of a careful attention to the state of the weather, and the advance of spring. The year commenced with south winds, changing to the southeast, west, and northwest, and attended with light snows.* The Delaware, Susquehanna, and the Hudson, as far as West Point, were frozen hard on the first of January. February gave a week of pleasant weather at the commencement, which was succeeded with high winds from the north, and northeast, and between the tenth and eleventh there was a heavy fall of snow, so that it lay four feet deep in the streets of New-York. This gave good sleighing for two weeks, when a thaw commenced, and the last days of the month were mild and pleasant. March commenced with unusual mildness, with varying and occasionally blustering wind, but no snow was to be seen on the fourth of that month, and an opinion was entertained, that the Hudson would open a fortnight before its usual period.† Every appearance indicated an early spring, an occurrence which we may, in our

* A meteorological register kept during this month in New-York, indicated an average heat of 18° at 7 A. M. 28° at 2 P M. and 16° at 9 P. M. Out of the month, thirteen days were marked "cloudy," and eighteen "clear." The wind blew south seven days, southeast six days, west five days, north four days, southwest three days, and northwest seven days. Snow fell on the 10th, 17th, 21st, 25th, and 29th.

† In the year 1755, noted for the defeat of Gen. Dieskau, at Lake George, the Hudson opened as far as Albany on the 14th day of January, and the following year it was open on the 14th of February, so that Gov. Fletcher sailed from New York on that day with 300 volunteers, to repel an irruption made by the French upon the Mohawks, and landed at Albany two days afterwards. These are the mildest winters of which any record has been preserved.—*Smith's History of New-York.*

climate, (latitude 40° to 44°) sometimes expect, and which by terminating our winter with the month of February, adds three or four weeks to our mildest and most delightful season. Under this impression, I left New-York on the 5th of March, in the citizens' post coach for Albany, a mode of conveyance which only exists during the recess of the running of the steam boats; and which by combining a good degree of comfort and convenience, compensates, so far as land stages appear capable of compensating, for the wonderful degree of celerity, comfort, and ease, afforded by the line of internal steam boat navigation, that connects New-York and Albany, nine months in the year.* Passing through Kingsbridge, Phillipsbourg, Tarrytown, Sing Sing, and Peekskill, we crossed the Highlands of the Hudson during the evening, and lodged at Fishkill, a post town of Dutchess county, sixty-five miles from New-York. On the 6th, we passed Poughkeepsie, Rhinebeck, and Hudson, and lodged at Kinderhook, and reached Albany† on the morning of the 7th. The entire distance is one hundred and sixty miles, which

* The invention of the steam boat is an event which will long render the year 1807 conspicuous in the annals of mechanical invention. It was during this year, after a long period spent in experiments on the application of the steam engine in propelling boats, that success crowned the efforts of Robert Fulton in the construction of the first steam boat called the *North River*, which performed a trip from New York to Albany, carrying a number of passengers to witness the nautical phenomenon of a vessel going at the rate of seven miles against wind and tide.

See Colden's Life of Fulton.

† By the census of 1820, Albany has a population of 12,541, being 1779 more than it had in 1810.

we accomplished in forty hours actual travelling, including detention at post-offices and taverns, giving an average of four miles per hour. This is about the rate of travelling in the *Trekschuits* of Holland,* and upon the frozen grounds in Russia.†

On our arrival at Greenbush, we found the ice in the Hudson too unstable to admit of crossing upon it, and were passed over in a boat propelled along a path cut through the ice.‡ There was some snow in the streets of Albany, and a cold wind from the north presaged a check to the advance of spring, which had a few days before, given such flattering proofs of an early development. On the succeeding day (the 8th) there arose a hail storm from the northwest, which continued, attended with rain and sleet, during the whole day and succeeding night, and on the morning of the 9th, the hail lay eight inches deep in the streets of the city, and upon the surrounding plains; and presented the novel spec-

* See Hall's *Modern Paris*, in the Literary and Philosophical Repertory.

† Clarke's Travels in Russia.

‡ To travellers, and others, who wish to study the topography of this route, the *map of the Hudson between Sandy Hook and Sandy Hill, with the post road between New-York and Albany*, recently published by A. T. Goodrich & Co. will prove a valuable document. In regard to the general geography and statistics of the country, *Spafford's Gazetteer of New-York* may be advantageously consulted. The history of the discovery of this river by Henry Hudson, in 1609, will be found in the *2d Vol. of the Collections of the New-York Historical Society*. Its geological character is detailed in *Ackerly's Essay on the Geology of the Hudson river*, a work which is accompanied by an excellent geological map; and in *Eaton's Index to the Geology of the Northern States, 2d edition.*

tacle of good sleighing produced by a fall of hail.—The storm had abated, but not ceased, in the evening, when I proceeded in the stage to Schenectady. The route lies by a well constructed turnpike of sixteen miles, across the *Pine Plains*, a district of sandy alluvion, bounded by the gravelly soil of Guilderland and Duanesburgh on the southwest, and by the river alluvions of Niskayuna and Watervliet, on the northeast, and covering an area of about seventy square miles. This tract is included in a triangle formed by the junction of the Mohawk with the Hudson, and of which the Helleberg, a lofty chain of highlands, visible from the plains at the distance of twenty miles, forms the southwestern boundary. Situated near the centre of a state, computed at 40,000 square miles, and containing a population of 1,200,000 souls,* this tract presents the topographical novelty of an unreclaimed desert, in the heart of one of the oldest counties in the state, and in the midst of a people characterized for enterprise and public spirit. Several attempts have lately been made to bring this tract into cultivation, and from the success which has attended the introduction of gypsum, and other improved modes of agriculture, it is probable the whole will, at some future period, be devoted to the cultivation of the various species of grasses, fruit trees, and esculent roots; three branches of agriculture to which its sandy soil seems admirably adapted. It is certainly an object worthy the attention of those societies whose efforts to improve the systems of cropping, to facilitate the progress of farming by the intro-

* This is an estimate warranted by partial returns of the census now taking. The population of New York in 1810, was 959,220. *Spafford's Gazetteer.*

duction of labour-saving implements and machines, and to emulate agricultural industry by the annual distribution of premiums, are already manifest in the improved state of farms, orchards, and breeds of domestic animals. After travelling fifteen miles through the Pine Plains, which present a succession of the most uninteresting views, the eye is relieved on emerging, somewhat abruptly, from the forest of pines, on entering the city of Schenectady,—a town which is characterized as the site of an Indian massacre in 1690,—the seat of the foundation of a College in 1794,* the residence of a population of 5,909 inhabitants in 1810, and the victim of one of the most terrible conflagrations in the fall of 1819.† As we entered the town, the snow, which had imperceptibly succeeded to the hail and sleet of the morning, entirely ceased, and was followed by a night of severe cold. The preceding day (the 10th,) I took the stage which left Albany at four in the morning, and reached Utica at seven in the evening, being a distance of ninety-six miles in seventeen hours. The road lies up the valley of the Mohawk, and the towns successively passed, are New Amsterdam, Caughnawaga, Palatine, Little Falls, and Herkimer. There is little

* See Smith's History of New-York, p. 115.

† "On the morning of the 17th inst. (Nov. 1819) at 4 o'clock, a most awful conflagration commenced its ravages in the city of Schenectady, and continued with unremitted violence, until about 11 o'clock in the forenoon. It broke out in a Currier's shop in Water-street, near the store of John Moyston, and destroyed about 100 stores and dwelling houses in State, Church, Union, Washington, and Front Streets. It was by the most extraordinary exertions only, that the bridge over the Mohawk was saved, having been on fire at every pier."—*Plough Boy*, Vol. I. p. 199.

either in the taste of buildings, condition of inhabitants, or state of improvements, to elicit description. A valley celebrated for the fertility of its soil, now covered with snow and chilled with a driving wind from the north, presented a scene of polar inclemency, and could not be distinguished from plains of irreclaimable sterility. The season was equally unfavourable for observing the physical productions and constitution of the country, or the labour that has been bestowed in rendering them subservient to the wants and the convenience of life. But the sites of towns, the banks of rivers, plains, or mountains, which have once witnessed the effects of human industry, whether in war or in peace, while they experience the most striking physical revolutions, preserve a moral character, which no change can obliterate; and we cannot pass through the country formerly possessed by the Mohawks, without recurring to the savage cruelties and murders, the battles, and the ambuscades, of which it was so long the conspicuous theatre. This powerful and warlike tribe was one of the principal members of the Iroquois confederacy, so long the terror and the glory of the North American Indians. The other members of it, were the Oneidas, the Onondagas, the Cayugas, the Senecas, and the Tuscaroras.* They inhabited the country, when first visited by Europeans, from the Highlands of the Hudson to the banks of the Niagara, and they had either pushed their conquests, or carried the terror

* The Tuscaroras did not originally belong to the confederacy, but inhabited the back parts of North Carolina, where having formed a conspiracy to destroy all the whites, they were defeated and driven away in 1712, and were subsequently received and adopted by the Iroquois.—*Smith's History of New-York.*

of their arms, from the island of Montreal to the banks of the Mississippi. The league was formed before their acquaintance with Europeans, and it is the only instance to be found in the history of the aborigines, of a permanent union for the general welfare and defence. There are two other instances of a temporary confederation of tribes, instituted through the energy of two chiefs, of similar character, at distant periods,—that of Pontiac, against the English, and that of Tecumseh, against the Americans. But these, although powerful, were temporary confederacies, and dissolved with the fall of the respective chiefs with whom they had originated. The Iroquois, on the contrary, had not united for any specific, but for general purposes; their compact was of immemorial standing, and is never known to have been broken, in a single instance. United by the ties of blood, speaking dialects of one language, inhabiting the same country and climate, and acting in one cause, they had acquired a national pride, and a national character; and when we reflect upon the advances they had made in the art of government, and the sound maxims of policy by which they were uniformly actuated, we cannot suppress the wish that the period of the discovery of the new world had been deferred a century longer, that we might have viewed the Northern Indian in a state of civilization, which it is not now probable we shall ever behold.* The ef-

* For an account of the numbers, government, exploits, and customs of the Iroquois, see Gov. Clinton's Discourse before the New-York Historical Society, 2d vol. of their Collections. Colden's History of the Five Nations. La Hontan's Voyages to Canada.—Journal of a voyage to North America, by Charlevoix. Smith's History of New-York.

fect we cannot doubt, would have been auspicious to the cause of the Indians, and gratifying to the friends of philanthropy.* Of this confederacy, which furnishes the strongest evidence of the intellectual vigour of the aborigines, and which has been entirely forgotten, as a confederacy, among the local names of the country which they once occupied, and still, in limited tracts, possess; the Mohawks were the most bloody, the most artful, the bravest, and the most powerful. They occupied the very extensive district of alluvial lands from Scaghticoke on the Hoosick river, to the banks of the Oriskany, in Oneida, and had such weight in the confederacy that it was sometimes even denominated by their name.†

From the time of my departure from New-York, the weather had gradually assumed a character of such severity, as to forbid the expectation of a speedy opening of the northern lakes, and left me at liberty to proceed with more leisure; a circumstance of which I availed myself by spending several days at Utica, and the villages adjacent. Standing at the head of the Mohawk, and at the intersection of the most important roads from the north and the west part of the state, Utica unites extraordinary advantages, as a point for the sale and exchange of the products of agriculture and domestic manufactures. It is the emporium of one of the most extensive and fertile districts of farming lands in the state, and the advantages of geographical position, will be still further augmented by the Erie canal, which is to pass

* Smith's History of New-York, p. 73.

† Governor Clinton's Discourse before the New-York Historical Society, 2d vol. of their Collections, p. 49.

through the centre of the town.* This village lies in north latitude 43° 6′ and occupies the ancient site of Fort Schuyler; a name that recalls the memory of a soldier and a patriot of the revolution.† It was first incorporated in 1798, under the name of the village of Fort Schuyler. In 1805, this act was repealed, and a new one passed conferring additional privileges, and its Asiatic name. In 1810, it contained a population of 1700 inhabitants, and consisted of 300 dwelling houses and stores, exclusive of churches and other public buildings. Its subsequent increase has been very rapid; and the style of architecture and general appearance of the town, indicate the taste and the public spirit which prevails. Fifteen miles

* Since that period, the canal has been finished from Utica to Seneca river, a distance of ninety-six miles, and the permanency of the works, the number of boats loaded with the produce of the country, which have constantly covered it, and other circumstances have been such as to realize the most sanguine expectations of the friends and projectors of that great work.

† My New-York readers will undoubtedly excuse me for presenting the following just and feeling tribute to the talents and patriotism of the late Gen. Schuyler, from the pen of a contemporary soldier and patriot, Col. Troup, of Geneva.

"I should outrage every feeling of my nature, were I to lay down my pen without paying, in the warmest language of the heart, the homage of my unfeigned gratitude to the memory of General Schuyler, for the patriotism which led him to devote to the *Lake Canal Policy*, that ardent zeal, and those extraordinary talents which marked his glorious career in our revolutionary contest; a career that justly entitles him to be ranked in the number of the illustrious founders of our republic. And, I hope to be pardoned for subjoining, that whenever imagination places this very distinguished man before me, I soon become confounded with shame for the extreme neglect—I will not call it ingratitude, with which the state has treated his venerable name."

Vindication of the Lake Canal Policy.

northwest of Utica, lies the site of Fort Stanwix, (now occupied by the village of Rome) the scene of one of the struggles of our revolutionary contest. This fort was first built about the year 1758, by the British, but falling into decay, was repaired and enlarged in 1776, and in the following year sustained, under the command of the late Major General Gansevoort, a siege of twenty-two days, from a combined force of British and Indians, under the command of Col. St. Ledger. It was in marching to the relief of this post, that the unfortunate Gen. Herkimer, falling into an Indian ambuscade on the banks of the Oriskany, lost his life, and the greatest part of his army. With the retreat of St. Ledger, (who, after a sortie from the garrison, led by Col. Marinus Willett, in which four stands of colours were captured,* was compelled to raise the siege) departed, the Mohawk Indians, then in alliance with the British, and they have never since appeared, as a nation, within our precincts.

On the 10th of April, I took the stage which left Utica at two in the morning, and passing through Vernon, Manlius, and Onondaga, lodged at Skeneatelas, a neat and airy village on the banks of one of those beautiful and transparent little lakes which cast such a charm over the scenery of western New-York.

* I do not find this sally of the besieged garrison recorded in any history, and it is here mentioned on the authority of a person (Col. Lawrence Schoolcraft, the father of the writer) who was present upon that occasion. This action is also characterized as affording one of the proofs of which the events of that war afforded many, of the triumph of militia, and raw recruits, acting under a strong sense of political oppression, and an enthusiastic love of liberty, over well disciplined and veteran troops, who were that day driven at the point of the bayonet.

On the eleventh, we passed Auburn* at an early hour, and crossing Cayuga lake by a wooden bridge of a mile in length, reached Geneva at one o'clock in the afternoon. The entire distance is ninety-six miles. The route lies across the important agricultural counties of Oneida, Sullivan, Onondaga, Cayuga, Seneca, and a part of Ontario, a part of the extensive country formerly occupied by the Iroquois, whose great council fire was fixed at Onondaga,† where a part of that tribe still remain. It is the scene of the operations of Gen. Sullivan's army in the summer of 1779, when the Iroquois tribes paid the price of their constancy to the British, in the destruction of their villages, the slaughter and expulsion of a great part of their population, and the total annihilation of their power as a confederacy and a people. There is no account of a general council held by them after the operations of this year, and the seat of their council fire, which is always sacred and im-

* The increase of this village, within the last ten years, is surprising, and may be cited from an hundred other instances, to convey an idea of the growth, population, and improvements of the western parts of New-York. In 1810, Spafford states it to consist of 100 houses and stores, mostly built within the last 6 years. The census of 1820 gives the following result.—*Auburn paper.*

Private Buildings.	Public Buildings.	Manufactures.	Inhabitants.
284 Dwelling Houses,	A State Prison,	3 Distilleries,	1026 free white males,
23 Stores,	A Court House,	2 Grist Mills,	927 do. females,
15 Offices,	Clerk's Office,	1 Brewery,	60 free blacks,
11 Groceries,	10 Schools,	3 Saw Mills,	12 slaves.
7 Inns.	A Theological Seminary,	1 Plaster Mill,	2025
340	1 Methodist Ep Church,	1 Oil Mill,	208 prisoners.
19	1 Presbyterian do.	1 Fulling Mill,	2233
16	1 Episcopal do.	4 Carding Machines.	
375 Total,	A Market House,	16	
	A County Jail,		
	19		

† Smith's History of New-York, p. 68.

moveable among Indian tribes, had fallen into the hands of their enemies. After this defeat, a great proportion of the tribes fled to Canada, and of two entire tribes, the Cayugas and the Mohawks, there is not an individual left. What remains of the tribes which were not then expelled, or have since expatriated themselves, is to be seen in the villages of the Oneidas and Onondagas, and such of the Senecas and Tuscaroras, as are located near Buffalo.* A county that was then the theatre of a frontier war, and the inheritance of a powerful nation of semi-barbarians, is now smiling under the hand of agriculture, and checquered with towns, and villages, roads and canals, the seats of learning, and the temples of religion. Perhaps no country presents so remarkable an instance of the progress of human settlements, achieved in so short a period of time.† A lapse of forty years

* The Stockbridge Indians settled on the Oneida reservation, are not of the race of the Iroquois. They migrated from the banks of the Hudson in 1734 to Stockbridge, in Massachusetts, and from thence about the year 1785 removed to the spot they now occupy. The Brothertown Indians are descendants of the Muhhekenow who formerly inhabited the country about Narraganset, in Rhode-Island.—*Clinton's Discourse before the Historical Society of New-York, p. 43, 2d vol. Collections of that Society.*

† *Increase of Population.*—In the year 1790, the then county of Ontario, according to the census then taken, contained but 205 families, and 1081 inhabitants. " In the same territory, (says the *Canandaigua Repository,)* in the year 1800 (except the county of Steuben, which was set off in 1796) the population was 12,584. The county of Genesee was erected in 1806, and the counties of Niagara, Chautauque, and Cataragus 1808 ; leaving for the county of Ontario, its present territory. In 1810, this county contained 42,032 ; in 1814, it contained 57,630 ; and the census now taking is expected to show about 90,000. Genesee and Niagara have in-

has already rendered it difficult to distinguish between those tumuli, ancient fortifications, and other antiquities which owe their origin to an anterior race of inhabitants, and those marks of occupation left by the Iroquois, or attributable to the French.

On passing through Oneida county on the 10th of April, there was still some snow to be seen in situations shaded by the buildings or fences, but it had entirely disappeared in the roads, and in the open fields. The roads continued muddy to Onondaga East Hill; on the West Hill, they were dry, and so continued with partial exceptions, to Geneva, where the clouds of dust by which we were enveloped, and the appearances of vegetation, indicated the benign climate which pervades the luxuriant country of the Genesee. Every appearance indicated a season ten days more advanced than the valley of the Mohawk, which is only separated by the distance of a hundred miles. The wild poplar put forth leaves on the 18th, the house popular (*populus dilatata*) on the 23d, apricots were in blossom on the 22d. The thermometer observed at one o'clock, P. M. varied, between the 11th and 28th, from 60°, to 78°, of Fahrenheit, during which period the weather was clear, mild, and pleasant, with the exception of a fall of rain on the 26th and 27th. The village of Geneva, occupying a beautiful eminence at the head of Seneca Lake, and surrounded by a district of country, under

creased nearly in the same proportion. The census in the several counties, for 1820, is not yet completed; but the total population in the territory, which, *only thirty years since*, contained but *ten hundred and eighty one souls*, doubtless exceeds TWO HUNDRED THOUSAND!!—We doubt whether a parallel can be found in the rise and progress of any country in any age."—*N. Y. Statesman.*

a high state of cultivation and improvement, presents a most picturesque appearance, on approaching it in a clear day from the east; and the display of the town, so highly favoured by local advantages, at the distance of a mile, creates an idea of wealth, taste, and business, which is not disappointed on beholding it the centre of a populous agricultural district, the mart of its produce and the theatre of its exchange, where the intersection of several important roads, and a branch of the Erie Canal, facilitate a ready intercourse with all parts of the state. A person of information who has had opportunities of occular comparison, is disposed to consider the natural advantages of this village and vicinity, as a place susceptible of rural embellishments, superior to that of the celebrated city of Switzerland, in allusion to which it has been named.

On the 28th of April, I left Geneva, and passing through Canandaigua, Bloomfield, and Lima, lodged at Avon, upon the banks of Genesee river. On the following day we passed through Caledonia, Le Roy, Batavia, Pembroke, and Clarence, and arrived at Buffalo in the evening, a distance of 210 miles from Utica. This route lies across the populous counties of Ontario, Genesee, and Niagara, colloquially known under the name of the Genesee country, and proverbial for the fertility of its soil.* We found

* At the annual fair and cattle show in Ontario county, in the fall of 1819, premiums were awarded on the following articles, viz:

Best winter wheat, 80 bushels 12 qts. on the acre.

Barley, 34 bushels on the acre.

Peas, 32 bushels 4 qts. on the acre.—*Canandaigua Paper.*

In Onondaga county at the agricultural fair of the same season, premiums were awarded on,

the peach, and the earlier varieties of apple tree, every where in blossom, and the beech (*fagus ferruginea,*) the wild poplar, or the American Aspen, and some other species of the early sprouting forest trees, already gave the forest a vernal aspect. These appearances continued until within eight or ten miles of Buffalo, where the influence of the lake winds, and the bodies of unmelted ice in the lakes, have a sensible effect upon the progress of vegetation, which appears to be retarded eight or ten days later on account of this exposure. The peach tree had there budded, but not yet blown. We found the lake still covered with floating ice, and no vessel had

The best Winter Wheat,	37 bushels	14lbs.	to the acre.
Spring	23	33	do.
Barley	41	17	do.
Flax,	350 lbs.		do.
Oats,	54	11	do.
Corn,	121	12 qts.	do.

Onondaga paper.

In Oneida County, at the annual fair and cattle show, of the same season, the following articles received premiums:

Winter Wheat, Reuben Gridley, of Paris, two acres 72 bushels per acre.

Spring Wheat, Jona. Wilcox, Paris, 44 bushels per acre.

Indian Corn, Samuel Cary, Deerfield, 119 bushels per acre.

Barley, R. Southworth, Paris, 56 bushels 28 quarts per acre.

Oats, Jed. Sanger, Whitestown, 84¼ per. acre.

Peas, D. Barton, Paris, 52 bushels. per acre.

Potatoes, A. Bartlett, Paris, 505 bushels per acre.

Butter, D. Barton, Paris, had already made 3107 pounds from 21 cows.—*Plough Boy and Journal of the Board of Agriculture by S. Southwick, Vol.* 1.

But the greatest product of Indian corn raised during this season, and perhaps the greatest ever known, was by Mr. Jedediah Dusenbury, of Portland, Chautauque county, which was 132 bushels 12 quarts from an acre.—*Plough Boy, Vol.* 1. *p.* 199

attempted the navigation. The steam boat had advertised to start on her first trip, on the first of May, but the backward state of the weather, and the ice in the lake, had induced the captain to defer it until the 6th, leaving me a week to visit the Falls of Niagara, and the battle grounds on the north banks of the Niagara.

The town of Buffalo contained a hundred houses, besides the county buildings, in 1810.* On the 30th of December, 1813, it was burnt by a party of British troops and Indians, who laid waste this frontier. It has since been rebuilt with increased elegance, and is now a town of about 200 buildings, a proportion of which are of brick. It occupies an eminence, which was recommended to the French government, as a commanding site for a garrison, by the Baron La Hontan, in 1693, and marked *Fort Suppose*, upon his map.† The first vessel which navigated Lake Erie, was built in this vicinity by La Salle, in 1679, being a vessel of sixty tons burden.‡ A part of the tribe of the Seneca Indians, about 700 souls, are located in this vicinity. The village of Black Rock, the residence of Gen. Peter B. Porter, is situated two miles below, at a spot which is supposed to unite superior advantages, as a place of trade, and a harbour for vessels.

On the first of May, I visited the celebrated Falls of Niagara,§ situated 22 miles below. Keeping the

* Spafford.

† La Hontan's New Voyages to Canada, p. 187, vol. 1.

‡ Smith's History of New-York, p. 80.

§ This is an Iroquois word said to signify *the thunder of waters*, and the word as still pronounced by the Senecas is *O-ni-áá-gáráh*,

American shore, the road lies over an alluvial country, elevated from ten to twenty feet above the water of the river, without a hill, or a ledge of rocks, and with scarce an undulation of surface, to indicate the existence, or prepare the eye for the stupenduous prospect which bursts, somewhat unexpectedly, into view. The day was clear and warm, with a light breeze blowing down the river. We stopped frequently on our approach to listen for the sound of the Fall, but at the distances of fifteen, ten, eight, and even five miles, could not distinguish any, even by laying the ear to the ground. It was not until within three miles of the precipice, where the road runs close to the edge of the river, and brings the rapids in full view, that we could distinctly hear the sound, which then, owing to a change of the wind, fell so heavy upon the ear, that in proceeding a short distance, it was difficult to maintain a conversation, as we rode along. On reaching the Falls, nothing struck me with more surprise, than that the Baron La Hontan, who visited it in August, 1688, should have fallen into so egregious a mistake, as to the height of the perpendicular pitch, which he represents at seven or eight hundred feet.* Nor does the narrator of the discoveries of the unfortunate La Salle, Monsieur Tonti, approach much nearer to the truth, when he states it at six hundred feet.† Charlevoix, whose work

being strongly accentuated on the third syllable, while the interjection O, is so feebly uttered, that without a nice attention, it may escape notice.

* La Hontan's Voyages, vol. I. p. 82.

† An Account of the last Expedition and Discoveries of Monsieur De La Salle.—*Collections of the New-York Historical Society*, Vol. II. p. 228.

is characterized by more accuracy, learning, and research, than those who had preceded him, and who saw the Falls in 1721, makes, on the contrary, an estimate which is surprising for the degree of accuracy he has attained. "For my own part," he says, "after examining it on all sides, where it could be viewed to the greatest advantage, I am inclined to think we cannot allow it less than a hundred and forty or fifty feet."* The latter, (one hundred and fifty) is precisely what the Fall on the Canadian side, is now estimated at. There is a rapid of two miles in extent above, and another of seven miles, extending to Lewiston, below the Falls. The breadth across, at the brink of the Fall, which is serrated and irregular, is estimated at four thousand two hundred and thirty feet, or a little more than three-fourths of a mile. The Fall on the American shore is one hunderd and sixty-four feet, being the highest known perpendicular pitch of so great a volume of water.† The fall of the rapid above, commencing at Chippewa, is estimated at ninety feet, and the entire fall of Niagara river from Lake Erie to Lake Ontario, a distance of thirty-five miles, at three hundred feet. Goat Island, which divides the water into two unequal sheets, has recently been called *Iris*, (in allusion to the perpetual rain bows by which it is characterized) by

* Charlevoix's Journal of a Voyage to North America, vol. I. p. 353.

† It is in the volume of falling water only, that Niagara claims a pre-eminence. There are many higher falls in various parts of South America and Europe. The greatest water fall in Europe, is on the river Lattin, in Lapland, which is half a mile wide, and has a perpendicular pitch of 400 feet.

the commissioners for settling the boundaries of the United States, acting under the treaty of Ghent. In approaching this cataract from Lewiston, the elevated and rocky description of country it is necessary to cross, together with the increased distance at which the roar is heard in that direction, must serve to prepare the mind for encountering a scene which there is nothing to indicate on approaching from Buffalo; and this impression unquestionably continues to exercise an effect upon the beholder, after his arrival at the falls. The first European visitors beheld it under this influence. Following the path of the *Couriers de Bois*, they proceeded from Montreal up the St. Lawrence, to Fort Caderacqui, and around the shores of Lake Ontario, to the alluvial tract which stretches from the mouth of Niagara river, to the site of Lewiston. Here the *Ridge*, emphatically so called, commences, and the number of elevations which it is necessary to ascend in crossing it, may, without a proper consideration of the intermediate descents, have led those who formerly approached that way into error, such as La Hontan, and Tonti fell into. They must have been deprived also of the advantages of the view from the gulph at the foot of the Falls, for we are not prepared to admit the possibility of a descent without artificial stairs, or other analogous labourious and dangerous works, such, as at that remote period, must have been looked upon as a stupendous undertaking; and could not, indeed, have been accomplished, surrounded as the French then were, by their enemies, the jealous and ever watchful Iroquois. The descent at the present period, with every advantage arising from the labours of mechanical ingenuity, cannot be performed without feeling some degree of personal solicitude. It is in this chasm that the sound of the water, falls heaviest upon the ear, and that the mind becomes fully impressed, with the appalling majesty of the Fall. Other views from the banks on both sides of the river, and from the Island of Iris, in its centre, are more beautiful and picturesque; but it is here that the tremulous motion of the earth, the clouds of irridescent spray, the broken column of falling water, the stunning sound, the lofty banks of the river, and the wide spreading ruin of rocks, imprint a character of wonder and terror upon the scene, which no other point of view is capable of producing. The spectator, who, on alighting at Niagara, walks hastily to the brink, feels his attention imperceptibly rivited to the novel and striking phenomenon before him, and, at this moment, is apt either to over-rate or to underratethe magnitude of the Fall. It is not easy to erect a standard of comparison ; and the view requires to be studied in order to attain a just conception and appreciation of its grandeur and its beauties. The ear is at first stunned by the incessant roar, and the eye bewildered in the general view. In proportion as these become familiarized, we seize upon the individual features of the landscape, and are enabled to distinguish between the gay and the sombre, the bold and the picturesque, the harsh and the mellow traits, which, like the deep contrasted shades of some high wrought picture, contribute to give effect to the scene. It was some time before I could satisfy myself of the accuracy of the accredited measurements of the height of the Fall, and not until after I had made repeated visits, and spent a considerable time in the abyss below. There appears a great disproportion between the height and the width of the falling sheet, but the longer I remained, the more magnificent it appeared to me; and hence it is, that with something like a feeling of disappointment, on my first arrival, I left the Falls, after a visit of two days, with an impression of the scene, which every thing I had previously read, had failed to create. At the time of my visit, the wind drove the floating ice out of Lake Erie, with the drift wood of its tributary rivers, and these were constantly precipitated over the Falls, but we were not able to discover any vestiges of them in the eddies below. Immediately in front of the sheet of falling water, on the American side, there was also an enormous bank of snow, of nearly an hundred feet in height, which the power of the sun had not yet been fierce enough to dissolve, and which, by giving an Icelandic character to the landscape, produced a fine effect. It appeared to me to owe its accumulation, to the falling particles of frozen spray.

What has been said by Goldsmith, and repeated by others, respecting the destructive influence of the rapids above, to ducks and other water fowl, is only an effect of the imagination. So far from being the case, the wild duck, is often seen to swim down the rapid to the brink of the Falls, and then fly out, and repeat the descent, seeming to take a delight, in the exercise. Neither are small land-birds affected on flying over the Falls, in the manner that has been stated. I observed the blue bird and the wren, which had already made their annual visit to the banks of the Niagara, frequently fly within one or two feet of the brink, apparently delighted with the gift of their wings, which enabled them to sport over such frightful precipices, without danger. We are, certainly, not well pleased to find, that some of the wonderful stories, we have read of the Falls, during boyhood, do not turn out to be the truth; but, at the same time, a little attention is only necessary to discover, that many interesting facts and particulars, remain unnoticed, which fully compensate for others, that have been overstrained or misstated. Among these, the crystalline appearances, disclosed among the prostrate ruins, and the geological character of the Fall itself, are not the least interesting.

The scenes where nature has experienced her greatest convulsions, are always the most favourable for acquiring a knowledge of the internal structure of the earth. The peaks of the highest mountains, and the depths of the lowest ravines, present the greatest attractions to the geologist. Hence this cataract, which has worn its way for a number of miles, and to a very great depth, through the stony crust of the earth, is no less interesting for the geological facts it discloses, than for the magnificence of its natural scenery. The chain of highlands, called *the Ridge*, originates in Upper-Canada, and running parallel with the south shore of Lake Ontario, forms a natural terrace, which pervades the western counties of New-York, from north to south, affording, by its unbroken chain, and the horizontal position of its strata, the advantages of a natural road, and terminates in an unexplored part of the county of Oswego, or thereabout. It is in crossing this ridge, that the Falls of the Niagara, of the Genesee, and of the Oswego rivers, all running into Lake Ontario, are produced; together with those of an infinite number of smaller streams and brooks.—

Through this, the Niagara has cut its way for a distance of seven miles, and to a depth of more than two hundred feet, disclosing the number, order of stratification, and mineral character, of the different strata of secondary rocks, of which it is composed. These are, beginning at the lowest visible point, red sand stone, fragile slate, and fetid limestone, the latter occupying the surface, and imbedding crystals of calcareous spar,* and foliated gypsum.† How far these formations, in the order in which they are here seen, continue towards the south, and extend laterally towards the east and the west, the want of more extensive observations, prevents us from determining. A similar formation exists at Genesee Falls, and the sand stone stratum, continues unbroken to Oswego, where it is quarried for the purposes of building.‡ It is probable, that the slate rock, variously modified, and combined, extends throughout the Genesee country, as it is found on the banks of the Seneca Lake,—the Cashong, Flint, and Allen's Creeks,—in the towns of Le Roy, and Clarence in digging wells,—on the banks of Lake Erie, at Ham-

* Kalk spath. Werner. Common spar. Kirwan. Calc spar. Jamison. Chaux carbonatée pure spathique. Brongnairt. *Cleaveland.*

† Selenite. Cleaveland. Fraueneis. Werner.

‡ The sand stone of Oswego, has been employed with some success, for the hearths, and lining of glass and iron founderies, where the intense degree of heat employed, renders the discovery of the most refractory rocks, an object of constant solicitude. Intelligent manufacturers will see the important application of geological science, in tracing the formations of rocks, upon which they are any wise dependant, into the vicinity of their manufactories.

burgh,—on Mud Creek, near Canandaigua—on the outlet of Honeyoye, and Caneseus Lakes, and on the Conostaga fork of the Genesee.* At the three latter places, it is so highly charged with bitumen, as to be capable of supporting combustion. The inflammable gas of the burning springs of Ontario, and the fountain of petroleum of Cattaraugus county, afford additional evidence of the existence of carbon and bitumen in the shistose rocks of the Genesee, and render it probable, that mineral coal, the discovery of which, has become so great a desideratum, will reward the future researches of the geologist, and the miner in this region. The secondary character of the Genesee slate, is particularly apparent upon the banks of the Cashong creek, in Ontario county, where it imbeds various species of *concholites* and *erismatolites*, together with globular masses of granular limestone. Along the southern borders of Seneca lake, it contains numerous impressions of univalve shells, and mollusca.

The surface rock of this region, (limestone) which is fetid at Niagara, either does not preserve a uniform character, or is succeeded by local formations of calcareous carbonats, of various character and extent. Thus, it is *compact shelly* (forming a shell marble,) at Wolcott, in Seneca county, and at Bath, in Steuben county; while the greater part of Ontario, Allegany, Chautauque, and Genesee, is charac-

* For several of these localities, I am indebted to the observations of Mr. C. K. Gu rnsey, of Lima, a gentleman whose habits of observation, during occasional excursions through that county, has led him to notice many of those mineral coinc dences and appearances, from which the geologist is enabled to draw the most important conclusions.

terized by an earthy, dull grey, compact limestone, which gives out no odour in breaking, contains shells, sparingly imbedded, and burns to a good quicklime. It is in this formation, that the gypsum beds of Caledonia, Vienna, and Waterloo, are situated; and which, also, appears in the vicinity of the sulphur springs, in Farmington,* and the beds of lenticular oxyd of iron,† in Palmyra, Williamson,

* For an account of these springs, see a Memoir, by J. H. Redfield, in the 2d vol of the Literary and Philosophical Repertory. Also, Dr. Mitchill's Descriptive Catalogue of Minerals, vol. I. p. 3. Bruce's Mineralogical Journal.

† During the session of the legislature of New-York, in the winter of 1820, a loan of $10,000, was made to A. Cole, and associates, to enable them to commence the manufacture of bar iron, from these beds of ore; and it is understood, that works are now in operation, at which a very malleable iron is manufactured. According to an analysis of this ore, by Professor Eaton, of Burlington College, (see Eaton's Geology, p. 266,) it yields thirty per centum of metallic iron, and the ore contains petrefied *volutites*, small and well characterized. I am indebted to Mr. Andrew M'Nab, of Geneva, for the following interesting account, of the locality of this mineral, accompanied by specimens of the ore.

"MEMORANDUM.

"*Lenticular Argillaceous oxyd of Iron.*

"TWO VARIETIES.

"VAR. 1st.—*A bright red, inclining to purple.*—Is found in the towns of Ontario, Williamson, Penfield, and Sodus, in Ontario county. The small rod of iron, accompanying it, was wrought from this ore, at forges erected, and now in operation, in the town of Ontario. The ore is found in great abundance, (quantity supposed to be inexhaustible) in a strip of country, about a mile in width, and midway between the Ridge (Niagara) Road, and the south shore of Lake Ontario, which are about an average of four miles apart, and nearly parallel with each other. The ore is found, generally, at the depth of three to five feet below the surface, and appears to extend downwards a considerable depth—

and Wolcott, in Ontario county. In the town of Caledonia it serves as the basis, to several varieties of madrepores, and corrallines, found in a state of petrefaction, and in the oak openings of Niagara county, it incloses nodules of hornstone.* This hornstone, is also found among the debris, of the Falls of Niagara, accompanied by radiated quartz, rhomboidal crystals of carbonate of lime, foliated and snowy gypsum, and slight traces of the sulphuret of zinc.†

These rocks, (sandstone, slate, and limestone)

perhaps 10 to 15 feet, growing better as it descends. The upper soil, is a reddish sandy loam—then a species of greenish clay, resting upon the ore. The ore is sometimes wrapt up in insolated roundish masses—sometimes in extended beds, similar to gypsum beds or quarries.

" VAR. 2d.—*A dark red, inclining to brown.*—Is found in the town of Wolcott, Seneca county, on the inlet of Port Bay, at the same distance from Lake Ontario, and lying in the same direction, as the above first mentioned kind. The soil, &c. are similar. The specimen herewith delivered, was taken from the surface of the ore bed, which lies naked at the bottom of the stream. The water has, probably, produced the difference in colour, which exists between this and the first kind. It is believed, that there is a continuation of the stratum in Ontario, extending east under Sodus Bay. A mile or two south of the ore, up stream, there is a perpendicular fall of 40 feet, over a bluish slaty rock ; still further south, the bed of the inlet, is a smooth rock, apparently limestone, of secondary formation, until the creek crosses the summit level, (a perfect bog) north of Cress lake, in Galen."—*Extract from a Com. by A. M'Nab, Esq.* 18*th Oct.* 1820.

* Considered as Flint, by Dr. Mitchill, in his Descriptive Catalogue. See Bruce's Mineralogical Journal. Also, Cleaveland's Mineralogy.

† Blende. Black-jack. Pseudo-galena.

however their properties may be found modified, by future discoveries, will probably be found, with a proper allowance for local formations, and disturbances, to pervade all that section of country, which lies between the Niagara and Seneca rivers,--between Lakes Ontario and Seneca,—and between the Allegany river and the south shore of Lake Erie, as general boundaries. All this section of country appears to be underlayed by a stratum of red sand stone, such as appears at the Genesee Falls, but which is imbedded at various depths, as the country happens to be elevated above, or depressed below the level of the Niagara stratum, in which no inclination, is visible.* No order of stratification, could have been affected by nature, which would have afforded greater facilities, to the wasting effects of falling water, so visible at these Falls. The slate which separates the calcareous from the sand stone rock, by a stratum of nearly forty feet in thickness, is continually fretting away, and undermining the superincumbent stratum of limestone, which is thus precipitated

*I find these observations, on the floeta rocks of the Genesee country, corroborated by those of an accurate observer of geological appearances, Samuel M. Hopkins, Esq of Genesee, who, in his Address, before the Agricultural Society of that county, (1819) and in allusion to the horizontal position of the rock strata, says: "This is not the only circumstance, in the geology of this country, which, according to the imperfect notions of the writer, is very remarkable. Not only does the whole level country, seem to have been once covered by lakes, but the deep chasms, which are formed by the Niagara, and other falls, disclose facts which would seem to prove, that the whole sub stratum, for several hundred feet beneath those former lakes, has undergone successive changes, by the action of water. These appearances, would well repay the labour of the geologist, who would investigate them."—*Plough Boy*, vol. I. p. 372.

in prodigious masses, into the abyss below. The most considerable occurrence of this kind, that has recently taken place, is, that of the *Table Rock*,* on the Canadian shore, which fell during the summer of 1818, disclosing a number of those crystallized substances, which have already been alluded to.—By these means, the falls, which are supposed by the most intelligent visitors, to have been anciently seated at Lewiston, have progressed seven miles up the river, cutting a trench through the solid rock, which is about half a mile in width, and two hundred feet in depth, exclusive of what is hidden by the water. The power, capable of effecting such a wonderful change still exists, and may be supposed to operate with undiminished activity. The wasting effects of the water, and the yielding nature of the rocks, remain the same, and manifest the slow process of a change, at the present period, as to position, height, form, division of column and other characters, which form the outlines of the great scene; and this change is sprobably sufficiently rapid in its operation, if minute observations were taken, to imprint a different character upon the Falls, at the close of every century. Nothing in the examination of the geological constitution, and mineral strata of our continent, conveys a more striking illustration of its remote antiquity, (still doubted by many) than a consideration of the time, it must have required for the waters of Niagara, to have worn their channel, for such an immense distance, through the rock. It

* The Table Rock, was a favourite point of view for many years, and the day preceding the night on which it fell with tremendous noise, a number of visitors, had stood with careless security upon it.

is true, we are in possession of no certain data, for estimating the annual rate of their progress, or for comparing the results with the Mosaic history of the earth. All that can be presumed is, that this progress, is now as rapid, as it was in former ages. The discovery of these Falls does not appear to have been made, until an hundred and eighty-six years after the first visit of Columbus to the American continent in 1492, or a hundred and eighty years after the discovery of North America by Cabot, in 1497. I assume the period of La Salle's visit, in 1678, as the basis of these deductions, but my opportunities of research, do not allow me to state with certainty that he was the first visitor, who has furnished a printed account of them. He was followed by La Hontan, in 1683, and by the Jesuit, Charlevoix, in 1721; but, they give no accounts which are sufficiently precise, to enable us to determine what changes have since taken place in the aspect of the Falls. It was not, indeed, until after the dismemberment of the Iroquois confederacy, that the path to the Falls, was opened to the English Colonies, the date of whose unmolested intercourse with this region, cannot, however, precede that of the ratification of the definitive treaty of peace, with Great Britain, in 1784. It is, therefore, only *thirty-six years*, since it has been the free and fashionable resort of all sections of the Union. Maps and descriptions are now extant, which will enable us to fix the rate of its progress, on the expiration of the present century, and we should not be disappointed in our anticipations, if its progress is found, greatly to exceed the prevalent expectation. To aid in the determination, the Island of Iris, which extends from the brink of the Fall, up the river, and which is now connected with the shore, by a wooden bridge, appears to present great facilities. A simple measurement of its length, with a monument for recording it at its head, would convert it into a graduated scale, and the point of the indentation of the Horse Shoe Fall, could, in like manner, be perpetuated on either shore, by a series of corresponding celestial observations, for determining the longitude of the extreme point of that incurvation. Distant ages would thus be furnished with data, the precision of which, would probably enable them to throw new and important lights on the history of the earth, and the changes it has undergone. Is this suggestion of too visionary a nature, to merit the consideration of geological societies?

On the third of May, I returned to Buffalo, and found the lake rapidly discharging its ice, which had been recently broken up by the wind. On the sixth, I embarked on board the Steam-Boat,* which left Black Rock at nine in the morning, and reached Detroit on the eighth at twelve at night. We were favoured with clear weather, and a part of the time with a fair wind. The Boat is large, uniting in its construction a great degree of strength, convenience, and elegance, and is propelled by a powerful and well cast engine, on the Fultonian plan, and one of the best pieces of workmanship of the origin-

* Called the "Walk-in-the-Water," J. Rodgers, master. This boat performed her first trip in 1818, eleven years after the first introduction of Steam-Boats upon the Hudson, and 139 years after the first vessel (larger than an Indian Canoe) was built upon Lake Erie. See page 33.

al foundry.* The accommodations of the boat are all that could be wished, and nothing occured to interrupt the delight, which a passage at this season, affords. The distance is computed at three hundred miles; the time we employed in the voyage was sixty-two hours, which gives an average rate of travelling of five miles per hour. The first two miles after leaving Black Rock, a very heavy rapid is encountered, in ascending which, the assistance of oxen is required. It terminates a short distance below the mouth of Buffalo creek, and immediately opposite the village of Buffalo, where we find ourselves on the level of the waters of Lake Erie five hundred and sixty feet above the tide waters of the Hudson river.† In passing through Lake Erie, the Boat touches at the town of Erie, in Pennsylvania, at the mouth of Grande River, and at the towns of Cleaveland and Portland, in Ohio, the latter situated on Sandusky Bay. On coming out of this Bay, we passed a large and well wooded island, which bears the name of Cunningham, and immediately came in sight of the rocky cluster of the Put-in-Bay or Bass Islands‡

* M'Queen's, New-York.

† See Report of the New York Canal Commissioners, to the Legislature, accompanied with a chart.

‡ "The Bass islands form a group of seven, lying about three miles from part of the Sandusky peninsula, and, as I have already observed, seven or eight miles northwest of Cunningham's island. Put-in-bay, is formed by a curve of the largest and most southern of the Bass groups, having two entrances, one from the east and the other from the west. The bay is very finely land-locked. The second large island of the group, stretching from east to west across the widest part at half a mile distant, and one of the smaller islands lying opposite each channel. The three main islands do not differ much in extent, though that in which is Put-in-bay is the largest. All are uninhabited, and covered with a dense forest I had no means to determine their area with certainty, but judged

which afford one of the best harbours in the lake, and have acquired some celebrity from the circumstance of Com. Perry's having been at anchor there on the morning previous to the memorable victory

the three main islands to average about one and a half miles long, and half a mile wide, and may cover from 2,500 to 3000 acres taken collectively, resting upon a solid mass of schistose rock in great part limestone. From here limestone, for the purpose of making lime, is carried as far as Detroit and Cleaveland. The soil is excellent. and would admit a settlement of thirty or forty families. But every object of utility to which the Bass islands could be applied, yields to the importance of Put-in-bay. This fine haven admits entrance and anchorage for vessels of any supposable draught, safe from all winds. It must become, from its position and depth of water. an object of great national value. No harbour in Lake Erie, or in its connecting waters, except in Erie strait, can in any respect compare with it ; its occupation as a naval and commercial station must one day take place."—*Darby's Tour to Detroit*, p. 185, 186.

In one of the smallest of these Islands, called Moss Island, a large quantity of crystalized sulphat of Strontian, has recently been discovered.

Having received several specimens of this mineral, from Mr. Wm. A. Bird, of Troy, one of which is the fragment of a crystal weighing two pounds, I wrote to him for some account of its locality and geognostic position, and shall here, although without having solicited his permission, make an extract from the reply, with which he favoured me.

"On our return down the lake last fall, (1820) we were becalmed near the Islands in Lake Erie—I took a boat and accompanied by Maj. Delafield, Mr. A. Stebenson, and Mr. De Russy (who was to be our guide) went in search of the Strontian to the *main* shore, where Mr. De Russy says, it was found in the summer of 1819. After an unsuccessful search of an hour, we gave it up and determined to return to our vessel—on our way we stopped at Moss Island, when immediately on landing, we found the mineral in question,—I wandered a little from the others, and found the large bed of which I spoke to you. We there procured large quantities, and some large crystals.

of the tenth of September, 1813. We passed through this cluster, and another, called the Three Sisters, which lie in the Steam-Boat track between Put-in-Bay and the mouth of Detroit river, and entered the latter at twilight on the eighth. We had a view of the Fort and town of Malden or Amherstburg, which lie a few miles above the entrance into the river, and immediately opposite the fertile islands of Bois Blanc and Grosse Isle. These were the last objects that could be distinguished; the night was dark, and we reached Detroit at a late hour, and

" This Strontian was found on the south side of Moss Island in a horizontal vein of three feet in thickness, and from 40 to 50 feet in length I had no means of judging its depth into the rock. The base of the Island is wholly compact limestone in which shells scarcely, if ever appear. The commissioner (Gen. P. B. Porter, acting under the treaty of Ghent, H. R. S.) has given his permission, and I shall name this Island on the maps, " Strontian Island," by which name I presume it will hereafter be known."

The same substance had been found upon another part of this island (as appears from Eaton's Geology, p. 234.) by the gentlemen attached to the boundary commission, during the preceding year, but not in the surprising quantity above stated. Professor Douglass, of West Point, and myself, have also noticed it upon Grosse Isle, in Detroit river, in the month of May, 1820, but found no crystals of more than a few ounces in weight. We found it lining concavities in a horizontal stratum of compact limestone destitute of organic remains. This locality is a stone quarry, which has been opened on the lands of Miss A. M'Comb of Detroit, and from which a great proportion of the building stone of that city is brought.

From these facts it appears, that this mineral, hitherto so very sparingly found either in Europe or America, exists abundantly in the region around the head of Lake Erie, and should the progress of the arts require it, it is probable that the compact limestone of the Erie and Detroit Islands, may hereafter be found to yield a sufficient and lasting supply.

without an opportunity of then witnessing the picturesque view, which the approach to that town, and the country adjacent, presents.

Detroit occupies an eligible situation on the west banks of the strait that connects Lake Erie with Lake St. Clair, at the distance of six miles below the latter, and in north latitude 42° 30′ according to the received observation. The town consists of about two hundred and fifty houses, including public buildings,* and has a population of fourteen hundred and fifteen inhabitants, exclusive of the garrison.† It enjoys the

* The following is a list of the public buildings of Detroit:

1. A Roman Catholic church, 116 feet in length, by 60 in breath—is 110 feet high with two steeples, has a chapel under ground 65 feet by 60, originally designed for a nunnery. Building—of stone and not entirely finished.

2. A Protestant Church, built of wood, painted and furnished with a dome supported by wooden pillars

3. An Academy of brick—is 50 feet long, by 24 in breath.

4. A Penitentiary—is built of stone, two stories high, and 88 feet by 44 on the ground.

5. The Council house—occupied by the Indian department, is built of stone 27 feet by 50.

6. The banking house of the bank of Michigan, 36 feet square, two stories high, built of brick.

7. A market house, 60 by 30.

8. Government store-house—of brick, 100 feet by 40.

9. Military Arsenal—is 50 by 38, two stories high, built of stone.

10. The Ordnance store-house, a spacious stone building.

11. To these may be added Fort Shelby, which stands in the town, and the adjoining barracks, capable of quartering several regiments.

† This is the result of the census of 1820, for the communication of which, together with the greater part of the details I publish respecting *modern* Detroit, I have to acknowledge my obligations to James D. Doty, Esq. attorney at law, of that place, and one of the members of the late expedition to the sources of the Mississippi,

advantages of a regular plan, spacious streets, and a handsome elevation of about forty feet above the river, of which it commands the finest views. Very few of the French antiquated buildings remain. There are several buildings of brick and stone, but the greatest number are painted wooden dwellings, in the style of architecture, which is prevalent in the western parts of the state of New-York. An air of taste and neatness is thus thrown over the town, which superadded to its elevated situation, the appearances of an active and growing commerce, the bustle of mechanical business, its moral institutions,* and the local beauty of the site, strikes us with a feeling of surprise which is the more gratifying as it was not anticipated.

The site of Detroit was occupied by an Indian village, called *Teuchsagrondie*,† when first visited by the French; and among the singularities of its history, we find that it is one of the most ancient European settlements in the interior of the new world, having been a stopping place for the *Couriers du Bois* and

* Societies at Detroit.

1. The Lyceum of the city of Detroit. Its object is the cultivation of general science and literature. Its meetings are popular.
2. A Society for the Promotion of Agriculture.
3. A Mechanics' Society.
4. A Bible Society.
5. Chapter of Royal Arch Masons.
6. Masters' Lodge of Free and Accepted Masons.
7. A Moral and Humane Society.
8. A Sunday School Association.

There are two catholic, a protestant and a methodist clergyman. 12 attornies, and 8 physicians.

† Colden's History of the Five Nations.

Jesuit Missionaries, as early as 1620. Quebec was founded in 1608; Albany, 1614. The New-England Pilgrims landed at Plymouth, in 1620. Regular settlements do not appear, however, to have been made at Detroit until the commencement of the seventeenth century. Charlevoix, who landed here in June, 1721, found it the site of a French Fort called Ponchartrain, under the command of La Salle's Lieutenant, M. Tonti. He speaks of the beauty and fertility of the country, in terms of the highest admiration. "It is pretended," he says, "that this is the finest portion of all Canada, and really, if we may judge by appearances, nature seems to have refused it nothing that can contribute to make a country delightful; hills, meadows, fields, lofty forests, rivulets, fountains, and rivers, and all of them so excellent in their kind, and so happily blended, as to equal the most romantic wishes. The lands, however, are not all equally proper for every sort of grain, but in general are of a wonderful fertility, and I have known some produce good wheat for eighteen years in succession, without any manure. The islands seem placed in the river on purpose to enhance the beauty of the prospect; the river and lake abound in fish, the air is pure, and the climate temperate and extremely wholesome."* There were then three bands of Indians located upon the west banks of the strait, between lakes Erie and St. Clair. The first on ascending, consisted of the Dionondadies,† a band of Wy-

* Charlevoix's Journal of a Voyage to N. America, vol. II, p. 6.

† Called Tionontatez by Charlevoix, and Amihouis by the French generally, but I follow the orthography of Colden.

andots,* having high pretensions to ancestry, and who were considered the radical stock of the Wyandot tribe.† Between these and Fort Ponchartrain, there was a settlement of Pottawattomies, and beyond the fort along the banks of Lake St. Clair, the Ottaways held possession. Charlevoix alludes to the labours of former missionaries among them, who appear to have been most successful with the Hurons, but of the French settlement which is stated to be of fifteen years standing, he adds, that "it has been reduced almost to nothing," and points out to the Dutchess de Lesdiguierés, to whom his letters are addressed; the advantages that New France would derive from a permanent settlement at that place.

The history of Detroit, during this early period is that of the territory of which it is now the capital. It was noted throughout the earliest settlements of the colonies, as the rendezvous of the *Couriers du Bois*, and the mart where the remote tribes of the North and West, called collectively the Far Indians‡ by early writers, exchanged their peltries for European manufactures; and when the fall of Quebec and Montreal in 1759, added the Canadas to the British crown, Detroit was a considerable French village, defended by a stockaded fort, and surrounded

* Called Hurons by the French. Quatoghies, by the Iroquois and English. This is one of the few Indian tribes in the U. S. who are called by the name which they have bestowed upon themselves as a nation.

† The council fire of this tribe, which is always the rallying point among our savages, is understood to be still fixed at the place indicated by Charlevoix, as the residence of the Dionondadies, viz. at Browntown, at the mouth of Detroit river.

‡ Colden's Five Nations.

with a farming population. In the year 1763,*(containing then a British garrison of three hundred men, under Major Gladwyn) it was besieged by a confederacy† of Indian tribes under Pontiac, an Ottaway‡ chief, who displayed such a boldness in his designs, such skill in negociation, and such personal courage in war, as to justify us in considering him one of the greatest men which have ever appeared among the Indian tribes of North America.§ He was the decided and constant enemy of the British government and excelled all his cotemporaries in both mental and bodily vigour. His conspiracy for making himself master of the town of Detroit, and destroying the garrison, although frustrated, is a masterpiece among

* Carver places the date of Pontiac's siege, in 1762, but I have followed Henry, who was an officer of the army of Gen. Bradstreet, which marched to the relief of the Fort in 1764. He says the siege had then been continued nearly twelve months and must consequently have began in 1763.

Henry's Travels and Adventures in Canada, and the Indian Territories between the years 1760 *and* 1776.

† The tribes composing this confederacy were the Miamis, Ottaways. Chippeways, Wyandots, Pottawatames, Mississagas, Shawnese, Ottagamies and Winnebagoes.

‡ Pontiac is considered by Carver as a Miami; but those persons best acquainted with the subject at Detroit, among whom is the present chief magistrate of the Michigan Territory, consider him to have been an Ottaway.

§ There is but a single individual in the history of aboriginal chiefs who will bear a comparison with Pontiac. This is Tecumseh, (a name still fresh in every body's recollection,) who, by his extraordinary powers, both of mind and body, formed a confederation of the same Indian tribes, under the British standard, whom Pontiac had formerly led against it.

Indian stratagems; and his victory over the British troops, at the battle of Bloody Bridge, stands unparalleled in the history of Indian wars, for the decision and steady courage by which it was, in an open fight, achieved.*

* I cannot resist the inclination I feel of giving in this place, an extract from the interesting account which Carver has given of the life and war of this extraordinary chief.

"The town of Detroit, when Pontiac formed his plan, was garrisoned by about three hundred men, commanded by Major Gladwin, a gallant officer. As at that time every appearance of war was at an end, and the Indians seemed to be on a friendly footing, Pontiac approached the Fort, without exciting any suspicions in the breast of the governor or the inhabitants. He encamped at a little distance from it, and sent to let the commandant know that he was come to trade; and being desirous of brightening the chain of peace between the English and his nation, desired that he and his chiefs might be admitted to hold council with him. The governor still unsuspicious, and not in the least doubting the sincerity of the Indians, granted their general's request, and fixed on the next morning for their reception.

"The evening of that day, an Indian woman who had been employed by Major Gladwyn, to make him a pair of Indian shoes, out of curious elk-skin, brought them home. The Major was so pleased with them, that, intending these as a present for a friend, he ordered her to take the remainder back, and make it into others for himself. He then directed his servant to pay her for those she had done, and dismissed her. The woman went to the door that led to the street, but no further; she there loitered about as if she had not finished the business on which she came. A servant at length observed her, and asked her why she staid there; she gave him, however, no answer.

"Some short time after, the governor himself saw her; and enquired of his servant what occasioned her stay. Not being able to get a satisfactory answer, he ordered the woman to be called in. When she came into his presence he desired to know what was the reason of her loitering about, and not hastening home before the gates were shut, that she might complete in due time the

The siege of Detroit was continued by Pontiac, for nearly twelve months together, during which time the garrison, although gallantly defended by the British commandant, had suffered severely, and the confederate Indians had been frequently on the point of

work he had given her to do. She told him, after much hesitation that as he had always behaved with great goodness towards her, she was unwilling to take away the remainder of the skin, because he put so great a value upon it; and yet had not been able to prevail upon herself to tell him so. He then asked her, why she was more reluctant to do so now, than she had been when she made the former pair. With increased reluctance she answered, that she never should be able to bring them back.

"His curiosity being now excited, he insisted on her disclosing to him the secret that seemed to be struggling in her bosom for utterance. At last, on receiving a promise that the intelligence she was about to give him should not turn to her prejudice, and that if it appeared to be beneficial she should be rewarded for it, she informed him, that at the council to be held with the Indians the following day, Pontiac and his chiefs intended to murder him; and, after having massacred the garrison and inhabitants, to plunder the town. That for this purpose all the chiefs who were to be admitted into the council-room had cut their guns short, so that they could conceal them under their blankets; with which, at a signal given by their general, on delivering the belt, they were all to rise up, and instantly to fire on him and his attendants. Having effected this, they were immediately to rush into the town, where they would find themselves supported by a great number of their warriors, that were to come into it during the sitting of the council, under pretence of trading, but privately armed in the same manner. Having gained from the woman every necessary particular relative to the plot, and also the means by which she acquired a knowledge of them, he dismissed her with injunctions of secrecy, and a promise of fulfilling on his part with punctuality the engagements he had entered into.

"The intelligence the governor had just received, gave him great uneasiness; and he immediately consulted the officer who was next to him in command on the subject. But that gentleman con-

carrying the town by assault. At length the approach of Gen. Bradstreet, with 3000 men,* struck the Indians with consternation, and they met him with offers of peace at Miami Bay. A few days afterwards, on the eighth of August, 1764, he arrived

sidering the information as a story invented for some artful purposes, advised him to pay no attention to it. This conclusion however had happily no weight with him. He thought it prudent to conclude it to be true, till he was convinced that it was not so; and therefore, without revealing his suspicions to any other person, he took every needful precaution that the time would admit of. He walked round the fort during the whole night, and saw himself that every centinel was on duty, and every weapon of defence in proper order.

"As he traversed the ramparts which lay nearest to the Indian camp, he heard them in high festivity, and, little imagining that their plot was discovered, probably pleasing themselves with the anticipation of their success. As soon as the morning dawned, he ordered all the garrison under arms; and then imparting his apprehensions to a few of the principal officers, gave them such directions as he thought necessary. At the same time he sent round to all the traders, to inform them, that as it was expected a great number of Indians would enter the town that day, who might be inclined to plunder, he desired they would have their arms ready, and repel every attempt of that kind.

"About ten o'clock, Pontiac and his chiefs arrived; and were conducted to the council-chamber, where the governor and his principal officers, each with pistols in their belt, awaited his arrival. As the Indians passed on, they could not help observing that a greater number of troops than usual were drawn up on the parade, or marching about. No sooner were they entered, and seated on the skins prepared for them, than Pontiac asked the governor on what occasion his young men, meaning the soldiers, were thus drawn up, and parading the streets. He received for answer, that it was only intended to keep them perfect in their exercise.

"The Indian chief-warrior now began his speech, which contained the strongest professions of friendship and good will towards

* Henry's Travels, p. 182.

at Detroit, and a general peace ensued. Pontiac, unable to control the events of a war in which he saw himself deserted by numbers of his followers, and unwilling to live on terms of friendship with a people to whom he had imbibed an early hatred, the consequence of his attachment to the French, fled to Illinois, where he afterwards paid the price of his enmity with his life.*

the English; and when he came to the delivery of the belt of wampum, the particular mode of which, according to the woman's information, was to be the signal for his chiefs to fire, the governor and all his attendants drew their swords half way out of their scabbords; and the soldiers at the same instant made a clattering with their arms before the doors, which had been purposely left open. Pontiac, though one of the boldest of men, immediately turned pale, and trembled; and instead of giving the belt in the manner proposed, delivered it according to the usual way His chiefs, who had impatiently expected the signal, looked at each other with astonishment, but continued quiet, waiting the result.

"The governor in his turn made a speech; but instead of thanking the great warrior for the professions of friendship he had just uttered, he accused him of being a traitor. He told him that the English, who knew every thing, were convinced of his treachery and villanous designs; and as a proof that they were well acquainted with his most secret thoughts and intentions, he stepped towards the Indian chief that sat nearest to him, and drawing aside his blanket discovered the shortened firelock. This entirely disconcerted the Indians, and frustrated their design.

"He then continued to tell them, that as he had given his word at the time they desired an audiance, that their persons should be safe, he would hold his promise inviolable, though they so little deserved it. However he advised them to make the best of their way out of the fort, lest his young men, on being acquainted with their treacherous purposes, should cut every one of them to pieces.

* Henry denies that the death of Pontiac is attributable to the influence of the British government, but admits that the account which Carver gives of it, is, in other respects, correct.

After the close of Pontiac's war, Detroit enjoyed a period of tranquillity, which continued until the breaking out of the American Revolution, at the close of which, it fell by the definitive treaty of peace of 1784, under the jurisdiction of the United States.

" Pontiac endeavoured to contradict the accusation, and to make excuses for his suspicious conduct; but the governor, satisfied of the falsity of his protestations, would not listen to him. The Indians immediately left the fort, but instead of being sensible of the governor's generous behaviour, they threw off the mask, and the next day made a regular attack upon it.

" Major Gladwin has not escaped censure for this mistaken lenity; for probably had he kept a few of the principal chiefs prisoners, whilst he had them in his power, he might have been able to have brought the whole confederacy to terms, and have prevented a war. But he atoned for this oversight, by the gallant defence he made for more than a year, amidst a variety of discouragements.

" During that period some very smart skirmishes happened between the besiegers and the garrison, of which the following was the principal and most bloody: Captain Delzel, a brave officer, prevailed on the governor to give him the command of about two hundred men, and to permit him to attack the enemy's camp. This being complied with, he sallied from the town before day-break; but Pontiac, receiving from some of his swift-footed warriors, who were constantly employed in watching the motions of the garrison, timely intelligence of their design, he collected together the choicest of his troops, and met the detachment at some distance from his camp, near a place since called Bloody-Bridge.

" As the Indians were vastly superior in numbers to captain Delzel's party, he was soon over-powered and driven back. Being now nearly surrounded, he made a vigorous effort to regain the bridge he had just crossed, by which alone he could find a retreat; but in doing this he lost his life, and many of his men fell with him. However, Major Rogers, the second in command, assisted by Lieutenant Breham, found means to draw off the shattered remains of their little army, and conducted them into the fort.

" Thus considerably reduced, it was with difficulty the Major could defend the town; notwithstanding which, he held out against

The continued hostility of the Indian tribes, however, prolonged the period of its surrender, for several years; and, according to Herriot,* the transfer of authority did not take place until 1796. The intermediate time was occupied by the Indian wars, suc-

the Indians till he was relieved, as after this they made but few attacks on the place, and only continued to blockade it.

"The Gladwin Schooner (that in which I afterwards took my passage from Michilimackinac to Detroit and which I since learn was lost with all her crew on Lake Erie, through the obstinacy of the commander, who could not be prevailed upon to take in sufficient ballast) arrived about this time near the town with a reinforcement and necessary supplies. But before this vessel could reach the place of its destination, it was most vigorously attacked by a detachment from Pontiac's army. The Indians surrounded it in their canoes, and made great havock among the crew.

"At length the captain of the schooner, with a considerable number of his men being killed, and the savages beginning to climb up the sides from every quarter, the Lieutenant (Mr. Jacobs, who afterwards commanded, and was lost in it) being determined that the stores should not fall into the enemy's hands, and seeing no other alternative, ordered the gunner to set fire to the powder-room, and blow the ship up. This order was on the point of being executed, when a chief of the Hurons, who understood the English language, gave out to his friends the intention of the commander. On receiving this intelligence, the Indians hurried down the sides of the ship with the greatest precipitation, and got as far from it as possible; whilst the commander immediately took advantage of their consternation, and arrived without any further obstruction at the town.

"This seasonable supply gave the garrison fresh spirits; and Pontiac being now convinced that it would not be in his power to reduce the place, proposed an accommodation; the governor wishing as much to get rid of such troublesome enemies, who obstructed the intercourse of the traders with the neighboring nations, listened to his proposals, and having procured advantageous terms, agreed to a peace. The Indians soon after separated, and return-

* See Herriot's Travels through the Canadas, in 1813.

cessively conducted by generals Harmer, St. Clair, and Wayne, in which the bad success of the two former, was amply compensated by the decisive campaign of the latter, who possessed the faculty of transfusing into the operations of his army, that wonderful energy, for which he was characterized. By the treaty of Greenville, of 1795, the post of Detroit was surrendered to the United States; and, from this period, there has been an American garrison kept here, with the exception of about eleven months, which elapsed between the surrender of general Hull, in 1812, and the re-occupation of the country, by general Harrison, in 1813.

The town was first incorporated by the Legislative Council and House of Representatives of the North-west Territory, on the 18th of January, 1802.

In 1805, when it consisted, according to Herriot, of upwards of two hundred houses, it was entirely destroyed by fire, not a house being left on the plat

ed to their different provinces; nor have they since thought proper to disturb, at least in any great degree, the tranquillity of these parts.

"Pontiac henceforward seemed to have laid aside the animosity he had hitherto borne towards the English, and apparently became their zealous friend. To reward this new attachment, and to insure a continuance of it, government allowed him a handsome pension. But his restless and intriguing spirit would not suffer him to be grateful for this allowance, and his conduct at length grew suspicious; so that going, in the year 1767, to hold a council in the country of the Illinois, a faithful Indian, who was either commissioned by one of the English governors, or instigated by the love he bore the English nation, attended him as a spy; and being convinced from the speech Pontiac made in the council, that he still retained his former prejudices against those for whom he now professed a friendship, he plunged his knife into his heart, as soon as he had done speaking, and laid him dead on the spot."

of the old town. This presented the opportunity of widening the streets, and laying out the town upon an improved plan, by which it has been much beautified, and eventually advantaged. The old town consisted wholly of wooden buildings, very compact, with the streets only thirty feet wide, resembling, in this respect, the antique French villages in Illinois, Missouri, and Louisiana.

In 1810, the act incorporating the town was repealed.

On the 16th of August, 1812, articles of capitulation were signed, by which the fort and town was surrendered to a British army under general Brock, who afterwards fell in the battle of Queenston.

On the 6th of October, 1813,* the town was reoccupied by a division of the American army under generals McArthur and Cass, and the latter subsequently appointed Governor of the Michigan Territory.

On the 24th of October, 1815, the town was again incorporated by the governor and judges of the territory, under the name of "the City of Detroit."

By the act of Congress, passed January 11th, 1805, it is declared to be the seat of the Territorial Government, until Congress shall otherwise direct.

The ordinance of Congress of 1787, prohibits slavery in the territory. This ordinance had respect to all that extensive tract of then unincorporated country, lying northwest of the Ohio river, and of which the present states of Ohio, Indiana, and Illinois form a part.

These are some of the prominent civil and military events of which Detroit has been the theatre, and

* See Fay's Battles of the late War, between 1812-15.

which, by eliciting, from time to time, the attention of the public, have conferred upon it a celebrity, which the most populous cities, barren of historic incident, never attain. This notoriety it has partaken of, in connexion with the surrounding country, which continued to be the rallying point of contending armies, and the scene of Indian warfare and Indian barbarity, during two of the most important campaigns of the late war. It has thus acquired an interest from the sword, which neither the pen of the poet, or the pencil of the painter, have been employed to excite.

It is gratifying, however, to behold, that Detroit does not acquire its principal charm from extraneous circumstances, and that the local beauty of the site, the fertile district of cultivated land by which it is surrounded, and the advantages it enjoys for the purposes of commerce, are calculated to arrest our admiration, and to originate a high expectation of its future destination and importance. A cursory examination of the map of the United States, will indicate its importance as a place of business, and a military depot. Situated on the great chain of lakes, connected, as they are, at almost innumerable points, with the waters of the Mississippi, the Ohio, the St. Lawrence, the Hudson, and the Red River of the North, it communicates with the ocean, at four of the most important points in the whole continent. And when these natural channels of communication shall be improved, so as to render them alike passable at all seasons of the year, the increasing products of its commerce and agriculture, will be presented with a choice of markets, at New-Orleans, New York, or Montreal, an advantage derived from its singular position on the summit level in which the most considerable rivers, lakes, and streams in America, originate. It is thus destined to be to the regions of the northwest, what St. Louis is rapidly becoming in the southwest, the seat of its commerce, the repository of its wealth, and the grand focus of its moral, political and physical energies.

CHAPTER II.

JOURNEY,

FROM DETROIT TO THE ISLAND OF MICHILIMACKINAC.

THE time which elapsed between my arrival at Detroit on the 8th of May, and the date of our departure on the 24th, was occupied in completing the preparations for the transportation, subsistence, and safe conduct of an expedition of forty men, through a country where the woods are not always to be relied upon for game, and among Indian tribes, where a welcome reception can only be certainly ensured by a respectable display of physical power. There is, perhaps, no instance in the history of voyages or travels, where the preparations have been wholly completed within the time originally contemplated. There is always some labour, the difficulty of accomplishing which, has not been duly estimated, or some untoward circumstance, wholly unforeseen, springs up to increase the number of obstacles to be surmounted, and to retard the period of departure. Hence several weeks elapsed, after the navigation of the lakes had opened, and after the time originally fixed for our departure, before we were, in reality, in a state of readiness. Our canoes, our arms, our camp and other equipage, our provisions, and the escort of soldiers destined to accompany us, all contributed to furnish causes of delay; and when no other obstacle remained, the winds blew so directly ahead, that no progress could be made against them. This delay, which was scarcely a cause of regret to any person, and from which the expedition eventually experienced not the slightest inconvenience, afforded us an opportunity of acquiring the most satisfactory knowledge of the town, the adjacent country, the climate, and the novelty of the water craft, in which we were to perform this journey; and, perhaps, this lapse cannot be more appropriately filled, than by some brief notices of such of the enumerated topics, as have not already been dwelt upon in the preliminary remarks. Among these, the Indian canoe, excited our earliest curiosity; and after examining it with scrupulous attention, and making a trial of its velocity upon the river, we were ready to say, with an eloquent writer, "that its slender and elegant form, its rapid movement, its capacity to bear burdens, and to resist the rage of billows and torrents, excited no small degree of admiration, for the skill by which it was constructed."* We were struck with the difference, both as to the form and materials of construction, between the canoe, by which the savages formerly navigated the Hudson, Connecticut, and Delaware, and that which is, at present, employed by the northern tribes. The former, as still remaining among us, is merely a log,

* Gouverneur Morris' Annual Discourse, before the New York Historical Society, in 1812. See their "Collections," 2d vol. p. 116.

which has been scooped out, and is, in every respect, analogous, according to Mr. Pennant,* to the *monoxyla* of the ancient Germans and Gauls, and to the pine canoe of the savages of Nootka Sound, except that the latter is supposed to exceed the ancient European canoe, in the elegance of its form. " The old Europeans, says Mr. Pennant, were content if they could but float." The northwest canoe, is, on the contrary, constructed wholly of bark, cedar splints, the roots of the spruce, and the pitch of the yellow pine, productions which are common, from the frozen ocean, situated within the arctic circle,† to the parallel of the forty-second degree of north latitude ; and these articles are fabricated in a manner uniting such an astonishing degree of lightness, strength, and elegance, and with such a perfect adaptation to the country, and the difficulties of northern voyages, as to create a sentiment of mixed surprise and admiration. Those of the largest size, such as are commonly employed in the fur trade of the north, are thirty-five feet in length, and six feet in width, at the widest part, tapering gradually towards the bow and stern, which are brought to a wedge-like point, and turned over, from the extremities, towards the centre, so as to resemble, in some degree, the head of a violin. See plate 2. fig. 1. They are constructed of the bark of the white birch tree, (*betula papyracea*) which is peeled from the tree in large sheets, and bent over a slender frame of cedar ribs, confined by gunwales, which are kept apart by slender bars of the same wood. Around these the bark

* See Pennant's Introduction to the Arctic Zoology, p. 235.

† See Hearne's Journey from Hudson's Bay to the Northern Ocean.

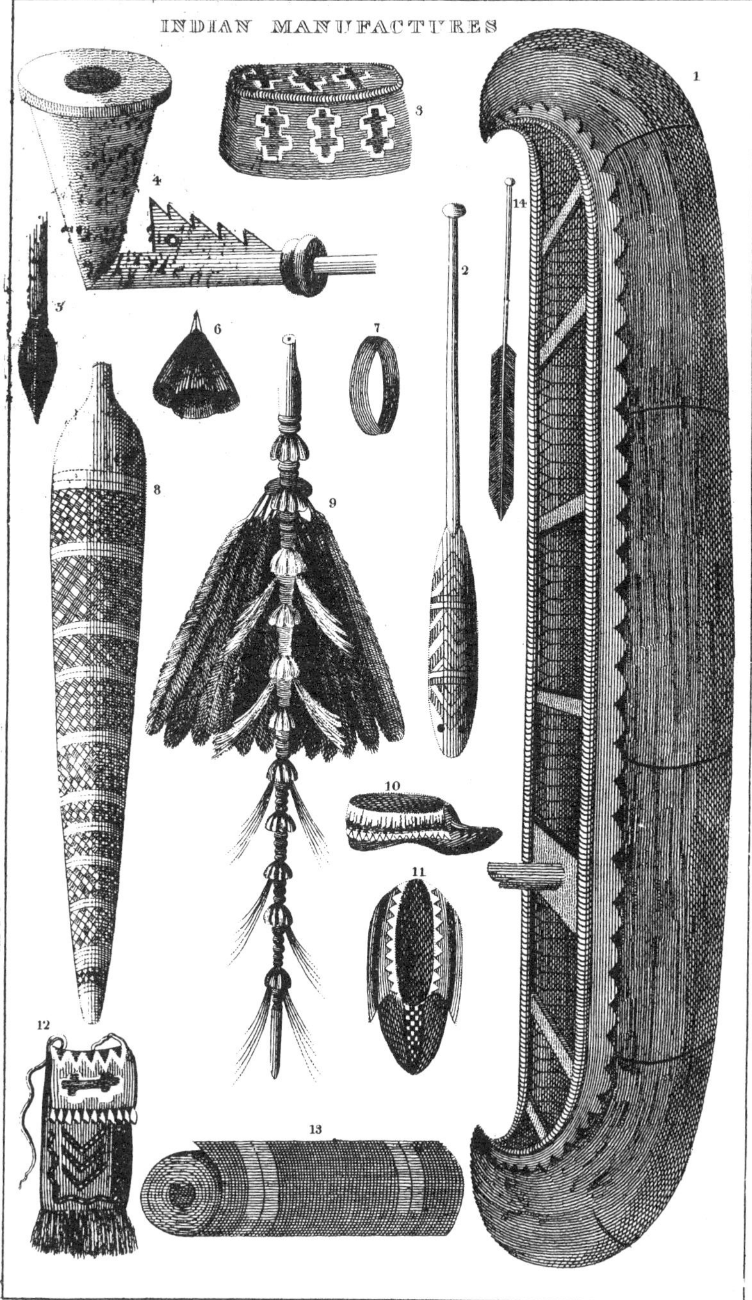

H.R. Schoolcraft d. Rawdon sc.

is sewed, by the slender and flexible roots of the young spruce tree, called *wattap*, and also where the pieces of bark join, so that the gunwales resemble the rim of an Indian basket. The joinings are afterwards luted, and rendered water tight, by a coat of pine pitch, which, after it has been thickened by boiling, is used under the name of *gum*. In the third cross bar from the bow, an aperture is cut for a mast, so that a sail can be employed, when the wind proves favourable. Seats for those who paddle, are made by suspending a strip of board, with cords, from the gunwales, in such a manner, that they do not press against the sides of the canoe. The Fur Companies have lately introduced the use of oars, in propelling the canoe; but the natives employ the cedar paddle, with a light and slender blade. See fig. 14. plate 2. In either case, they are steered with a larger paddle, having a long handle, and a broad blade. See fig. 2. plate 2. A canoe of this size, when employed in the fur trade, is calculated to carry sixty packages of skins, weighing ninety pounds each, and provisions to the amount of one thousand pounds. This is exclusive of the weight of eight men, each of whom are allowed to put on board, a bag or knapsack, of the weight of forty pounds. In addition to this, every canoe, has a quantity of bark, wattap, gum, a pan for heating the gum, an axe, and some smaller articles necessary for repairs. The aggregate weight of all this, may be estimated at about four tons. Such a canoe, thus loaded, is paddled by eight men, at the rate of four miles per hour, in a perfect calm—is carried across portages by four men—is easily repaired at any time and at any place, and is altogether one of the most eligible modes of conveyance, that can be employed upon the lakes, while in the interior of the northwest—for river navigation, where there are many rapids and portages, nothing that has been contrived to float upon water, offers an adequate substitute. Every night the canoe is unloaded, and, with the baggage, carried ashore; and if, during the day, a storm should arise, such is the activity of the Canadian voyageurs, that ten minutes time is sufficient to effect a landing, and secure both vessel and cargo. Recommended by these advantages, we felt an avidity to test them by experience; and, after a long voyage, in which we have had occasion to complain of the confined posture of sitting, and of the frequency of injuring the canoes, by striking against hidden rocks and logs of wood, we have, nevertheless, returned, with an unaltered opinion of their superior utility and adaptation for northern voyages. Such is the vessel in which Europeans, adopting the customs of the savages, first entered the great chain of American lakes, and in which they have successively discovered, the Mississippi,—the Columbia, and the Arctic Sea; and the coincidence is deserving of remark, that it has been employed by every traveller of the region, from the time of Father Marquette, the Jesuit, to the discoveries of Sir Alexander McKenzie.*

* The order of travelling, in this region, is as follows:

1. Father Marquette.
2. La Salle.
3. Hennepin.
4. La Hontan.
5. Charlevoix.
6. Henry.
7. Carver.
8. McKenzie.

With respect to the climate of Detroit, the result of our observations will allow us to speak in a very favourable manner. Situated in the longitude of Chillicothe, in Ohio, and on the parallel of latitude which embraces Prarie du Chein, on the Mississippi, and Albany, on the Hudson, it falls under that temperate medium of climate, which is found so favourable to the cereal gramina, the grasses, and the fruit trees of the United States. This we first witnessed in the early development of spring, always one of the best tests of the benignity of a climate. On leaving Buffalo, on the 6th of May, the blossoms of the peach tree were not yet fully expanded, and the petals of the apple were just beginning to swell. On reaching Detroit, two days afterwards, the leaves of the peach blossom had fallen, and those of the apple had passed the heighth of their bloom. Gardening also, which had not commenced at Buffalo,* we found finished at Detroit, and the half grown leaves of the beach, the maple, the common hickory, (*juglans vulgaris*), and the profusion of wild flowers on the commons, gave to the forests and to the fields the delightful appearance of spring. These facts will go farther in determining upon the differences of climate, than meteorological registers, which only indicate the state of the atmosphere, without noticing whether a corresponding effect is produced upon vegetation. During ten days of the period of our detention at Detroit, of which I kept a meteorological register, the mean daily temperature of the atmosphere, (for a period of ten days,) as indicated

* The thermometer observed at Buffalo for seven days, namely, from April 29th to May 6th, indicated a mean temperature of 44° at 8 o'clock in the morning, and 65$\frac{9}{2}$ at 2 in the afternoon.

by a Fahrenheit thermometer, was 61°.* The average temperature of the whole month of May, at Albany, according to the observations of Dr. Beck,† was 58°.

By a journal of the weather kept at the garrison of Detroit, (Fort Shelby), in obedience to orders from the War Department, for a period of one hundred and five days, namely, from the 15th November, 1818, to the 28th February, 1819, forty days are remarked to be "clear," forty "cloudy," thirteen "variable," and twelve "cloudy, with rain or snow." The average monthly temperature as noted by a Fahrenheit thermometer during the same period, was, for November 43°, December 25°, January 30°, and February 33°.‡ According to a meteorological journal, kept at Albany, during the same time,§ the ave-

***Meteorological Observations, at Detroit.**

Date.	A. M. 6.	8.	10	P.M. 12	6.	8.	Daily Temp.	Prevail. Winds.	State of the Atmosphere.	REMARKS.
May 15	50			61	51	47	52	N. E.	Fair.	
16	49	51		62	50	46	51	N. E.	Fair.	
17	50			64	51		55	N. E.	Fair.	
18	52			64	50	47	55	N. E.	Fair.	
19		60		68	60		62	N. E.	Fair.	
20		64	67	68	63	61	64	N. N. E.	Fair.	
21		67		82	66	62	69	W.N.W	Fair.	Th. 85° at 2 pm.
22		64		88	82	65	74	S. W.	Fair.	89° at 2.
23		72		84	76	62	73	W.N.W.	Cloudy.	Some rain.
24		53		64			53	N. W.	Cloudy.	Left Detroit at 4pm
						10	612			
							61° average daily temperature of May.			

† See Meteorological Register, for the month of May, 1820, in the Plough Boy.

‡ See notes to "The Emigrant," printed by Shelden and Reed, at Detroit, 1819.

§ Dr. T. R. Beck, Plough Boy, vol. I, pages 303, 343.

rage temperature of the atmosphere was in January 22°, and in February 29°. These facts, while they indicate a remarkable difference of climate between two places whose received latitudes only vary nine degrees,* are calculated to justify a remark which we have frequently heard from intelligent persons at Detroit, that they are favoured with a summer atmosphere of uncommon serenity, and that their winters are not so severe as those experienced in the same latitudes east of the Alleghany mountains.

The winds which are expected at this season to prevail here, as in the valley of the Ohio,† from the southwest, had blown from the northeast, shifting to the north and northwest, (points unfavourable to those who are ascending through the lakes,) during the whole period of our stay at Detroit. This gave us no uneasiness so long as the preparations for the journey were going forward, but when, on the 23d of May, these were completed, and the canoes ready for embarkation, all felt the utmost anxiety to proceed, and the governor, although suffering from an attack of the fever and ague, fixed the following day for our departure.

I. Day.—(*May 24th*, 1820.)—It was late in the day before our baggage could be embarked. At four o'clock in the afternoon, all was in readiness. A large concourse of people had collected upon the shore to offer us their good wishes, and to witness our departure, when, upon the word being given, the voyageurs, with one impulse, struck their pad-

* Lat. of Albany, 42° 39′. Detroit, 42° 30′.

† Drake's Natural and Statistical View of Cincinnati.

dles in the water, and instantly chanting one of their animated songs, we passed rapidly along the town, and in two hours time, landed at Grosse Point, on the west shore of Lake St. Clair, nine miles from Detroit, where it had previously been determined to encamp. To this place Governor Cass and suite, accompanied by Gen. M'Comb of the army, and a party of gentlemen and ladies from Detroit, who honoured the expedition with this mark of attention, proceeded by land. Feeling an anxiety to witness the picturesque scenery presented from the river, I embarked on board the canoes at Detroit, but had nearly repented of my choice before reaching the place of our encampment, for the wind, which gave us no inconvenience of leaving the shore, soon shifted directly ahead, and blew with such violence, that the waves broke over the canoes, and gave us a severe drenching. Immediately on leaving Detroit a canoe race, and trial of skill, was witnessed between the French voyageurs and the Indians, (who occupied a separate canoe,) of our party, in which the expertness and spirit of the latter, for sudden and short exertions, and the superiority of the former for labours long continued, were handsomely and clearly manifested. The banks of the river present a compact settlement along the American shore, in which the succession of farm houses, orchards, and cultivated fields, is in no place interrupted by forests, or even by detached copses of woods. Every thing bears the appearance of having been long settled and well improved. The soil is a deep, black alluvion, of the richest quality, and disclosing on the water's edge, pebbles of limestone, granite, and hornblende rock, mixed with silicious sand, and, in small quantity, with iron sand. Farms are laid out with a width of only four acres in front, and extending eighty acres in depth, which gives a compactness to the settlement that was formerly very advantageous in defending the early settlers against the attacks of the aborigines. The appearance of extensive orchards, the wind-mills which occupy every prominent point along the river, the clearness of the water, the woody islands in the river, already covered with green foliage, and the distant view of Detroit, every moment receding in the landscape, all served to imprint a character of mildness and beauty upon the scene, which was perhaps heightened by the reflection, that it presented the last glimpse of a refined population which we were for some time to witness. On reaching Grosse Point, we found the party, that proceeded by land, already there; several of the citizens of Detroit had previously returned, and the rest departed in the evening.

II. Day.—(*May 25th.*)—A strong head wind prevented us from quitting our encampment. The mean daily temperature of the air, and the water of Lake St. Clair, at six inches below the surface, have been equal at 51° of Fahrenheit, which is 5° lower than the mean *annual* temperature of the Ohio at eight inches below the surface.* Large masses of granite, hornblende, limestone, hornstone jasper, mica slate, and quartz, are lying upon the margin of the lake. The banks are alluvial, elevated about twenty feet above the water, and with an undulatory surface. Lake St. Clair is by far the smallest of the chain of

* Drake's Statistical View, p. 14.

lakes, which, by their intercommunications connect Lake Superior with the river St. Lawrence Its greatest length is computed at 30 miles, by a breadth of 25 miles, with an inconsiderable depth. It receives a number of tributary streams, the largest of which are the river Huron, from the American, and the rivers Chenal Ecarte, and Thames,* from the Canadian shore. The latter runs parallel with the north shore of Lake Erie, for a considerable distance, and is noted as the scene of General Harrison's victory over the British army, on the 5th of October, 1813. Considered as a decisive field battle,—as securing the safety of our extensive northwestern frontier,—and as breaking up a powerful Indian confederacy, in the death of their celebrated leader, Tecumseh,†

* Called by the French, "La Rivière à la Trenche," and by the aborigines, Escann-Seebe.

† This noted warrior, was first made known to the public as the leader of the Indians at the battle of Tippacanoe, (7th Nov. 1811.) He burst suddenly into notice, but from that time, until his fall upon the river Thames, the attention of the American people was constantly rivetted upon him. He possessed all the energy, bravery, sagacity, and fortitude, for which the most distinguished aboriginal chiefs have been celebrated, and the terror of his name alone kept the whole line of our northwestern frontier in a constant state of alarm. He projected every enterprize which the savages executed against the whites, and took a conspicuous part in every massacre, in every murder, and in every siege He was no less an orator, than a soldier, and by the persuasive power of his eloquence formed one of the most powerful confederacies which has been attempted by the Indians within the last century. His watchful mind was ever on the alert, his hatred never slumbered, and he held himself a stranger to personal fatigue. Such was Tecumseh, who is reported to have fallen towards the close of the battle upon the Thames, in a personal combat with Col. R. M. Johnson, of Kentucky. He was a Shawanee.

this victory may be looked upon as one of the most important events of the late war.

It is gratifying to the expedition, to reflect, that they are proceeding under the orders of a person, whose participation in that engagement, and in the general dangers and fatigues of the operations of that arduous campaign, affords a pledge of that decision of character, foresight, and personal courage, so necessary in the safe conduct of the voyage before us.

III. Day—(*May 26th.*)—The wind, which continued unfavourable in the morning, abated about eleven o'clock, when we commenced loading the canoes. At twelve the Governor embarked, and we proceeded along the southern shore of the lake, to the entrance of St. Clair river, and up that, a distance of six miles where we encamped, having proceeded twenty-five miles. The expedition consisted, on leaving Grosse Point, of the following persons:

His Ex: Lewis Cass, *Governor of the Michigan Territory.*

Alexander Wolcott, M. D. *Indian Agent at Chicago, Physician to the Expedition.*

Capt. David B. Douglass, *Civil and Military Engineer.*

Lieut. Æneas Mackay, 3*d Regiment U. S. Artillery, commanding the soldiers.*

James D. Doty, Esq. *Secretary to the Expedition.*

Maj. Robert A. Forsyth, *Private Secretary to the Governor.*

Mr. Charles C. Trowbridge, *Assist. Topographer.*

Mr. Alexander R. Chace.

Also,—ten Canadian voyageurs,—seven U. S. soldiers,—ten Indians of the Ottaway and Shawanee tribes, an interpreter and a guide, making thirty-seven persons exclusive of myself, and all embarked in three canoes. Provisions were only taken to serve the party to the island of Michilimackinac, to which place, the stores, arms, Indian goods, and other principal outfits had been sent by vessels in order to facilitate our passage through lake Huron. The Indians occupied one canoe, under the direction of an Ottaway chief. The baggage and men were divided equally. The canoes were moved wholly with paddles, but a sail provided to each, as well as a small standard, bearing the arms of the United States. Each canoe had also a tent or marque, and an oil cloth, to secure baggage from the effects of rain, together with the necessary gum, bark, and apparatus for mending canoes. Thus equipped, we took our final departure from Grosse Point about noon, with a double feeling of pleasure, from the reflection of the termination of a delay, which had so early retarded our progress, and the anticipation of the novel and interesting scenes, we were to encounter. A glow of satisfaction, beamed on every countenance, which was heightened by the serenity of the atmosphere, and by the temperate warmth of the day. About two o'clock, we passed the mouth of Huron river, which enters behind a point of land, projecting some distance into the lake, and is a stream of sixty yards wide, and navigable with boats, of a small class, for sixty or seventy miles. Upon this stream, stand the towns of Mount Clemens and Pontiac, both recent, and in a state of rapid improvement; the lands upon the banks of this river, are represented as fertile and well adapted to the growth of wheat, rye, and Indian corn. Its principal forest trees, are oak, maple, and blackwalnut. From Point Huron, it is necessary, in order to strike the mouth of St. Clair river, and to save a tedious voyage around the shore, to traverse across a large bay, or arm of the lake, but before we had reached half the distance, the wind arose and continued to blow with such violence, that with every exertion, little head way could be made, while the waves were frequently breaking across our canoes, which rendered it necessary for one man to be continually employed in bailing out the water. It was dark before we reached the entrance of the river, which consists of a number of channels, separated by islands partly under water, and covered with a heavy growth of rushes, reeds, and tall coarse grass, affording no advantages for encampment, so that we were compelled to ascend the river to the upper end of Lawson's island, a distance of two leagues where we arrived two hours before midnight, wet and cold, and passed an uncomfortable night.

IV. Day.—(*May* 26*th.*)—Embarked at seven o'clock in the morning, and passed up the river thirty miles, which brought us to Fort Gratiot, at the foot of Lake Huron. The principal tributary streams of St. Clair river are Belle river, and Black river, both entering on the United States shore, the former at the distance of fourteen, and the latter at the distance of two miles below Fort Gratiot. The banks of the river St. Clair are handsomely elevated, and well wooded with maple, beach, oak, and elm. Settlements continue for a considerable part of the way on the American shore, and contribute very much to the effect of a district of river scenery, which is generally admired. The lands are rich, and handsomely exposed to the sun. The river is broad, and deep, with a gravelly shore and transparent water, and its surface is chequered with a number of the most beautiful islands. Indeed, the succession of interesting views, has afforded us a continued theme of admiration, and we can fully unite in the remark of the Baron La Hontan, who passed this strait in 1688, "that it is difficult to imagine a more delightful prospect, than is presented by this strait, and the little Lake St. Clair."* In ascending the river, we have successively passed nine vessels at anchor, being detained by head winds. They were laden with merchandise, military stores, and troops, for Michilimackinac, Green Bay, and Chicago. We also passed a number of Indian canoes, in which were generally one family, with their blankets, guns, fishing apparatus, and dogs. On conversing with them, through our interpreter, we found they belonged to the Chippeway and Ottaway tribes, who are on a footing of the most perfect friendship with each other, and with the United States. There are some of these tribes permanently settled on the Canadian shore of the river, which is generally in the state of nature, and presents a striking contrast with the improvements on the opposite shore. The white inhabitants are chiefly French, who profess the Roman catholic religion. The river maintains an average width of about three quarters of a mile, with a gentle current until we approach within three miles of Lake Huron, where there is a rapid in which the

* La Hontan's Voyages, vol. I. p. 83.

water runs with a velocity, of from six to seven miles per hour. Fort Gratiot stands at the head of this rapid, and commands the entrance into Lake Huron. The site appears to have been judiciously selected, and must always, in the event of a war, command the commerce of the upper lakes, and sérve as a check to the incursions of the savages. So important did the French formerly consider this, that at a very early period the *Coureurs du Bois*, had erected a Fort at this spot at their own expense.—This was afterwards occupied by the French Government, under the name of *Fort St Joseph*, and finally abandoned and burnt by the commandant, La Hontan, on the 27th August, 1688.* This measure was adopted upon the occasion of a Peace. concluded by the Marquis de Denonville, Governor of Canada, in consequence of which, Fort Niagara had been abandoned to the Iroquois. The present Fort is understood to have been built about the close of the late war, (1814.) It consists of a stockade inclosing a magazine, barracks, and other prerequisites, calculated to accommodate a garrison of one battalion. We found it occupied by a company of sixty men, under the command of Major Cummins, a prompt officer, who under the recent order of the War Department, is cultivating an extensive plantation and kitchen garden. The expedition was received with a national salute, and welcomed to the hospitality and conveniences of the garrison. We here returned two soldiers who were sickly, and received an accession of five able bodied men to supply their places. To cover any arrangements of this kind,

* La Hontan's Voyages.

which the exigencies of our situation might render necessary, an order had been issued by the war department, and transmitted by General Macomb throughout the northwestern division of the army to afford the expedition every necessary assistance either in men, boats, or other facilities.

In passing up the river, we have constantly observed ducks, plovers, and snipe ; and while walking along the shore had an opportunity to witness the manner in which certain snakes prey upon inferior reptiles. In the present instance a common green snake (*coluber æstivus*) had seized upon a frog and succeeded in swallowing it alive, saving a small part of the hinder legs, which were visible when we discovered it. A blow at the snake was sufficient to relieve the frog, which fled towards the water without having received much apparent injury. The mean temperature of the air, since leaving Detroit has been 51°, that of the water, 52°.* The wind has varied little from northwest, blowing at times with some violence, and so as to retard our progress.

No change in the geological character of the country, has been noticed, the shores of the river continue alluvial, and the detached stones strewed along the beach, are of the same kinds formerly men-

* *Meteorological Observations on the Lake and River St. Clair.*

Date	AIR.								WATER.						Mean daily temp Of water	Mean daily temp. Of air.	Prevailing Winds	Weather.
	A. M.				P. M.				A. M.			P. M.						
1820	[illegible]	8	[illegible]	[illegible]	1	2	6	8	6	8	12	2	6	3				
May 24.								51								51	N N W	Fair
25	47	[illegible]		[illegible]		59	46		49		54			47	50	52	N W	Fair.
26		52		53		[illegible]	[illegible]			53		[illegible]			55	51	N W	Fair.
27		54		55				44		54	55			50	53	51	N. W.	Fair.
															158	205		
															52° water	51° air.		

tioned, among which, hornblende and granite predominate:—no rock strata appear. There are some traces of iron sand along the shore On ascending the rapids between Black river and Fort Gratiot, where the current washes hard against the south shore, we perceive a tenaceous stratum of blue clay of fifteen feet in depth, covered by a layer of sandy alluvion of thrice that depth. What strikes us as particularly deserving of attention is, a number of trees imbedded at the point of contact between the clay and the overlaying stratum of sand, and which the falling in of the bank has caused to project horizontally several feet over the water These trees are also seen at various depths below the surface of the sand bank, together with fragments of granite and limestone; but no such imbedded substances either vegetable or mineral, are found in the stratum of clay! Is not, therefore, the sub-stratum of sand a posterior formation? And do not the imbedded substances furnish data for determining the relative geological ages of the two alluvial deposites? These considerations lead us further to inquire into the impropriety of confounding all earthy strata under the broad and indistinguishable name of alluvion, and whether they do not, like other mineral depositions, admit of a classification according to composition, the imbedded substances, and the order of superposition.*

* The views which I have f rmerly suggested with regard to alluvial formations, and the ligh in which they have been ·onsidered by Professor Eaton, of Bur'ington College, may be seen by a reference to his valuable work, entitled *An Index to the Geology of the Northern States, second edition, p.* 262.

V. Day.—(*May 28th.*)—We left Fort Gratiot, at eight o'clock in the morning. For the first half mile, a strong rapid is encountered, on reaching the head of which, we find ourselves on the level of Lake Huron, at an elevation of twenty-nine feet above Lake Erie, and five hundred and eighty-nine feet above the ocean.* Here the lake spreads amply before us, and we shortly find the prospect, on the right, bounded by an expanse of water, terminated on the line of the horizon, and on the left by an alluvial shore, covered chiefly with a growth of white pine, poplar, and birch, and skirted on the water's edge, by a broad beach of gravel and sand. In coasting along this, there is little to interest. The view of the lake, which, at first, pleases by its novelty, soon becomes tiresome by its uniformity, and the eye seeks in vain to relieve itself, by some rock bluff, or commanding elevation, upon the shore. One or two species of duck, the plover, and a small kind of gull, with white feathers and sharp pointed wings, have

* These facts are deduced from the following estimates:

Fall of Detroit river, twenty miles, at six inches per mile	10 feet.
Fall of St. Clair river, thirty miles, at four inches per mile . . .	10 feet.
Rapid of St. Clair river, extending three miles	9 feet.
	29 above L. Erie.
Elevation of Lake Erie, above the tide waters of the Hudson, according to the survey of the New-York Canal Commissioners	560 feet.
	589

appeared, to variegate the scene. In landing, at one or two places along the shore, we found the pebbles and loose stones to consist, principally, of hornblende, granite, sienite, and limestone. Among the latter, are several large masses, containing numerous species of petrified remains—(*concholites* and *erismatolites.*) The soil, after leaving the head of St Clair river, appears to degenerate, grows sandy and sterile, and in some places marshy, and a marked difference in the forest trees is observable. Maples, and the beech, and elm, become rare, and, in their stead, we perceive pines, poplars, the birch, and the hemlock We have passed several considerable indentations in the shore, and other places which have names known to the voyageurs, or to the Indians, but as most of them are trifling or ludicrous, and I cannot conceive the bare enumeration of the names of unimportant points and places, either useful or interesting, I have omitted to record them, a practice, which I purpose to adhere to, during the future progress of the expedition. The Canadian voyageurs, have passed the greatest part of their lives along these coasts, and in scenes of hardship and danger. These people are continually pointing out to us places where they have formerly encamped—broke their canoes—encountered difficulties with the natives, or met with some other occurrence, either pleasant or disagreeable, which has served to imprint the scene upon their memories. There is, perhaps, not two miles along the whole southwestern shore of Lake Huron, which is not the scene of some such occurrence. It is by no means certain, however, that such points are designated by names in universal use, even among themselves; and in a country, where there are no permanent settlements, local appellations are necessarily subject to be changed, or fall into disuse. There are, however, certain prominent points and features, in the topography of every savage country, which are universally known by established names among themselves, and deserve to be perpetuated in the permanent geography of the country. Such are the names of all rivers, streams, bays, promontories, and mountains, which are proper subjects to enrich our maps, and to employ the pen of the tourist.

We progressed thirty-five miles during this day, in a general course northwest, and encamped upon the open beach of the lake. The wind has been lightly ahead. The greatest observed heat of the atmosphere, has been 55°; the water of Lake Huron standing, at the same time, at 58°.

VI. Day.—(*May 29th.*)—In passing along the margin of the lake, for a distance of thirty miles, little diversity in the natural appearances of the country, has been presented. At the distance of about fifteen miles beyond our encampment of the twenty-eighth, the shore of the lake assumes an elevation of thirty or forty feet, terminating in a perpendicular bank at the water's edge, which continues six or eight miles. While passing along this coast, at the distance of one or two miles, it was difficult to determine, even with the aid of an excellent magnifying glass, whether this bank consised of a ledge of rocks, or a stratum of compact clay. Its dark colour led us to suppose it was bituminous slate, fragments of which had been observed upon the shore, at no great distance beyond the point of its termination; but this doubt was satisfactorily solved upon our return, when that part of the shore was found to consist of a stratum of dark tenacious blue clay, the colour of which was rendered more intense, by the dashing of the waves against the foot of the bank, and which thus kept it continually wetted, for eight or ten feet above the common level of the water. A few miles beyond the termination of this clay bank, (about fifty-five miles above Fort Gratiot,) we passed the White Rock, an enormous detached mass of transition* limestone, standing in the lake, at the distance of half a mile from the shore. This is an

* Notwithstanding the objections which have been urged against this class of rocks, by Greenough, Maccullough, and other late geological writers, I find it necessary to employ the term "transition," as a generic for those rocks, which possess characters intermediate between the floetz and the primary strata. Of this intermediate character, the White Rock of Lake Huron, presents an example, which is the more worthy of remark, as the entire mass appears to be unconnected with any continuous stratum, and with respect to original position, is out of place. I shall not here stop to enquire, by what means it has been transported into a region, to which it appears foreign. The limits of this note will barely permit me to mention the fact of its apparent translation from its original and parent bed A glympse of the recent fracture is sufficient to satisfy us, that it is not a secondary rock, while the crystalline and granular structure, and the absence of organic reliqua, appear equally conclusive of its primary character. In the haste of the moment, we had, therefore, referred it to the class of primitive limestone; but a recent examination of the specimens we procured, shews. that the crystallization is not perfect, and the fracture discloses numerous small cavities, which have not been observed in the alpine limestone. It will not bear a comparison with any specimens of well characterized granular limestone in my possession; but the most conclusive circumstance, is a petrified madrepore, recently noticed in one of the specimens. What, therefore, is neither decidedly primordial, or floetzose, we must be permitted still to consider, "transition."

object looked upon as a kind of mile-stone by the voyageurs, and is known to all canoe and boat travellers of the region. It has already found a place upon some maps. The White Rock is an object which had attracted the early notice of the Indians, who are the first to observe the non-conformities in the appearances of a country; and it continues to be one of the places at which offerings are made. How far these offerings are to be considered as partaking of the nature of religious worship, will admit of great diversity of opinion. We have heard much speculation concerning the religion of the Indians, and the subject has recently called forth the talents and research of a very interesting writer,* but the want of opportunities of personal observation, has led him into some conclusions, which we do not think warranted by the existing state of society among the northern Indians. In the true acceptation of the term, the Indians have no religion; but they believe in the existence of a great invisible spirit, who resides in the region of the clouds, and by means of inferior spirits, throughout every part of the earth. It is not ascertained, however, that they acknowledge the gift of life from this spirit, or pay him the homage of religious adoration. *Manito*,† in the Indian lan-

* Dr. Jarvis. See the Annual Discourse before the New-York Historical Society, 1819.

† This word is employed to signify the same thing, by all the tribes extending from the Arkansaw to the sources of the Mississippi: and, according to Mackenzie, throughout the arctic regions. It may, with many others, (the collection of which would form the subject of a very interesting work,) be quoted to strengthen an opinion, for which there appears ample grounds, that the erratic tribes, of the northwestern region, and of the valley

guage, signifies "spirit." They have good and bad manitoes; great and small manitoes; a manito for every cave, water-fall, or other commanding object in nature, and generally make offerings at such places. These tributary acknowledgments, however, we have observed, are such things as, in their nature, are perfectly useless to the savages;—a broken gun barrel, a pair of old mockasins or leggins, a broken paddle, or other useless or trifling article. Small bits of carrot tobacco are the only valuable offering we have observed, but they never leave a silver arm band, a beaver skin, a knife, a hatchet, or other substance of utility. Neither is there that solemnity observed in making these deposites which has been represented;—nor does there appear to be any obligation upon individuals to make them, or to renew them, at any regular periods. The thing ap-

of the Mississippi, are all descendants from one stock, which is presumed to have progressed from the north towards the south, scattering into different tribes, and falling from the purity of a language, that may have originally been rich and copious. Among those who are disposed to make great allowances, for the corruptions that have crept into the languages of the aborigines of America, we find the most celebrated traveller of the age. "What some learned writers have asserted, from abstract theories, respecting the pretended poverty of the American languages, and the extreme imperfection of their numerical system, is as doubtful as the assertions which have been made respecting the weakness and stupidity of the human race, throughout the new continent—the stunted growth of animated nature, and the degeneration of those animals, which have been transported from one hemisphere to the other. Several idioms, which now form the language of barbarous nations only, seem to be wrecks of languages, once rich, flexible, and belonging to a more cultivated state."—*Humboldt's Researches*, vol. I. p. 20.

pears entirely optional, and is often accidental. Offerings are made when they happen to pass by any scene capable of exciting wonder; but they seldom, if ever, undertake journies to perform them. Their bad manitoes answer to our Devil, but I have not learned, that their bad manitoes are considered to be subservient to one great bad manito. Neither do I know, that the connexion existing between the good manitoes, from the most inferior up to the great spirit, is precisely what I have stated it to be, or that there is any fixed and uniform understanding among them respecting it; but my impression is, that an understanding of this kind is universal.

All are more or less superstitious, and believe in miraculous transformations, ghosts, and witchcraft. They have jugglers and prophets, who predict events, who interpret dreams, and who perform incantations and mummeries. Great solemnity is observed on occasions of this kind, when men and women are ceremoniously arranged around the walls of a cabin appropriated to these mysteries, and while they alternately assist in the performance of a round of unintelligible ceremonies, the spectator finds a difficulty in restraining his laughter. A magic rod suddenly darted at the person who is the subject of operation, causes him to fall as if struck dead. A whiff from a tobacco pipe communicates new spirit to him, and he arises reinstated in his former health of body or mind. The most remarkable of these ceremonies, is called the medicine dance, where all sorts of bodily ailments, are affected to be cured; and persons in the last stages of existence are sometimes brought out to undergo these ceremonies, who die while they are performing. Yet their faith is not destroyed; it is considered the signal interposition of some bad spirit who has prevented the operation of the medicine, that is, *the ceremony*, for physical aids are not relied upon in these cases; and if one in ten who have been subjects of operation, recover, the success in that case is alone dwelt upon, and the nine unsuccessful ones disregarded. Such is the religion,—the superstition, and the knowledge of medicine of the lake savages, blended as they appear. It is difficult to separate them, and to say how much may be considered religious, or mere mummery. Much allowance, however, is to be made on account of our ignorance of their languages,—on account of bad interpretation, and the unfavourable sentiments we may entertain from early prejudices, or from other causes, which are apt to influence our opinions and views.

As to the success which has attended the attempts to introduce christianity among them, it is difficult to perceive, that any material change has been worked among the tribes so remote. The French Missionaries were the most successful, particularly with the Hurons, and many of the Indians still retain some of the signs and symbols of the Catholic religion. Silver crosses delivered to them a century ago by Jesuit priests are still preserved and worn, and they profess a great veneration for them. This religion, striking as it has always appeared to the illiterate and vulgar, by its splendid ceremonies and external signs, appears to have presented great attractions for the Indians. They do not appear, however, to retain any notions of the doctrines taught, and so far as I have been able to learn, do not wish to be disturbed by the introduction of any religion, prefering, in their emphatic language "to follow the religion of their fathers." They may not, however, be the proper judges in this case, and it requires the attention and perseverance of christians and religious societies to effect a moral reform among them. Of the feasibility of well directed efforts, there can be no doubt; but hitherto the little attention which has been bestowed upon them, seems to have reached them through missionaries badly selected for the task. The savage mind, habituated to sloth, is not easily roused into a state of moral activity, and is not at once capable of embracing and understanding the sublime truths and doctrines of the evangelical law. It is necessary that letters, arts, and religion should go hand in hand. It is probable, also, that a plainer and more familiar mode of explanation than that commonly practised in refined society, would be found productive of its advantages, at least, in the commencement of moral and religious instruction.

On embarking this morning we had the wind lightly ahead, which continued during the forenoon, but changed so that we were able to make use of our sails in the afternoon. About four o'clock the weather became cloudy and hazy, and the wind increased in violence, attended by thunder. A storm was hastily gathering, and the lake became so much agitated that it was thought prudent to land and encamp. We effected a landing, with some difficulty, on a very shallow shore, and dangerous from the number of detached stones projecting above the water, or merely hid beneath it; and pitched our tents on a narrow neck of land nearly separated from the main shore, and covered with a beautiful growth of forest trees. Shortly after our arrival at this place a vessel hove in sight, and afterwards came to anchor within half a mile of the land, the wind blowing a gale ashore. We were apprehensive the vessel would be driven from her mooring, but the night passed without accident. In the course of the day we passed several canoes of Indians, and uniformly found them in want of provisions.

VII. Day—(*May* 30*th.*)—Detained by unfavourable winds. The shore of the lake is strewed with water worn masses of rocks of the same kinds already mentioned, and we still find granite and hornblende to predominate. No rock has, however, yet appeared *in situ.* The lands adjoining our encampment, are generally low and swampy, and the forest consists of hemlock, birch, ash, oak, and some maple. Among the plants the *convallaria augustifolia*, and a species of Indian *Brassica*, have been noticed. The margin of the lake is skirted with bull-rushes, quake grass, (*briza canadensis*,) and other aquatic plants. The greatest observed heat of the air has been 53°, wind N. E.

VIII. Day.—(*May* 31*st.*)—Still detained by head winds. In loitering along the shore of the lake, examining the loose stones, I discovered in a detached block of mica slate, several large and well defined crystals of staurotide,* of a dark reddish brown colour, moderate

* To prevent a misapprehension arising from the variety of names which have been applied by mineralogists to the same sub-

hardness, and perfectly opaque. Near the same spot a number of petrifactions (*celleporites* and *madreporites*,) were observed in the detached fragments of limestone, found along the coast; but what excited a particular interest, was a large block of granitic rock imbedding globular pebbles of hornblende. This rock, as being a quarternary compound of feldspar, quartz, mica, and hornblende, would be considered a *granilite* according to the suggestions of Kirwan. The masses of hornblende, which are in most instances pure and unmixed, in others contain feldspar and quartz, thus indicating a transition of one substance into the other which does not admit of a ready explanation. Will the present state of mineralogical science, justify us in considering this substance as a primitive breccia? or is it a granitic porphyry?

stance, an introduction of synonomies has become necessary in all elementary works on mineralogy; nor does it appear less requisite in books of general information, which are often read by those whose business or leisure does not permit a reference to elementary treatises. It must moreover, be considered a fault in every book, which compels its readers to hunt over scarce or voluminous works for insulated facts, which are the only parts of such works, that happen at the time, to interest them. I shall, therefore, perhaps accumulate a body of notes, which will not recommend this narrative to readers of a certain class, but I shall aim to introduce no more than appears to me necessary to a correct understanding of the subjects brought into view. In the present instance I have followed Cleaveland in designating a certain crystalline combination of alumine, silex, and oxide of iron, *staurotide*. The same substance is called *Granatit* by Werner, and *Grenatite* by Jameson and Brochant. An analysis of this mineral, by Klaproth, gave alumine 52.25, silex 27, oxide of iron 18.50, oxide of manganese 0.25.=98.

IX. Day.—(*June 1st.*)—The wind abating, we embarked this morning at six o'clock, but on proceeding about one league, it again arose to such a pitch, that it became necessary to effect a speedy landing. Such are the delays to which our voyage is continually exposed. Shortly after landing the Indians were sent into the woods in quest of game, and a party of soldiers and engagées went to an adjacent river for the purpose of fishing, but after an absence of four or five hours, both parties returned without success. In the mean time, the agitation of the lake had ceased, and the wind sprung up in our favour; we, therefore, embarked again at three in the afternoon, and proceeded under sail to Saganaw Bay, a distance of twenty-five miles, where we encamped after twilight, having successively passed Elm creek, Black river, and Point aux Barques,—the latter forming the southeastern cape of Saganaw Bay.

At the distance of a league before reaching Point aux Barques, we perceive the first stratum of rock in situ, which consists of a secondary sandstone of a greyish white colour and very friable texture. It forms a horizontal ledge of from ten to twenty feet in height, immediately upon the lake shore, but the continuity of the stratum is interrupted by small bays and inlets, worn into the rock by the violence of the storms and tempests, which prevailing from the north, have an uninterrupted sweep from the Straits of St. Mary, across the widest part of the lake, until they are opposed by the perishable sandstone of Point aux Barques. Here the waves beat with the utmost fury, and by prostrating the opposing barrier into heaps of sand, have manifestly extended the dominions of the lake, while the winds have heaped the disintegrated ruins into vast sand hills and ridges, that skirt the borders of the lake, and exhibit all the fanciful forms which a tempest is capable of communicating to the drifting sands of the ocean. These ridges are now covered with a growth of the pitch pine, the American aspen, and the pyrola rotundifolia;—productions, which delight to grow upon the most sterile sand banks. Insulated masses of the rock covered with forest trees, form several islands in the lake along this coast at the distances of one, and two miles, and by the perfect similarity of the stone,—its horizontal position, and other geological correspondences remain as the monuments of their former connexion with the main land. These operations give to this part of the lake, and particularly to the outer shores of Saganaw Bay, a broad beach of sand intervening between the woods and the water, which affords innumerable harbours for encamping, and one of the safest shores for boat and canoe navigation. The frailty of these vessels is not here threatened by those hidden blocks of granite and other primary stones, which we have found so very annoying along the coast between Fort Gratiot and Point aux Barques,—for with the commencement of the sand rock, and sand beaches, these substances have entirely disappeared. If, as along other parts of this lake, these detached masses of primary formation, once lined the shores of Saganaw Bay and the adjacent coast, the subsequent inroad of the lake upon the main shore, has left them at the bottom of the water at the distance of a mile or two off land.

As the sand stone of Point aux Barques, has no overlaying stratum of rock, and the water prevents us from ascertaining that upon which it rests, some difficulty would arise in pointing out its geological character, were it not indicated by the organic remains (erismatolites) which we find in a state of petrifaction, in the most compact parts of it.

Saganaw Bay is by far the largest of the numerous inlets which serve to indent the very irregular shores of Lake Huron. It is computed to be sixty miles in depth, and thirty in width, and has a number of small islands, the most considerable of which is Shawangunk Island, situated nearly in its centre. The navigation is safe for vessels of any burden, and its numerous coves and islands, present some of the best harbours in the lake. At its southern extremity it receives Saganaw river, a large and deep stream with bold shores, and made up of a great number of tributaries, which irrigate an extensive country, reputed to be one of the most fertile and delightful in the Territory of Michigan. The banks of this stream are now inhabited by detached bands of Chippeway and Ottaway Indians,* who have long enjoyed the advantages of an easy subsistance, from the fine hunting grounds in that vicinity, and the abundance of fish afforded by the bay and other tributary waters. These lands have recently been disposed of

* It is understood that the northern missionary society of the city of Albany are about to establish a missionary family upon some of the tributary streams of Saganaw river, and that an agent has been sent out to explore the country, and to report upon the feasibility of the design.

to the United States government, and will shortly be thrown into market. From the terms ot high admiration of which all continue to speak of the riches of the soil, and the natural beauty of the country, and its central and advantageous position for business, we are led to suppose that it presents uncommon incitements to enterprising and industrious farmers and mechanics.

X. Day—(*June 2d.*)—In order to cross Saganaw Bay with safety in a canoe, it is necessary to pass up the eastern shore from Point aux Barques to Point aux Chenes, a distance of eighteen miles. Here, if the lake be calm, the voyageur crosses by a stretch of twenty miles to the opposite shore, with the advantage of landing on the island of Shawangunk, should a storm overtake him in the centre of the Bay, which is frequently the case. On gaining the opposite shore, it is necessary to pass down the bay about the same distance that was formerly ascended, before the open lake is again reached. The entire crossing can easily be performed in one day if the weather is favourable, but this does not always happen, and the fatal accidents that have formerly befallen those who were too venturesome, have operated as a severe caution to voyageurs and canoe-travellers of the present day. so that it is difficult to induce the former to attempt it, unless the weather be perfectly clear and the bay calm. Fortunately, we were not detained by these causes, and effected the crossing and re-entry of the lake at so seasonable an hour, that we were allowed time to proceed two leagues beyond, and encamped at the mouth of the river aux Sablés, making an entire distance of fifty-six miles. In crossing the bay we landed a few moments upon Shawangunk island which is found to be based upon compact limestone, and contains imbedded masses of Chalcedony, and calcareous spar. I also picked up, during the short period we remained, a lump of the argillaceous oxyd of iron, and some detached fragments of a coarse striped jasper. These discoveries created a strong desire to make a geological survey of the island, but we were prevented from attempting it, by the necessity of an expeditious progress across the bay while the weather favoured. On reaching the river aux Sablés, we found a number of Chippeway Indians upon the shore, and a permanent village at the distance of two miles above its discharge. They appeared friendly, and as soon as our tents were pitched came formally to the Governor's marque. A chief of the Chippeways then addressed the Governor in a speech in which he told him that he was glad to see him there—that he had heard of his coming—and hoped he would see, and relieve their wants, &c. The pipe of peace was then smoked in the usual style of Indian ceremony, by handing it to all present, each one taking a whiff, which is all that is required: when this ceremony was ended, they commenced that of shaking hands,*

* The practice of shaking hands we afterwards found universal among the northwestern tribes, but were unable to ascertain whether it is an ancient custom, or has been introduced by their intercourse with Europeans. To ascertain that a custom so ancient and so universal in the Old World, and which is one of the most striking characteristics of civilized nations, was also prevalent among the abor igines of America, at the period of its discov-

beginning with the Governor, and passing round in a circle to each individual composing his suite. They afterwards presented some fresh sturgeon (*accipenser*) which are caught in abundance in that river, and received in return some tobacco and whiskey, and then departed to their villages. We were anxious to witness how our Indians, on first landing, would conduct themselves towards those of the river aux Sablés, and whether they would demonstrate any feeling of joy or satisfaction upon the interview, and were somewhat disappointed to see a total indifference, or reserve, maintained. They appeared neither to see, or know each other, nor could we learn that any familiarity ensued between them during our stay at that place. Nothing appeared to give them so much satisfaction as the whiskey they received, and when it was drank they presented a request for more. We have since observed, that the passion for drinking spirits is as common to the tribes of this region, as it is to the remnants of the Iroquois, inhabiting the western parts of New-York. To procure it they will part with any thing at their disposal, and if they have no furs or dried venison to exchange, they will sell their silver ornaments, their guns, and even parts of their dress. They generally become intoxicated whenever an opportunity is presented, and a trader or traveller can present nothing which is of half so much value in their estimation. We have generally

ery, would establish a coincidence of the most important nature. But the period for making this observation has long gone by.—There are probably, no tribes now in America, who have not some knowledge of Europeans, or their American descendants.

found it the *first*, and the *last* thing enquired for. It appears this habit was contracted at an early period by the lake Indians, and the anecdote* that Charlevoix relates of an intoxicated Indian, is a proof that it was common in his time. It is due, however, to the tribes of Lake Superior, and the heads of the Mississippi, to say, that we found them far less eager for whiskey than the more contiguous tribes, and that cases were presented, in which it was not relished.

XI. Day.—(*June 3d.*)—The distance from the river aux Sablés to Thunder Bay,* is forty miles, reckoning to the island,—thence to Flat Rock Point, called by the Chippeways, Sho-she-ko-naw-be-ko-king, eight miles. These form the extreme points of our journey during this day. After leaving the aux Sablés five or six miles, a ridge of highland appears visible from the lake, at some distance back, and continues in a general direction north northwest, which is that of the lake coast, to Thunder Bay, and then bears further west, and becomes invisible. In crossing Thunder Bay, we halted at an island which lies in the track of the usual traverse, for a short time, and while there, observed a kind of Indian altar erected beneath a tree near the water's edge. This consists

* "An Ottaway, called John Le Blanc, who was a bad christian and a great drunkard, on being asked by the Count De Frontenac, what he thought the brandy of which he was so fond, was made of, he said of tongues and hearts, for, added he, after I have drank of it I fear nothing, and I talk like an angel."—*Charlevoix's Journal*, vol. II. p. 83.

* *L'Anse du Tunneré*, of the old French writers.

of a block of quartzy granite, worn, apparently by the water, into a columnar shape, terminated by a kind of cornice, and on account of its remarkable shape and appearance, had probably been carried from the water's edge and set up at that spot. It is probable also that this column of granite is dedicated to one of their numerous local gods or manitoes, and that he is supplicated for prosperous voyages across the Bay.

What has been so often reiterated, as to the highly electrified state of the atmosphere at this Bay, seems to have no foundation in truth. There is nothing in the appearance of the surrounding country,—in the proximity of mountains,—or the currents of the atmosphere, to justify a belief that the air contains a surcharge of the electric fluid. In no place does the coast attain a sufficient altitude to allow us to suppose that it can exert any sensible influence upon the clouds, nor is it known that any mineral exhalations are given out in this vicinity, as has been suggested, capable of conducing towards a state of electrical irritability in the atmosphere. From the northwest cape of Saganaw Bay, to the vicinity of Flat-Rock-Point, we find the shore of the lake an alluvial bank, edged with a beach of sand, with masses of primary and floetzose rocks, sparingly scattered along the shore, or projecting above the water. In no instance do the rock strata jut out along the shore, until we reach Thunder Bay, and here they are not elevated more than two or three feet above the level of the water, but generally very much shattered by the violence of the storms, so as rather to present a bed of rubbish, than a ledge of rock. This rock, where it can be examined, is a compact limestone, abounding in petrified remains, and is seen, although the stratum is occasionally interrupted, from Thunder Bay to Shoshe-Konawbekoking, the site of our present encampment, where the number and variety of reliquæ, the perfect state of petrifaction they present, and the facility with which they are disengaged from the rock, are very surprising.*

XII. Day.—(*June 4th.*) We embarked at six o'clock, but after proceeding about a league were driven ashore by a thunder storm, which suddenly arose, attended with a violent wind and rain. In the course of a few hours the storm abated, and we again took the lake, but a renewal of the storm, on going seven or eight miles, again compelled us to the shore, where we were detained during the remainder of the day. A noted island of Lake Huron, called *The Middle Island*, now bears from our encampment due north, and is distant six or eight miles from the shore. This island affords a shelter to vessels en-

* Among these relics, we find various species of concholites, erismatolites, and helmintholites. We particularly recognize the cornu-madreporite, the conite, and the cellepcrite; and the *cornu-ammonite*, which has so often been mistaken for the petrified snake, is found abundantly along this part of the coast. Many of these relics have already been noticed in the floetz rocks of the United States, particularly by Dr Drake, in the valley of the Ohio, by Mr. Eaton, in the valley of the Hudson, and by J. G. Bogert, Esq. along the southern shore of Lake Ontario, and it is believed an increased attention to the subject, is all that is required to render our Fossil Zoology, as rich as that of any other country. Geologists have yet to learn, however, that the *fleshy part* of snakes or other amphibious animals, has ever been discovered in a state of petrifaction!

gaged in the lake trade, and is occasionally resorted to by canoe-travellers.

XIII. Day.—(*June 5th.*) The wind still continuing ahead, it was concluded to send the canoes along the shore, with the soldiers and voyageurs, while the remainder of the party proceeded on foot. At ten o'clock we reached Presque Isle, and carried our canoes and baggage across the portage, which is about two hundred yards, over a low sandy neck of land, connecting the peninsula with the main shore. By this portage, we save a voyage of six or eight miles around a point of land which projects, at this place, into the lake. On reaching the head of the portage, we found that the wind had increased to such a degree as to render it impossible to proceed, and we encamped upon the sand. Here our Indians brought in a brown rabbit,* a species of water turtle, and some pigeons; being the only success met with in hunting since leaving Detroit, with the exception of a partridge, (a species of grouse,) killed a few days previous. It is not to be inferred, however, that the country is destitute of game, or the savages lack skill in hunting it, but the plentiful supply of provisions which they have derived from the

* This is presumed to be a variety of the *American Hare*, of zoologists, and may be distinguished by the following characters: Body about eighteen inches long,—colour of the hair greyish-brown on the back,—greyish-white beneath—neck and body rusty and cinereous,—legs pale rust colour,—tail short, brown above, white beneath—hind legs longest, and callous a short distance from the paws up.—ears tipped with black,—covering of the body, rusty fur, beneath long coarse hair,—probable weight six pounds.

home-stock of the expedition, takes away much of the usual incitements to hunting, while either the rapidity of our movements, or the momentary expectation of re-embarking, while detained by head winds, has prevented them from straying any considerable distance from camp. In these short excursions, they have frequently observed the tracks of the deer, and black bear, too of the largest animals now remaining in the forests along Lake Huron. Circumstances have been equally unpropitious in their attempts upon the ducks, and other aquatic birds, which have occasionally, although not in large flocks, been seen along the shores; for the noise occasioned by our paddles has served to alarm them long before we could approach within shooting distance.

At five o'clock in the evening the wind abated, and we left Presque Isle with the design of continuing in our canoes all night, but at eleven o'clock the wind had freshened to such a degree, and the night become so dark, that we were compelled to encamp, after having gone about twenty miles.

XIV. Day.—(*June 6th.*)—From the place of our encampment on the 5th, to the island of Michilimackinac, is computed at fifty-two miles. Our ardent desire of reaching that place, and the spirit manifested among the voyageurs, on seeing themselves within a day's journey of it, produced a very early embarkation, and notwithstanding a moderate head wind, we advanced against the current at the rate of five miles per hour, and entered the harbour of the northwestern metropolis at four o'clock in the afternoon. The intermediate shore of Lake Huron, presents no change of character worthy of remark; the same kind of soil, the same trees, the same rock strata and pebbly shore, and the same unvaried expanse of water towards the north, serve to imprint a character of uniformity upon the scene. Among the forest trees, pine, hemlock, and spruce predominate, mixed with some maple, oak, birch, and poplar. No bluffs appear along the shore, but the rock, where apparent, is a compact limestone with organic remains. Fragments of hornblende, granite, breccia, and trap, all very much water worn, and not *in place*, continue along the shore. On approaching within four leagues of Michilimackinac, we perceive ourselves opposite the foot of the island of Bois Blanc, which is about ten miles in length, and takes its name from the Liriodendron tulipifera by which it is in a great part covered. It is here necessary to cross over a channel of three or four miles in width to the island, and to pass up around its southern margin to its northwestern extremity. We accomplished this part of the voyage with great labour, and at some hazard ; the lake being so much agitated as frequently to throw the waves into our canoes. In passing around the southwestern curve of the island of Bois Blanc, we leave the site of old Michilimackinac, and the entrance into lake Michigan, on our left, and it is here that the island of Michilimackinac first bursts upon the view. Nothing can present a more picturesque or refreshing spectacle to the traveller, wearied with the lifeless monotony of a canoe voyage through Lake Huron, than the first sight of the island of Michilimackinac, which rises from the watery horizon in lofty bluffs imprinting a rugged outline along the sky, and capped with two fortresses on which the American standard is seen conspicuously displayed.

A compact town stretches along the narrow plain below the hills, and a beautiful harbour chequered with American vessels at anchor, and Indian canoes rapidly shooting across the water in every direction. There is no previous elevation of coast to prepare us for encountering the view of an island elevated more than three hundred feet above the water, and towering into broken peaks which would even present attractions to the eye of the solitary traveller, among the romantic and sublime scenes of the wilderness of Arkansaw. Independent of its imposing features, and its pleasing novelty, we feel an inexpressible degree of delight, after traversing an Indian wilderness of nearly four hundred miles in extent, to find ourselves once more approaching the seat of a civilized population, with all its concomitant blessings. It can only be known to those who have traversed savage regions—who have subsisted long without the most common conveniencies of life—with what feelings the traveller approaches scenes, where, even for a few days, he is to renew former modes of living, and to partake of the advantages of a refined society. At an intermediate distance between Bois Blanc and Michilimackinac, lies Round Island, a well timbered islet, that serves to land-lock the harbour of Michilimackinac, which we immediately entered, on clearing the northern cape of this island, and encamped on the narrow plain below the fort, and in the immediate vicinity of the town. The expedition was received with a national salute from the garrison, and we landed amid the congratulations of a number of the citizens who had assembled on our arrival. Thus terminates the first part of our journey, after a tedious voyage of fourteen days, in which we have encountered an almost continual head wind, with showers of rain, and very little weather that can be considered as warm for the season, the highest point at which the thermometer has been observed being 70°, and the mean daily temperature 51°.* We have also found the natural history of the country, less interesting in the main, than was expected; and the scenery has not been sufficiently diversified to keep up a general interest. Particular scenes have attracted admiration, but it has arisen wholly from the mildness and beauty of their outlines, and the pleasing effect of the water; and not from any features of boldness or sublimity. The islands along the shore, have served to give relief to the eye, when often there was nothing else to excite an interest. The quadrupeds, the birds, and the plants, would furnish very interesting objects to the land traveller, but can only be glanced at by the hasty voyageur. The chalcedony of Shawangunk, and the staurotide procured near Elm creek, are the principal substances that reward a mineralogical search of the shores. It is the geology of the region only that sustains a general interest, and promises a rich reward, and we have been enabled to make

* *Meteorological Observations on Lake Huron.*

Date.	Air.								Water.								Mean temp. of wat	Mean temp. of air.	Prevailing winds	
L. Huron	A. M.				P. M.				A. M.				P. M.							
1820.	6	8	10	12	2	4	6	8	6	8	10	12	2	4	6	8				Weather.
May 28th.		54		55				44	55			58			56		56	51	N. W.	Clear.
" 29th.		44			70		53		54			60			63		59	55	N W.	Thunder.
" 30th		46		53			48											49	N. W	Clear.
" 31st.			54	55		54	48											53		
June 1st	46	57		61				54	42			52			44		45	54		
" 2d.				55			50											52		
" 3d	50				61			47	48				56			46	47	52		
" 4th.	52		51			49		45										49	W.	Rain.
" 5th	48			57			44											49	WNW	Cloudy.
" 6th.		49		57			46			50		52			49		50	50	WNW.	Clear.
																	5)258	10)516		
																	51°	51°		

very ample collections both of hand-specimens of rock strata, and of imbedded fossils. The soil until reaching the head of St. Clair river, is an alluvion, that may be considered equal in quality with the valley of the Ohio or the Mississippi, but from thence to Michilimackinac partakes too much of the sand of the shore, and is in many places swampy, with the exception of the fine region about Saganaw, and the extreme point of the peninsula of Michigan.

The distance from Detroit to Michilimackinac, is computed at three hundred miles, by those who perform the route in vessels of a large size, but is considerably more, as will appear from the following table, when all the indentations of the shore are followed.

TABLE

OF THE STATIONARY DISTANCES BETWEEN DETROIT AND THE ISLAND OF MICHILIMACKINAC.

	Miles.	Total Miles.
To the upper end of Peach Island, and entrance into Lake St. Clair. - - - -	6	
Grosse Point, - - - - - -	3	9
Mouth of Huron River, of Lake St. Clair,	15	24
Mouth of St. Clair River, - - - -	8	32
Belle Rivière, at St. Clair settlement, -	18	60
Black River, - - - - - -	9	69
Fort Gratiot, - - - - - -	2	71
White Rock, - - - - - -	55	126
Elm Creek - - - - - - -	10	136
Black River, - - - - - - -	12	148
Point Aux Barques, - - . -	12	160
Point Aux Chènes, on Saganaw Bay, -	18	178
Shawangunk Island, - - - - -	11	189
River Aux Sablés, - - - - - -	30	210
Thunder Bay Island, - - - -	40	250
Flat Rock Point, near Middle Island, -	18	268
Presque Isle - - - - - -	20	288
Lower end of the Island of Bois Blanc, -	60	348
Michilimackinac, - - - - - -	12	360

CHAPTER III.

SIX DAYS RESIDENCE AT MICHILIMACKINAC, INCLUDING A VISIT TO THE ST. MARTIN'S ISLANDS.

XV. Day.—(*June 7th.*)

THE island of Michilimackinac is nine miles in circumference, and covers an area of about seven thousand six hundred and eighty acres. Its extreme elevation above the lake is three hundred and twelve feet, according to the observations of the garrison, and nine hundred feet above the Atlantic ocean, which is something more than half the height of the Highlands of the Hudson.* Although its

* The altitude of the following points has been ascertained by admeasurement:

HIGHLANDS OF NEW-YORK.	
West-Point, above the Hudson	188 feet
Fort Putnam,	598
Bare Mountain,	1350
Crow's Nest,	1418
Butter-Hill,	1529
New-Beacon, (east side)	1582
The highest peak of the Catskill mountain, as calculated by Capt. Partridge,	3804
Highest peak of the Alleghanies, in Pennsylvania,	1300

Ackerly's Essay on the Geology of the Hudson.

bluffs present the appearance of sterility, they are covered with a strong soil, which is continually renovated by the spontaneous decomposition of calcareous rock, and the island has been long, and we are led to believe, very justly, celebrated for the salubrity of its atmosphere. It contains three objects of natural curiosity which are generally visited by strangers, *The Giant's Arch,—The Natural Pyramid,* or, sugar loaf rock, and *The Scull Rock.* The former is a natural arch projecting from the precipice on the northeastern side of the island, about a mile from the town, and elevated one hundred and forty feet above the level of the water. Its abutments are the calcareous rock common to the island, and have been created by the falling down of enormous masses of the rock, leaving a chasm of eighty or ninety feet in height and crowned with an arch of fifty or sixty feet sweep, having the usual curve of factitious arches. The best view is from the beach, at the water's edge. On viewing it from above, you are obliged to approach within ten or twelve feet of the chasm by which it is produced, before it can be distinctly seen, so that the effect of perspective is lost. The natural pyramid is a lone standing rock, upon the top of the bluff, of probably thirty feet in width, at the base, by eighty or ninety in height, of a rugged appearance, and supporting, in its crevices, a few stunted cedars. It pleases chiefly by its novelty, so wholly unlike any thing to be found in other parts of the world, and on first approaching it, gives the idea of a work of art. Its appearance is readily explained by perceiving it to be a calcareous carbonat of the same character as that upon which it is based, and retaining its original geological situation, and by supposing it to be the relic of a stratum which formerly extended to that depth over the whole island. There is every appearance to justify the conclusion, that such a decay and removal of rock matter has taken place.

The Scull Rock is chiefly noted for a cavern which appears to have been an ancient receptacle of human bones, many of which are still to be observed about its mouth. The entrance is low and narrow, and seems to promise little to reward the labours of exploration. It is here that Alexander Henry was secreted by a friendly Indian, after the horrid massacre of the British garrison, at *Old* Michilimackinac, in 1763.*

The present town of Michilimackinac is pleasantly situated around a small bay, on the southern extremity of the island, and consists altogether of about one hundred and fifty houses, several of which are handsomely painted. Its permanent population does not differ far from four hundred and fifty, but is sometimes swelled by the influx of traders, voyageurs and Indians, to one or two thousand. The harbour is safe in all winds, and sufficiently large to accommodate a hundred and fifty vessels. Fort Michilimackinac stands on a rocky eminence, immediately above the town, and is at present garrisoned by a company of infantry, under the command of Capt. Peirce. Fort Holmes occupies the apex of the island, and is not at present garrisoned. This fortress was erected by the British while they held possession of the island, during the late war, and by them named *Fort George*. But after the surrender of

* See Henry's Travels and Adventures, p. 110.

the island, the name was altered in compliment to the memory of Major Holmes, who fell in the unfortunate attack upon the island, by Col. Croghan. The town of Michilimackinac is now the seat of justice for a county of the same name, which has recently been erected in this part of the Michigan Territory. According to the observation of Lieut. Evileth, it lies in north latitude 45° 54′—which is only 23′ north of Montreal, as stated by Professor Silliman.* It is in west longitude from Washington city, 7° 10′.

XVI. Day.—(*June 8th.*) In consequence of a reported discovery of gypsum upon the St. Martin's islands, which belong to the Michilimackinac cluster, I was directed by Gov. Cass to make a mineralogical survey of those islands, and to report upon the quantity and the quality of the gypsum found. To convey me thither an arrangement had been made with Capt. Knapp, commanding the United States revenue cutter on this station, and accompanied by Capt. Douglass, of the expedition, and Lieut. Pierce, of the army, I went on board the cutter this morning, at ten o'clock. We were favoured with a wind, and after accomplishing the object of the voyage, returned to the harbour of Michilimackinac before dark. The St. Martin's islands lie about ten miles northeast of Michilimackinac. The largest is about nine miles in circumference, by three broad at the widest part, and consists of alluvial soil, covered partly with a forest of oak, maple, and poplar. In no place does it attain an

* Lat. of Montreal, 45° 31′. *Silliman's Tour from Hartford to Quebec, p.* 341.

elevation of more than twenty feet above the level of the lake, and it is subject to a partial inundation in the spring, when the sudden melting of the northern snows produces a rise of water in the lake. Imbedded in this soil, which appears naturally fertile, we found large detached masses of gypsum, of a very fine quality, and unconnected with any adhering rock, so that no expense of blasting is necessary. The principal body of this mineral noticed, consists of the *granularly foliated* sulphate of lime of mineralogy, mixed with scattered masses of the *fibrous* kind, very white and beautiful. A great variety in the colour, and its varying degrees of intensity is found, among which white, red, and dark chesnut brown predominate. Altogether the specimens bear a greater resemblance to the Nova Scotia gypsum, of which such quantities are annually imported into the United States, than any of the numerous beds hitherto discovered in New-York, and other sections of the Union. And, if an opinion may be drawn from external characters, we may venture to consider the St. Martin's, or, as it is already called, the '*Mackinac gypsum*, of a superior quality for agricultural purposes. As to the quantity in which it exists, nothing can be decisively stated, as the earth has not been much explored ; but from the abundance which is scattered over the surface of the ground, and from other geological appearances, it is probable that the quantity will prove exhaustless.

XVII. Day.—(*June 9th.*) The island of Michilimackinac, and the adjacent coasts, have been the theatre of some of the most interesting events in the history of the settlement of the northwestern regions of our continent. In adverting to them, I shall apply the term *modern* to the present town of Michilimackinac, in order to distinguish it from the ancient town, which was situated on the extreme point of the Peninsula of Michigan, about three leagues distant from the island. It appears from Herriot,* that the settlement of the old town, is due to the exertions of Father Marquette, a French missionary, who came here in 1671, with a party of Hurons, whom he prevailed on to locate themselves at that spot, where a fort was constructed, and it afterwards became an important post. This was *eight* years before La Salle's expedition through the lakes, and was the first point of European settlement made northwest of fort Frontenac, or Cadaracqui, on Lake Ontario.†

M. Tonti, Hennepin, Charlevoix and other ancient French writers, when they speak of Michilimackinac, allude to the old peninsular fort. It continued to be the seat of the fur trade, and the undisturbed rendezvous of the Indian tribes during the whole period that the crown of France exercised jurisdiction over the Canadas. After the fall of Quebec in 1759, it passed by treaty into the possession of the British government, but much against the wishes of the Indian tribes, who from long habits of intercourse with the French, entertained an attachment and a partiality which it was not easy to counteract. Such was the spirit of animosity entertained by the Indians,

* See Herriot's Travels through the Canadas, p. 196.

† Neither Fort Niagara, or Fort Ponchartrain, (the present site of Detroit,) was then in existence. The foundation of the former was laid by La Salle, in 1678,—the latter had not been erected when La Hontan passed through the country, in 1688.

that one of the first English traders, (Alexander Henry,) who ventured to visit Michilimackinac, found it necessary on his arrival at that place in 1761, to conceal the circumstance of his nativity, and to conduct his trade under the name of a French assistant whom he had employed. When the deception was a few days afterwards discovered, his goods were only saved to him, by the fortunate arrival of a British garrison of 300 men, who gave protection to the English trade, and compelled the Indians, for a time, to smother the flame of their animosity. It was only, however, to break forth with redoubled violence, and the massacre of this garrison, which ensued about eighteen months afterwards, (1763) while it exhibits one of the most shocking instances of Indian barbarity, is at the same time, a striking proof of the sagacity and dissimulation of the Indian character. It appears from the very interesting account which is given of this transaction by Henry, who was an eye witness, that the Indians were in the habit of playing at a game called *bag-gat-iway*, which is played with a ball and bat, on the principles of our foot-ball, and decided by one of the party's heaving the ball beyond the goal of their adversaries. The king's birth day, the 4th of June, having arrived, the Sacs and Chippeways, who were encamped in great numbers around the fort, turned out upon the green, to play at this game, for a high wager, and attracted a number of the garrison and traders to witness the sport. "The game of baggatiway, is necessarily attended with much violence and noise. In the ardour of contest, the ball, as has been suggested, if it cannot be thrown to the goal desired, is struck in any direction by which it can be diverted from that designed by the adversary. At such a moment, therefore, nothing could be less liable to excite premature alarm, than that the ball should be tossed over the pickets of the fort, nor that having fallen there, it should be followed, on the instant, by all engaged in the game, as well the one party as the other, all eager,—all struggling,—all shouting, in the unrestrained pursuit of a rude athletic exercise; nothing, therefore, could be more happily devised, under the circumstances, than a stratagem like this; and it was, in fact, the stratagem which the Indians employed to obtain possession of the fort, and by which they were enabled to slaughter and subdue its garrison, and such of the other inhabitants as they pleased. To be still more certain of success, they had prevailed upon as many as they could, by a pretext the least liable to suspicion, to come voluntarily without the pickets; and particularly the commandant and garrison themselves."*

This event finally sealed the fate of the fort and the town, after having been the seat of the fur trade for ninety-two years. The Indians, after butchering the garrison, burnt down the fort, and the English afterwards took possession of, and fortified the island of Michilimackinac, which had previously given name to the fort on the Peninsula. No event of importance appears to have disturbed the tranquility, or retarded the growth of the modern town, for a long period, during which its trade and size, were both considerably increased. During the American revolution we hear nothing of it, except as the rendezvous of hostile tribes. By the treaty of Paris, of 1783, acknowledging the independence, and fixing

* Henry, p. 85.

the boundaries of the United States, it fell under the jurisdiction of the American government, and was surrendered, according to McKenzie, in 1794. During the late war, (1812—14) the fort was surprised by a body of British troops, and maintained until surrendered by the treaty of Ghent of 1814. In the meantime an unsuccessful assault was made upon it, by Col. Croghan, who had distinguished himself in so conspicuous a manner in the defence of Fort St. Stephens, at Lower Sandusky. This assault was marked by the death of the gallant Maj. Holmes, who fell at the head of his column in attempting to drive the enemy from a commanding position.

XVIII. Day.—(*June* 10*th.*)—Few persons have visited this Island without being struck with the variety and the delicacy of the fish, which are caught in the vicinity. Among them we see two species of trout, the lake herring, black and white bass, sturgeon, mosquenonge, white fish (*ticamang* of the Indians) pike, gar, perch, and catfish, with several other species of cartilaginous, and shell fish. Of these the white fish is most esteemed for the richness and delicacy of its flavour, and there is a universal acquiescence in the opinion formerly advanced by Charlevoix, "that whether fresh or salted, nothing of the fish kind, can excel it." We cannot, however, agree with the Baron La Hontan in the remark "that it has one singular property, namely, that all sorts of sauces spoil it." This fine fish is very abundant around the island, and is taken with the hook and line. It has not heretofore been described in ichthyological works, but Governor Clinton is disposed to consider it a non-descript species of the *salmo* genus.*

XIX. Day.—(*June* 11*th.*)—The geological character of the island of Michilimackinac, presents some features, which so far as observations have enabled us to judge, are peculiar to it. It consists of a stratum of limestone of immense thickness, based upon a calcareous rock, in which the semi-crystalline structure, and almost entire absence of fossil remains, prove its intermediate age. This formation is not elevated more than a foot above the level of the lake, and extends horizontally under the island. It is overlayed by the rock forming the bluffs which have so commanding an appearance on the approach to the island, and attaining various elevations from one hundred to three hundred feet. Its compact structure, and imbedded fossils leave no doubt as to its posterior deposition, but what strikes us as peculiar in this formation is the circumstance of its being made up of fragments of both transition, and compact limestone, with cavities of carbonat of lime in the powdery form, (agaric mineral) together with small fragments of a species of striped flinty agate, and innumerable small crystals of calcareous spar, thus giving it a breccioidal appearance. It is to be observed, however, that no fragments of primitive rock, are found in its composition, and that the calcareous fragments are acute-angled, and bear no marks of attrition. This formation is handsomely exposed at the bluff, called Robinson's Folly, not quite a

* Memoir on the fishes of the western waters of the state of New-York, appended to Mitchill's Ichthyology. 1st vol. Transactions of the Literary and Philosophical Society.

mile east of the town. The organic relics found in it are generally in the state of chalcedony, and sometimes covered with minute crystals of quartz. Of this the best instance is afforded at Fort Holmes, where the British garrison attempted to procure water by sinking a very deep shaft, but without success. This formation has not been traced on the adjoining shores. We shall content ourselves with the bare mention of these facts, without attempting, in this place, to apply them to existing theories, or received classifications. The town of 'Mackinac, stands on a strip of alluvion below the bluff, consisting of small smooth water worn pebbles of calcareous rock, covered with a deposit of black soil about one foot in depth. On the west side of the island, at the water's edge, there is a bed of light blue clay which is said to *burn white*, and to be well adapted for pipes, and other articles of pottery. Among the detached minerals of the island, I have noticed the brown oxyd of iron, and radiated quartz upon a basis of limestone, together with fragments of the flinty agate of the 'Mackinac limestone, which has just been mentioned. *Detached blocks of granite and hornblende rock, are scattered over the alluvial soil of this island.* These are the leading traits of its mineralogy and geology.

XX. Day.—(*June* 12*th.*)—Hitherto, very little attention has been paid to agriculture on the island, although the soil is not deficient in strength. Garden vegetables grow in great perfection. We have particularly remarked the dry and mealy quality of the potatoe, and have no where observed finer beets and cabbages. The little depth of soil, is, however, unfavourable to forest trees, and there is a scarcity of fire wood and building timber upon the island. A supply of these articles is procured chiefly from the neighbouring islands of Bois Blanc and Round Island. Stone for building, and for quicklime, is abundant. There are a number of sheep, cattle, and horses upon the island, all of which thrive well. There is neither school or preaching upon the island. The town has a post-office, a small jail, and a council house, in which the courts of justice are held. There is no regular bred attorney, although two persons, occasionally practice. The only physician is the one attached to the garrison. There appears therefore in the present society of 'Mackinac the want of a preacher, a school-master, an attorney, and a physician,—of merchants there are always too many. The etymology of the word *Michilimackinac*, admits of a ready explanation. It is a compound of the word *missi* or *missil*, signifying "great," and *mackinac* the Indian word for "turtle," from a fancied resemblance of the island to a great turtle lying upon the water. These are words of the Chippeway language. Herriot derives this name, but without much probability, from *Imakinakos*, an Indian spirit supposed to have formerly inhabited the island. Since our arrival here, there has been a great number of Indians of the Chippeway and Ottaway tribes, encamped near the town. The beach of the lake has been constantly lined with Indian huts and bark canoes. The savages are generally well dressed, in their own costume, and exhibit physiognomies with more regularity of features and beauty of expression, than it is common to find among them. This is probably attributable to a greater intermixture of blood

16

in this vicinity. These savages resort to the island for the purpose of exchanging their furs, for blankets, knives, and other articles. Their visits are periodical, being generally made after their spring and fall hunts, and their stay is short. Some of the tribes also bring in for sale several articles of Indian manufacture, particularly a kind of rush mat of a very handsome fabric, (see Plate 2, Fig. 13,) bark baskets filled with maple sugar, called *moke-ocks*, (see Plate 2, Fig. 3,) with quilled mockasins, (10 and 11,) shot pouches (12,) and other fancy goods of Indian fabric, which are generally in demand as articles of curiosity.

During our detention here, vessels have been constantly entering or leaving the harbour, giving the town an appearance of bustle and business, which was not expected. This appearance of trade has, perhaps, recently assumed a partial activity, by the concentration of a considerable military force on this frontier, which has furnished employment to a number of vessels in the transportation of troops, military stores, and provisions. The Indian trade is chiefly conducted by the American, or South West Fur Company, under the direction of Messrs. Stuart and Crooks. Indeed the ware houses, stores, offices, boat yards and other buildings of this establishment, occupy a considerable part of the town plat, and the company furnishes employment to a great number of clerks, engagés, and mechanics, and contributes very largely to the general business, activity, and enterprise of the town. The trade and operations of this company are confined principally to the northwestern territories of the United States. As to the amount of capital vested, and the quantity of furs annually returned into their ware houses, we have no means of accurate information. It is said to be less profitable now, than at a former period. The following account of the produce of the fur trade for one year, given by McKenzie, will serve to give an idea of its former extent:

" 106,000	Beaver skins,	" 6,000	Lynx skins,
2,100	Bear skins,	600	Wolverine skins,
1,500	Fox skins,	1,650	Fisher skins,
4,000	Kitt Fox skins,	100	Raccoon skins,
4,600	Otter skins,	3,800	Wolf skins,
16,000	Musquash skins,	700	Elk skins,
32,000	Martin skins,	750	Deer skins,
1,800	Mink skins,	1,200	Deer do. dressed,

500 Buffaloe Robes, and a quantity of castorum."

Whether the skins of these animals continue to form the staple articles of the trade—whether the proportion of skins varies greatly in different years—and whether there is an increase or diminution of the total amount, are the secrets of a business of which we are ignorant.

The weather since our arrival upon the island, has been cooler and more variable, we are informed, than is common during this month. Out of six days, two have been rainy and cloudy. The wind has prevailed from the S. E. The highest point at which the thermometer has been observed, as will be seen by a reference to the following meteorological register, is 68°, and the average daily heat for the week 55°. which is eleven degrees lower than the mean temperature of June at Quebec, according to the observations of the late Duke of Richmond.*

During the afternoon of this day we beheld a striking instance of the singular manner in which the island is frequently enveloped in a fog, which is so dense as to obscure objects at the distance of two hundred yards. Being at the moment engaged, in company with Lieutenant Mackay, in sketching a view of the fort and town, from Round Island, we were compelled to relinquish our designs unfinished, and it was with some difficulty we reached the harbour of 'Mackinac. These fogs are common upon the lakes during the summer season. They rise suddenly, without any previous indications of a hazy atmosphere,—move with great velocity, and sometimes prove disastrous to canoe-travellers, and voyageurs.

* Silliman's Tour to Quebec, p. 294.

Meteorological Observations at Michilimackinac.

1820.	Atmospheric temp.						Mean temp.	Winds.	Weather.
	A. M.			P M.					
	7	8	12	2	6	8			
June 7th.	46	47	62	62	59		55	W. N. W.	Clear.
" 8th.		59	64	68	52		66	W. N. W.	"
" 9th.	41	53	56	57	4		49	S. E.	Rain.
" 10th.		55		6[illegible]		54	56	S. E.	Rain.
" 11th.	52			54		51	52	S. E.	Clear.
" 12th.		54		55		52	59	S. E.	"
" 13th.	53						53	S. W.	Clear, quit Mack. at 10.
							7)385		
							55° Mean daily temperature.		

CHAP. IV.

JOURNEY,

FROM MICHILIMACKINAC TO THE SAULT DE ST. MARIE.

XXI. Day.—(*June 13th.*)

THE provisions and stores shipped from Detroit, did not reach 'Mackinac until the 10th instant. We also found our canoes deficient both in size and construction, and that to embark the provisions of the expedition, an additional number would be required. To secure our corn, flour, bacon, &c more completely from exposure, it was considered advantageous to get the principal part of these articles packed up in ten gallon kegs, an arrangement that would also very much facilitate the loading and unloading, which must, at least, be performed every morning and evening. Additional sources of delay arose from military equipments, the tardiness of mechanics, and unfavourable winds, which prevented us from quitting 'Mackinac, until this morning. Our whole force now consisted of forty-two persons, embarked in four canoes, exclusive of a detachment of twenty-two soldiers from the garrison of 'Mackinac, under the command of Lieut. Pierce, which occupied a twelve oared barge. This escort was deemed necessary to accompany us to the Sault, where the Indians were reported to entertain a spirit of hostility towards the United States, and some even went so far as to affirm that they would attempt to stop our passage through Lake Superior. We left the harbour of 'Mackinac at ten o'clock in the morning, with a favourable breeze, which carried us at the rate of five miles per hour, and passing the *De Tour* before sun-set, ascended the straits of St. Mary, five miles, and encamped on the west shore, opposite Drummond's Island. The entire distance is forty-five miles. The intermediate places of most note, are Outarde Island, at the distance of three leagues from Michilimackinac, and the mouth of Rapid river, which is passed at the distance of twenty miles.

The banks of Lake Huron are generally low and swampy ; in some places there are sandy plains, covered with pine. The shore is strewed with fragments of limestone, granite, and hornblende ; and the former, in the compact form, appears *in situ*, at the few places where we had an opportunity to examine it. A ridge of highland appears on the main land east of 'Mackinac, stretching off towards the Sault de St. Marie, in a general course, northeast. This ridge apparently belongs to that mountain chain of which the island of Michilimackinac is, probably, one of the disjointed links ; but we are not enabled to say that this remark will be justified by geological correspondences.

The Detour is the western cape of the Straits of St. Mary, distant forty miles from Michilimackinac, and situated, according to McKenzie, in north latitude 45° 54′. Here our course is suddenly changed from E. to N. and N. W. consequently the wind, which was favourable thus far, proved a serious inconvenience at the moment of our turning the point. No current in the Strait has, however, as yet, been experienced. The mercury has not risen over 63° in the shade, although standing at 82° in the sun. In the course of the afternoon of this day, on landing in a small cove, on the Huron shore, we saw a large porcupine upon the beach, on which one of the voyageurs immediately jumped out of the canoe, and killed it with a hatchet. This animal has generally been confounded, by the travellers of the region, with the hedge-hog, which is entirely different in its characters and habits, and is not supposed to inhabit the northern regions of America, although it is frequently found in high northern latitudes in Europe,—as in Norway, Sweden, and Russia. Buffon gives two engravings of the porcupine, as distinct species, under the name of *L'Urson*, and *Le Coendou*, both said to inhabit the Canadas. But there is some reason to suppose that he has described the same animal in its summer and winter dress, as the thinness and scarcity of hair on his *L'Urson*, is the principal characteristic difference. The porcupine is known to shed a great portion of its hair as the warm season approaches. This animal is called *Caqua*, by the Indians, by whom it is highly valued for its quills. The skin does not form an article of traffic, but it serves them as a vessel to hold bears oil, and as medicine bags or short pouches. The quills are dyed, with indigenous plants, of various beautiful colours, and employed to trim the edges of their mockasins, leggons, skins, and dresses. The colours, which are red, blue, green, black, and yellow, are very bright and permanent, and a mockasin or Indian shoe, which has been thus ornamented, may be worn any length of time, in mud and water, without perceiving that the colouring matter of the quills is any way obliterated or discharged. The Indians are also very fond of the flesh of this animal, which is said to be delicious, and to resemble in flavour a young pig. It fixes its habitation under the roots of trees, but being provided with sharp claws, also ascends their boughs in quest of fruit. There are four claws on each fore paw, and *five* on the hinder ones. It has small ears, hid in the hair, and a long bushy tail covered with coarse hair, white and black. It is a lazy animal, seldom going more than a mile from its habitation ; has a slow motion, and is easily overtaken and killed. When attacked it appears to rely, with a foolish confidence, upon its quills, which are, in reality, a very inefficient defence. It has no power to eject them, but when touched, they easily leave the skin, but will not work their way into the flesh, as has been represented. The Indians, however, employ them for boring their ears and noses. They seldom make use of the rifle in killing this animal, but run up and despatch it with the tomahawk. The one now killed would probably weigh eight pounds.

XXII. Day.—(*June 14th.*) We embarked at five o'clock in the morning, and reached the Sault de St. Marie, in season to pitch our tents before sun set. The distance is forty-five miles. The country continues low and swampy, until you come within three or four miles of the Sault, where it is handsomely elevated. There are two rapids in the intermediate distance, which are ascended with loaded canoes. The lake or strait, may be supposed to cease, and the river to commence, at the foot of the first rapid called *Miscoutin* or *Nibish*, as there is no perceptible current below it, where the strait assumes a great width, and is filled with innumerable islands. Keeping close to the western shore, these islands constantly bound the view on the east until within five miles of the Sault, where the different channels unite. The ship channel lies on the east side of the islands, where the great body of water passes, and the rapids are less formidable. In passing up the rapid of Nibish, in the west channel, which is generally taken by canoes, we experienced a very swift current, and shallow water, and injured our canoes so much that we were compelled on reaching the head of it, to unload, and repair. It was one o'clock when we passed the rapid, and this accident consumed a couple of hours. In the meantime the sky became overcast, the wind arose and blew ahead, and very heavy peals of thunder, indicated an approaching storm. After waiting sometime, however, without getting any rain, we reloaded the canoes and embarked, and had proceeded five or six miles when a heavy shower of rain commenced. It did not compel us to land, and at six o'clock in the evening the sky was clear. We now passed the site of the village of St. Joseph, upon the island of the same name, where the British maintained a garrison before the late war, but it was demolished by Col. Croghan previous to his attack upon the island of Michilimackinac, and the village burnt. Since that period the English have fortified Drummond's island at the entrance of the straits, which is now the depot of their Indian trade. The island of St. Joseph is large and fertile, and was considerably cultivated previous to the late war. It is computed to be seventy-five miles in circumference, and to cover an area of fifty-seven thousand six hundred acres, which is seven times the size of the island of 'Mackinac. The site of the demolished fort, is elevated about fifty feet, and is extremely beautiful and commanding. It was first occupied by the British in 1795, preparatory to the surrender of 'Mackinac which took place the following year. The stone chimneys of the former houses are still standing to attest the barbarous policy of war. At eight o'clock we passed the second rapid, but without injury to our canoes. This is situated two miles below the village of the Sault, and on reaching the head of it, we have a handsome view of that village, with the intervening river and shore, and the dense forest of elm, sugar maple, ash, and pine, which lines this part of the river. In passing up this river from the Detour no change in the geological appearances of the country are seen, until we approach the head of the island of St. Joseph, where the compact limestone disappears, and is succeeded by a red sand stone. The latter rock is particularly apparent, at the ensuing rapid in the bed of the river, and continues from that onward.

XXIII. Day.—(*June 15th.*)—The Sault de St. Marie, is the largest of three rapids which impede the navigation of the river St. Mary between Lake Superior and Lake Huron, and puts a final stop to the ship navigation of the northern lakes. It is situated fifteen miles below the foot of Lake Superior, and ninety northwest of the island of 'Mackinac, in N. latitude 46° 31′ according to McKenzie. The fall of the river, at this rapid, as ascertained by Col. Gra-

PLATE III.

H. R. Schoolcraft del. Rawdon sc.

SAULT DE S^T. MARIE

ALBANY, PUBLISHED BY E. & E. HOSFORD 1821

tiot, is twenty-two feet ten inches, in little more than half a mile, which is nearly the same as the fall of the Ohio at Louisville in the distance of two miles.* Unlike that, however, it can never, at any season of the year, be ascended with large vessels. Canoes and barges usually go up with half a load, the balance being carried over the portage, but in returning, descend with a full load. The bed of the river consists of horizontal strata of red and variegated sand stone, which have been much worn, broken, and carried away, and large fragments of it, together with blocks of mixed granite and hornblende, out of place, are thickly strewed throughout the rapid, and by opposing the rush of water, throw it violently in all directions, and at the distance of half a mile give it the appearance of a bank of foam. Several wooded islands upon the inclined plane of the falls, by contrasting the deep green foliage of the hemlock, spruce, and pine, with the snowy whiteness of the rapids, produce a contrast which has a pleasing effect; and with the shadowy outlines of the distant mountains of Lake Superior, the singular mixture of forest trees upon the shores, and the fishing canoes of the savages, which are constantly seen at the foot of the falls, render it one of the most picturesque views of northern scenery. I have attempted to seize upon some of the prominent features of this scene in the accompanying sketch, (Plate 3,) which may also serve to convey an idea of the unusual manner in which the maple, and the pine,—the elm, and the hemlock, are intermingled in the forests upon the banks of this beautiful stream.

* See Dr. Drake's Natural and Statistical View of Cincinnati, and the Miami country, p. 15.

The village of the Sault de St. Marie, is on the south or American shore, and consists of from fifteen to twenty buildings, occupied by five or six French and English families. Among the latter is that of J. Johnston, Esq. a gentleman of rank, who, in the prosecution of the northwest fur trade, settled here shortly after the close of the American revolution, and married the daughter of a Chippeway chief. In the hospitality and politeness, which during our stay at the Sault, we experienced in this family, we have been made to forget our insulated situation, and to observe how short a participation in the blandishments of refined society, is sufficient to obliterate the effect of the fatigues and privations of travelling. The site of the village is elevated and pleasant, and a regular plan appears to have been observed in the buildings, though some of them are in a state of dilapidation, and altogether it has the marks of an ancient settlement fallen to decay. Such indeed it is, having been settled by the French shortly after the occupation of *old* 'Mackinac, and it continued for a long time the site of a French fort and Jesuit mission. Charlevoix, in 1721, speaks of this mission as one of no recent date,* and Henry, in 1762, found here a stockaded fort, with a small garrison, under the command of a French national officer, who was colloquially addressed by the title of *Governor.*† There were then four houses, two of which had been occupied as barracks, and the fort is described as "seated on a beautiful plain, of about two miles in circumference, and covered with luxu-

* Charlevoix's Journal, Vol. II. p. 45.

† Henry's Travels, p. 58.

riant grass, and within half a mile of the *Rapids*." Although no vestiges of the old fort remain, this description of the site is perfectly accurate at the present moment. It has always been the residence of Indian tribes, who are drawn to this spot in great numbers, by the advantages of taking the white-fish, which are very abundant at the foot of the rapid. There are, at present, about forty lodges of Chippeway Indians, (called *Saulteurs*, by the French,) containing a population of about two hundred souls, who subsist wholly upon the white-fish. "The method of taking them is this:—Each canoe carries two men, one of whom steers with a paddle, and the other is provided with a pole, ten feet in length, and at the end of which is affixed a scoop net. The steersman sets the canoe from the eddy of one rock to that of another; while the fisherman, in the prow, who sees, through the pellucid element, the prey of which he is in pursuit, dips his net, and sometimes brings up at every succeeding dip, as many as it can contain. The fish are often crowded together in the water in great numbers, and a skilful fisherman, in autumn, will take five hundred in two hours. This fishery is of great moment to the surrounding Indians, whom it supplies with a large proportion of their winter's provision; for, having taken the fish in the manner described, they cure them by drying in the smoke, and lay them up in large quantities." (*Henry*.) These fish are preferred by most of our party to the 'Mackinac trout. Their abundance may hereafter render them an important article in the commerce of the upper lakes.

On the north, or Canadian shore of the river, there are also six or seven dwelling houses, occupied by

French and English families, exclusive of the Northwest Company's establishment, which is seated immediately at the foot of the Falls, and consists of a number of store and dwelling houses, a saw mill, and a boat yard. These are represented on the right side of the View of the Sault de St. Marie. Plate No. 3. This company have also constructed a canal, with a lock at its lower entrance, and a towing path for drawing up barges and canoes. At the head of the rapid they have built a pier from one of the islands, forming a harbour, and here a schooner is generally lying to receive the goods destined for the Grand Portage, and the regions northwest of Lake Superior.

XXIV. Day.—(*June* 16*th*.) The commanding position of the Sault de St. Marie, on the outlet of Lake Superior, and at the head of ship navigation, had early pointed it out to the French as an advantageous site for a military and a trading post, and we accordingly find that it was occupied as such at an early period of the settlement of Canada. By this place all the fur trade of the northwest is compelled to pass, and it is the grand thoroughfare of Indian communication for the upper countries, as far as the arctic circle. Independent of these circumstances, the advantages of taking the white-fish, at the foot of the Rapids, have always rendered it a place of resort to the Indian tribes of the region, particularly during the summer season, when the hunting is most precarious. No place could, therefore, be better adapted to acquire an influence over the savage tribes, to monopolize their commerce, and to guard the frontier settlements against their incursions. It is, indeed, surprising to reflect upon the early enterprize and sound judgment of the French in seizing upon the points, commanding all the natural avenues and passes of the lakes, particularly when it is considered that these selections must necessarily have been the result of an intimate acquaintance with the geographical features of the country. This is yearly proved by the re-occupation of posts and places long neglected, but the importance of which has become apparent in proportion as we have set a just value upon the Indian trade, and the natural advantages of the country. Perhaps in no instance is this more strikingly exemplified than in the Sault, the commanding position of which, although always known to the traders, has but lately been perceived by our government. The advantages which a rival nation has taken of this neglect, could not fail to excite attention at a period when such laudable exertions are making in all parts of the Union to explore the geography, and to call into action the hidden resources of the country; and it appears to have been among the primary objects of the expedition to prepare the way for the introduction of an American garrison at this place. To attain this object, a council of the chiefs of the Chippeway tribe was this morning summoned at the Governor's marque, and the views of the government explained to them. By the treaty of Greenville, of 1795, a saving clause had been inserted by Gen. Wayne, covering any gifts or grants of land in the Northwest Territories, which the Indians had formerly made to the French or English governments,* and this clause has been renewed or

* In the third article of this treaty, after reciting a number of particular cessions of lands, posts and carrying places, number

confirmed by treaties with the same tribes since the conclusion of the late war.* Under this treaty, the United States claimed the concession formerly made at the Sault, to the French, by virtue of which it had been occupied as a military post. It was now proposed to treat for settling the boundaries of the grant, and in this way obtain an acknowledgment and renewal of it. These things were distinctly stated through the interpreter. The Indians, seated in their usual ceremonious manner, listened with attention, and several of the chiefs spoke in reply. They were evidently opposed to the proposition, and first endeavoured to evade it, by pretending to know nothing of the former grant, but this point being pressed home, was afterwards given up.—still they continued to speak in an evasive and desultory manner, which amounted to a negative refusal. It was also observable that there was no great unanimity of opinion among them, and some animated discussion, between themselves, took place. Some appeared in favour of settling the boundary, provided it was not intended to be occupied by a garrison, saying, that they were afraid in that case, their

ed from one to eleven, it also cedes, "12th. The post of Detroit, and all the land to the north, the west, and the south of it, of which the Indian title has been extinguished by gifts or grants to the French or English governments," &c. *Treaty with the Wyandot, Delaware, Shawanee, Ottaway, Chippeway, Pottawatami, Miamie, Eel-river, Weea, Kickapoo, Piankashaw and Kaskaskia nations. Greenville, 3d August*, 1795.—*Land Laws of the United States*, p. 56.

* By the treaty of Detroit, or Spring Wells, of the 8th September, 1815, and by the treaty of Fort Harrison, of the 4th June, 1816.

young men might prove unruly, and kill the cattle and hogs that should stray away from the garrison. This was intended as an insidious threat, and I was particularly struck with the reply of Gov. Cass, to the chief who had thrown it out, in which he said,—that as to the establishment of a garrison at the Sault, they might give themselves no uneasiness, for that point was already settled, and so sure as the sun, which was then rising, would set, so sure would there be an American garrison sent to that place, whether they renewed the grant or not. Such decision has always great weight with the Indians, and in the present instance was particularly so, as a casual, but indiscreet and unauthorised conversation which had been held by some officers of our party with one of the chiefs, before the council assembled, had given them to understand that the United States did not wish to occupy the Sault as a military post. They were, however, determined not to accede to our wishes, and in seeing ourselves surrounded by a brilliant assembly of chiefs, dressed in costly broadcloths, feathers, epaulets, medals, and silver wares, of British fabric, and armed from the manufactories of Birmingham, all gratuitously given, we could not mistake the influence by which they were actuated in this negociation. When, therefore, several hours had been spent, during the latter part of which the Indians employed a very animated language, and strong gesticulation, the council broke up, somewhat abruptly, without coming to any final decision, at least, without assenting to the proposition. The last chief who spoke, called "the Count,"(a brigadier in the British service,) in the course of his speech, drew his war-lance and stuck it furiously in the ground before him, and assumed a look of savage wildness, which appeared to produce a corresponding effect upon the other Indians, for there was an evident agitation among them, during the latter part of the council; and when he left the marque kicked away the presents which had been laid before him. On breaking up, they proceeded directly to their encampment, and we dispersed to our tents. A few moments only had, however, elapsed, before it was discovered that the Indians had hoisted the British flag in the midst of their encampment. On being informed of this, Gov. Cass immediately ordered the expedition under arms, and calling the interpreter, proceeded, with no other escort, to the lodge of the chief, before whose door it had been erected, took down the insulting flag, and carried it back to our camp. Upon this occasion he entered the lodge of the chief who had raised it, (the same who had before drawn his war-lance in council,) and told him it was an indignity they were not permitted to offer upon the American territories,—that we were their natural guardians and friends, and were always studious to render them strict justice, and to promote their peace and happiness; but the flag was the distinguishing token of national power, connected with our honour and independence,—that two national standards could not fly in peace upon the same territory,—and that they were forbid to raise any but our own, and if they should again presume to attempt it, the United States would set a strong foot upon their necks, and crush them to the earth.* This intrepid

* I do not pretend to quote the exact language of the Governor, or to be positive as to every sentiment uttered, not having heard him, but rely upon my recollection of the account given by the

conduct struck the Indians with astonishment, and produced an effect,—which we were not at the moment sensible, was all that prevented an open rupture. In ten minutes from the Governor's return to our camp, the Indians cleared their lodges of every woman and child, covering the river with canoes, and expecting so decisive a step to be followed by a general attack of their camp. In the mean time it was looked upon by the expedition, as a preparatory movement to the savage war whoop, and we stood prepared to encounter the shock. Our number, at this time, including Lieut. Pierce's command, was sixty-six men, well armed and prepared ; about thirty of whom were United States soldiers. The number of Indian warriors then upon the ground was between seventy and eighty, being also well armed in the Indian manner. Our encampment was regularly formed upon the green, near the banks of the river. The Indians occupied an eminence which was formerly the site of the French fort, at the distance of five or six hundred yards, and separated from us by a small ravine. We were kept in this state of alarm for some time, when the Indians having ceased to hold themselves in a hostile attitude, the soldiers were dismissed to their tents. In the mean time, an overture was proposed by some of the older chiefs, who had not been present at the council in the morning, and about seven o'clock in the evening a treaty was concluded and signed, by

interpreter, (the only person with him,) on his return to camp. I should not take the liberty of quoting it at all, were it not necessary to shew the feeling of resentment with which the insult was received, and to explain our critical situation upon that occasion.

which they cede to the United States a tract of land four miles square, commencing at the Sault, and extending two miles up, and the same distance down the river, with a depth of four miles, including the portage, and the site of the village and old fort, but reserving the right of fishing at the falls, and of encampment upon the shore. When the agreement was concluded, the Indian ceremony of smoking the pipe of peace, and shaking hands, as mentioned in DAY X. was performed, and their signatures by mark, were afterwards obtained. For this cession of land they were paid on the spot, in blankets, knives, silver wares, broadcloths, and other Indian goods.

CHAP. V.

JOURNEY,

FROM THE SAULT DE ST. MARIE TO THE ONTONAGON RIVER ON LAKE SUPERIOR.

XXV. Day.—(*June 17th.*)

DURING our stay at the Sault, eleven barges and canoes from the upper lakes descended the rapids affording us a handsome opportunity to witness the skill of the voyageurs in conducting canoes over this dangerous leap. They were principally laden with furs and skins for the North West and American companies. At nine o'clock in the morning, we commenced the ascent of the Sault, the canoes carrying half loads, while the soldiers were employed in carrying the remainder of the baggage across the portage, which is a little more than half a mile in length. It was six o'clock in the afternoon, before this labour was finished, when we embarked and proceeded six miles to Point aux Pins, on the Canadian side of the river; and this is the only night during the whole expedition which we passed in the Canadian territory. Point aux Pins was formerly noted as the site of a ship yard, and had a few buildings to accommodate the workmen, but the vestiges of these only remain. The width and depth of the river at this place, must have rendered it a favourable spot for launching vessels. The current is very gentle, and the shore sandy, and entirely free from rocks. The thermometer this day at 3 P. M. stood at 82°, being the highest point at which it has been observed upon the river St. Mary.*

XXVI. Day.—(*June 18th.*)—We embarked at six o'clock in the morning. The distance from Point aux Pins to the entrance into Lake Superior, was now three leagues, the river spread broadly before us, and the highlands which had been dimly seen from the Sault, presented their imposing outlines distinctly to the view, and were every moment assuming a new and more interesting character. The morning was clear and pleasant, with a gentle breeze blowing up the river, which, while it filled our sails and relieved the voyageurs from labour, produced an exhilerating effect upon our spirits, by its refreshing coolness; and we approached the lake with a feeling of impatient delight. The most enchanting views were presented in every direction, and we fully realized the justice of the remark made by Carver "that the entrance into Lake Superior affords one of the most pleasing prospects in the world." Suddenly, however, a storm arose, and compelled us precipitately to land, and we were here detained from five

* *Thermometrical observations on the journey from Mackinac to Lake Superior.*

DATE. 1820.	Place of observation.	A. M. 6	8	10	12	P. M. 1	3	4	7	9	Mean heat.	Wind and Weather.
June 13th	Mack. to Detour.	53			61	63				58	59	Wind, S. W.
" 14th.	St. Mary's River	55		60		73			57		61	Rain.
" 15th.	Sault de St. Marie.		66		67		69		56		64	Clear.
" 16th.	" "		59	70	76		81		66		69	Clear.
" 17th.	" "		[illegible]8		77		82	80		78	75	Clear.
" 18th.	Head Riv. St. Mary		56		70	76			68		67	RainThunder&c
											395	
											66° mean dai. heat.	

to six hours. In the mean time the rain fell in torrents, attended with very frequent peals of the most severe and appalling thunder. At one in the afternoon, the weather was perfectly clear and delightful, when we again embarked. The entrance into Lake Superior was now in full view, presenting a scene of beauty and magnificence which is rarely surpassed, even amid the rugged scenery of the north. The river St. Mary here issues from a deep bay of the lake, and passes out between two high promontories called Point Iroquois,* and the Grand Cape, which appear, at some remote period of the creation, to have been rent asunder, by one of those unaccountable convulsions which have produced so much confusion upon the surface of the earth. This opinion is rendered probable from the general course, elevation, and other appearances of the chain of mountains which here runs parallel with the lake shore, and I regret that we were not permitted to land and examine the geological appearances of the rock strata on both sides, in order to detect a physical analogy which is now only conjectural. I felt this regret the more sensibly, as my expectations had previously been excited by the account of an important mineral discovery, which Henry states to have been formerly made at the foot of the southern promontory, which is Point Iroquois.† But these considerations, were merged

* This point takes its name from the circumstance of a large party of Iroquois Indians having suffered a signal defeat upon it, from a body of Fox's, Ottagamies, and Chippeways. So say Carver and Henry.

† The following extract embraces the notice alluded to. "Mr. Norburg, a Russian gentleman, acquainted with metals, and holding a commission in the 60th Regt. and then in garrison at Michi-

in objects of greater moment, and after our long detention by the storm, and the favourable wind we now enjoyed, the advantages of a speculative enquiry, or the chance of falling upon a useful discovery, opposed too feeble an argument for a further, and to be useful, a more considerable detention. On passing this point, the lake spread like a sea before us. Towards the north, we could discern across the bay the distant highlands which border the Canadian shore of the lake, while on the south the mountain chain extending from the head of the river St. Mary, westward, towered majestically into the air, and presented a fine contrast to the boundless expanse of waters at its base. In coasting along the shore for fifteen miles we passed the mouth of Tanquamenon river, with a small island of the same name lying off its mouth, and proceeded three leagues beyond where we encamped at eleven o'clock at night, at the mouth of Shelldrake river, having advanced altogether a distance of thirty-four miles. We generally kept within a mile of the shore, and often much nearer so that it was constantly in plain sight. The shore of the lake thus far is sandy, without large pebbles, and with no bluff rocks at the water's edge, although the highlands a few miles back, rise to a great height. The growth of timber is pine, hemlock, (pinus canadensis) oak, aspen, and birch. At Shelldrake river, we found se-

limackinac, accompanied us on this expedition. As we rambled among the *shods* or loose stones in search of minerals, Mr. Norburg chanced to find one of eight pounds weight, of a blue colour, and semi-transparent. This he carried to England, where it produced in the proportion of sixty pounds of silver to a hundred weight of ore. It was reposited in the British Museum."

Henry's Travels, p. 231.

veral lodges of Chippeway Indians, who are drawn to this spot by the advantages of taking fish at the mouth of the river; they appeared friendly—presented us some dried white fish, and received in return, some tobacco.

XXVII. Day.—(*June 19th.*)—At the moment we were prepared to embark, a number of northwest barges, worked with oars, were descried approaching from the west, and we concluded to await their arrival. It proved to be Mr. Morrison, an agent of the American Fur Company, with five heavy barges laden with furs from the Fond du Lac department, on his annual return to Michilimackinac. From him we obtained information respecting the best route of communication from the head waters of Lake Superior to those of the Mississippi, with some valuable topographical memoranda, and in consequence did not leave Sheldrake river until eight o'clock. We had scarcely gone a league when we met eighteen or twenty canoes of Chippeway Indians on their way to the Sault de St. Marie and Michilimackinac. Always expecting some presents on such occasions, they were anxious for a conference and made signs for us to stop, and some of their canoes came along side, but sailing with a good wind, we passed on. At the distance of nine miles we turned White Fish Point, which is a barren peninsula of sand, stretching a considerable distance into the lake, with a few aspen trees, and rising in some places in naked hills of sand, which the wind is continually whirling into the air, and depositing in banks and ridges, like drifting snow. Here a considerable alteration of course brought the wind directly ahead, so that we were compelled to lower sail, and in a short time, a storm approaching from the west, drove us to land. While thus detained an express from the Sault de St. Marie, overtook us bringing letters for the Governor, &c. It was a bark canoe, very light, and strongly manned, and after tarrying a couple of hours, was despatched back. In the mean while, the wind had subsided, and after progressing ten miles we encamped upon the sand. The shore of the lake has been, thus far, a perfect sand bank, without a pebble to variegate the beach, but with patches of iron-sand, (the black paper sand of commerce) abundantly dispersed over a broad and level beach. At a short distance back from the lake, a thin stratum of vegetable mould has accumulated upon the sand and sustains a forest of pines, spruce, birch, and aspen, but the humble growth indicates the sterility of the soil.

XXVIII. Day.—(*June 20th.*)—We left our encampment this morning at half past five. In going twelve miles, we reached the mouth of Two-Hearted river, a small stream not navigable with canoes; and seven leagues beyond passed the outlet of a very extensive marsh, called the Grande Marráis. Immediately west of this commences the Grand Sablé, a lofty ridge of naked sand extending nine miles along the shore, and presenting a steep acclivity towards the lake. Its medium height, as estimated by Dr. Wolcott of the expedition, is three hundred feet, and it presents a novel and interesting appearance from the lake. The views, however, although generally commanding, present a great uniformity, and leave upon the mind a strong impression of bleakness and desolation. Even the few bushes and trees which are occasionally seen, serve to increase this effect by their impoverished growth, while the birds of prey which we observed hovering around these bleak sandy heights, could hardly be considered as ameliorating the dreariness of the prospect. The bald eagle perched upon a shattered tree half buried in the sand, looked down upon us in security, from a height of three hundred feet, while the noisy raven, and the slow sailing falcon, were perpetually upon the wing. These birds are generally drawn together upon elevated bluffs and barren heights, that they may more easily discover and be directed to their prey, either in the adjoining waters or upon the land, and at the same time they are thus protected from the unseen approach of their enemies. But it may be doubted whether they do not always add to the forbidding appearances of such scenes as are naturally sterile, and destitute of vegetation. There is, however, no scene wholly without attractions, and by an admirable arrangement in the works of nature, what is denied to bleak places in vegetable beauty, is often supplied in the rarity of animated nature, or in the order of the unorganized strata of mineral matter; and it is in the latter respect, that the Grand Sablé affords an interesting object of consideration. It is composed of three layers of sand, lying horizontally, and distinctly marked as separate deposits. The first stratum rising from the water, is a light yellow silicious sand, unmixed, and about one hundred and fifty feet in depth; then succeeds a deposit of the same substance, very much mixed with pebbles of granite, hornblende, limestone, and quartz; and this forms the distinguishing mark of the middle stratum, which may be eighty feet in thickness. The upper stratum is loose yellow sand, in every respect similar to the first or lower deposit, except that it is continually acted upon by the winds, and contains imbedded trunks of trees, some of which remain in the position in which they grew, but have been buried by drifting sand nearly to their tops, and thus killed. The depth of this top-stratum may be estimated at sixty or seventy feet. I have made all these estimates, however, on the assumed altitude of the entire bank, as before stated, and although this may be incorrect, yet the relative thickness of the three strata, may thus, with tolerable accuracy, be judged. It is impossible to view these stupendous sand hills, without being at the same time strongly impressed with the idea that they owe their arrangement and present order of superposition to the agency of water, and that this fluid has at some former period covered their highest tops. Dr. Wolcott, who with considerable labour ascended these sandy eminences, discovered a small lake of pure water, at no great distance back, and on his return presented me several mineral specimens, picked up during the excursion, which bear the appearances of volcanic origin, together with a couple of specimens of corralline petrifactions. The specimens which suggest the idea of volcanic production, appear to be granitic aggregates semi-vitrified, at least, on the surface, which possesses the smoothness and gloss of common glass. Some of these specimens are black, without gloss, harsh to the touch, and vesicular, resembling certain lavas, but all possess a considerable specific gravity, and will sink in water.*

* I have not been able since my return to submit these specimens to the examination of any accurate mineralogist, or to un

These hints may serve to direct the attention of future travellers to this subject, which I have only to regret other objects of the expedition did not allow us leisure to investigate.

On passing along the coast of the Grand Sablé, we observed, through the water which is very transparent, large tabular rocks, in situ, at the bottom of the lake beneath our canoes, and on encamping a short distance west of the termination of these sand banks, at *La Pointe La Grand Sablé*, we found, apparently, a similar rock, jutting out upon the shore of the lake, and rising to an elevation of eight or ten feet above the water. On examination, this proved to be a variegated sand stone in horizontal strata, tolerably compact, and consisting of coarse grains of silicious sand, united apparently by an argillaceous cement. Its colour is white or red, arranged in spots and stripes. No traces of shells or corrallines, could here be detected in the rock. It is covered by an alluvial deposit of a few feet in depth bearing cedars, pines, hemlock, and birch, with some beech, oak, and maple interspersed. We encamped on a beach of sand, near the entrance of a small creek, which, from a violent storm that raged during the night, was called Hurricane creek. This storm had threatened us before reaching the land, and in a short time after, the wind raged with the utmost violence, and threw the lake into such disorder, that the water drove into the Governor's

dertake myself any experiment upon their composition, and am not therefore prepared to decide upon their mineralogical character. There is some reason to conclude, that the glossy specimens owe their lustre to the effects of water, although from their indented surface, it could not have been effected by common attrition.

marque, pitched fifty yards from the margin, and lashed it down. At the same time the thunder was very frequent and severe, and when the fury of the gale abated, a heavy rain drenched every part of our camp.

XXIX. Day.—(*June 21st.*)—The rain still continued at early day light, and the sea-like swells of the lake broke furiously upon the shore long after the wind had entirely ceased. At sun-rise the atmosphere began to assume its usual serenity, the clouds broke away rapidly, and before eight o'clock we had the most delightful weather. It was eleven, however, before the lake regained sufficient tranquillity to permit us to embark. A perfect calm now reigned in the atmosphere, and we continued the voyage with renovated spirits. On going three leagues, we reached the commencement of the Pictured Rocks, (*La Portaillé, of the French Voyageurs,*) a series of lofty bluffs, which continue for twelve miles along the shore, and present some of the most sublime and commanding views in nature. We had been told, by our Canadian guide, of the variety in the colour and form of these rocks, but were wholly unprepared to encounter the surprising groupes of overhanging precipices, towering walls, caverns, water falls, and prostrate ruins, which are here mingled in the most wonderful disorder, and burst upon the view in ever-varying and pleasing succession. In order to convey any just idea of their magnificence, it is necessary to premise, that this part of the shore consists of a sand stone rock of a light grey colour internally, and deposited stratum super-stratum to the height of three hundred feet, rising in a perpendicular wall from the water, and extending from four to five leagues in length. This rock is made up of coarse grains of sand, united by a calcareous cement, and occasionally imbedding pebbles of quartz and other water-worn fragments of rocks, but adhering with a feeble force, and, where exposed to the weather, easily crushed between the fingers. Externally, it presents a great variety of colour, as black, red, yellow, brown, and white, particularly along the most permanent parts of the shore, but where masses have newly fallen, its colour is a light grey.* In no place does the recent fracture disclose any traces of red, and the variety of outward colouring is owing partly to mineral waters which appear to have oozed out of the crevices of the rock, but mainly, to the washing down of the banks of coloured clay from the superincumbent soil. Thus, although a great variety of surface is presented, there is, in reality, none in its geological character.† This stupendous wall of rock, exposed to the fury of the

* Adhering too rigidly to the definitions of those geologists who consider graywacke as consisting "essentially of grains of quartz, cemented together by indurated clay," I was inclined, at the moment, to apply the term to this stratum of rock. But a subsequent examination of my specimens proves that it is composed essentially of grains of quartz cemented by a *calcareous* substance. It preserves also the granular structure, friability, and uniformity of composition of common sand stone, although the *white colour and limey consistence* of the cementing matter, gives it, on the first glance, an appearance foreign to this class of rocks.

† In this respect, (the variety of external colours,) it resembles the *Calico Rock,* which I have formerly noticed upon the banks of White River, in Arkansaw Territory.—*See the New-York Monthly Journal and Belles Lettres Repository.*

waves, which are driven up by every north wind across the whole width of Lake Superior, has been partially prostrated at several points, and worn out into numerous bays, and irregular indentations. All these front upon the lake, in a line of aspiring promontories, which, at a distance, present the terrible array of dilapidated battlements and desolate towers.

> " Their rocky summits split and rent,
> " Form'd turret, dome, or battlement,
> " Or seemed fantastically set
> " With cupola or minaret,
> " Wild crests as pagod ever decked,
> " Or mosque of eastern architect."

In some places the waves have lashed down the lower strata, while the upper ones hang in a threatening posture over the lake; in others, extensive caverns have been worn into the rock, and in this way rocky bluffs, nearly severed from the main, or left standing upon rude and massy pillars, between which barges and canoes might with safety sail. All that we have read of the natural physiognomy of the Hebrides—of Staffa,—the Doreholm, and the romantic Isles of the Sicilian coast, is forcibly recalled on viewing this scene, and it may be doubted whether, in the whole range of American scenery, there is to be found such an interesting assemblage of grand, picturesque, and pleasing objects. Among many striking features, two attracted particular admiration,—the Cascade La Portaille, and the Doric Arch. The cascade is situated about four miles beyond the commencement of the range of bluffs, and in the centre of the most commanding

PICTURED ROCKS, LAKE SUPERIOR

ALBANY, PUBLISHED BY E. & E. HOSFORD 1821.

part of it. It consists of a handsome stream, which is precipitated about seventy feet from the bluff into the lake at one leap. Its form is that of a rain bow, rising from the lake, to the top of the precipice. We passed near the point of its fall upon the surface of the lake, and could have gone, unwetted, between it and the rocks, as it is thrown a considerable distance into the lake. The Doric Rock, of which a profile is given on the title page, is an isolated mass of sand stone, consisting of four natural pillars, supporting a stratum or entablature of the same material, and presenting the appearance of a work of art. On the top of this entablature rests a stratum of alluvial soil, covered with a handsome growth of pine and spruce trees, some of which appear to be fifty or sixty feet in height. To add to the factitious appearance of the scene, that part of the entablature included between the pillars is excavated in the form of a common arch, giving it very much the appearance of a vaulted passage into the court yard of some massy pile of antiquated buildings. A little to the west of this rock, the *Miner's River* enters the lake by a winding channel, overshadowed with trees, and intersected by a succession of small rapids.

The annexed view, (Plate IV.) represents a range of bluffs, immediately west of the Doric Rock, as viewed from the lake, and embraces some of the wonderful excavations which diversify this part of the coast. Grand Isle appears in perspective.

In passing these rocks, one of our voyageurs picked up, upon the shore, and brought to me, a green translucent pebble, of a spheroidal figure, and two ounces in weight. A subsequent examination of this mineral induces me to consider it as Prase, which is arranged by Cleaveland, as a sub-species of quartz. Its colour is a light uniform leek green, and fully translucent. It has a quartzy hardness, and somewhat of a waxy lustre, but exhibits no appearances of a crystalline structure,—its spheroidal shape is owing to attrition. This mineral is stated to owe its colour to actynolite, or epidote, and to be sometimes employed in jewelry. May not the oxyd of copper be the colouring ingredient in some cases?

In landing in one of the coves to examine the geological appearances, and procure specimens of the rock, I found, among an infinite variety of pebbles, which are washed up on the beach, several fragments of carnelian, and a species of hornstone jasper, in alternate bands of red, black, &c. These appearances created a desire, which it was impossible, however, to satisfy, of making a more minute examination of the mineralogy of the coast. It is considered a dangerous pass when there is any wind on the lake, as there are very few places where a landing can be effected. The day, however, notwithstanding the boisterous weather of the morning, proved calm and pleasant, and we proceeded two leagues beyond the termination of this picturesque shore, and encamped on Grand Island, in a large, deep, and beautiful bay, completely land-locked. Here we found a village of Chippeway Indians, who, as soon as we landed, came from their lodges to bid us welcome. They manifested the most friendly disposition towards the party, and towards the United States; and when they were told of our objects in visiting their country, appeared highly pleased. The promptitude with which they offered the pipe of peace, left no doubt of their sincerity, and their subsequent conduct evinced that they felt themselves flattered by our visit. In the evening they assembled in our camp, to shew their skill in dancing, upon which they all pride themselves, and spent sometime in this amusement, which is also done as a mark of respect. In these festive feats, they were accompanied by their own music, consisting of a kind of tambarine, and a hollow gourd, filled with pebbles, while one of the number beat time upon a stick, and all joined in the Indian chant. There is something animating in the Indian chorus, and at the same time, it has an air of melancholy, but certainly nothing can be more monotonous, or farther removed from our ideas of music. These ceremonies lasted sometime, and were rather an annoyance to the party, to whom they presented nothing novel, and as is usual, were only a prelude to the customary presents of whiskey and tobacco. We found these Indians very poor, both as to clothing and provisions, but were struck with their manly figure and beautiful proportions. During the evening several speeches were addressed to the Governor, in the course of which we were told that they had lately returned from a war excursion against the Sioux, in which they had lost a number of warriors. but that they had fallen like brave men, and were worthy of being called Chippeways. It appears that the Indians of Grand Island had been reproached by the northern bands of the tribe for not taking a more active part in the war which has been so long waged between the Chippeways and the Sioux. To wipe off this stain, they determined to make an irruption into the Sioux country, without giving notice to any other part of the tribe, that they might claim the exclusive merit of their warlike deeds. Accordingly, a party of thirteen warriors proceeded, by the most unfrequented paths, into the midst of the Sioux territories, without meeting with any opposition, or exciting any premature alarm. Here, however, at a time when they did not expect it, they suddenly encountered a large war party of their enemies, amounting to ten times their number. As a negotiation of peace had been commenced between the two tribes, the Sioux were disposed to receive them as friends, and were very much surprised to hear them declare that they had left their homes on a war excursion,—that they had come a great way to meet them,—that they wanted to test their courage,—and that they rejoiced there was now an opportunity presented. The Sioux replied that they thought the Chippeways were tired of a long war, in which so much blood had been spilt,—that they were too few in number to hope for any success, and had better retire in peace to their own territories, as their destruction was otherwise inevitable. The Chippeways were, however, determined in their hostility, and had prepared themselves to die, and to sell their lives at the dearest rate, and the next morning attacked the Sioux in their camp. In a short time they were driven back to the place where they had determined to make a final stand, and which they had previously fortified by digging two large holes or intrenchments in the ground, capable of affording them a partial shelter. Into these intrenchments they retired, and maintained the unequal contest until they had expended their ammunition, and killed more than double their number, when the Sioux surrounded their intrenchments, and dispatched the survivors with their tomahawks. Of the number that retired into these holes, not one escaped, but they kept up a destructive fire upon their enemies, while their ammunition lasted, for they were protected during the time they retired to reload their guns. To transmit the fame of this exploit to their nation, they had appointed the youngest warrior of their number to watch on an adjoining hill, and when their fate was terminated, to carry the news to their friends. By this it seems that they had previously determined to die in their intrenchments. This messenger had not been long returned, when we reached Grand Island, where he sung the exploits of his departed friends. He was a tall and beautiful youth, with a manly countenance, expressive eyes, and formed with the most perfect symmetry,—and among all the tribes of Indians whom I have visited, I never felt, for any individual, such a mingled feeling of interest and admiration.

XXX. Day.—(*June 22d.*)—We embarked at six o'clock in the morning, the weather clear and calm. On coming out of the bay of Grand Island, we passed a small wooded island on the right, and on turning a point of land, traversed a bay of four leagues across, in the centre of which is situated the Isle aux Trains, and opposite to it, in the extremity of the bay, the River aux Trains discharges into the lake. On turning the next point, we put into a little bay and entered the mouth of Laughing Fish river, which is twenty yards wide, deep,—with reddish water, and a sandy shore. Near it are several large swamps, which maintain a connexion with Lake

Superior, through this little river, and a singular ebbing and flowing of its tide, is produced by the swells of the lake. This flux and reflux, was observed three times during our stay, a space of thirty or forty minutes. On leaving this we turned a prominent point of land, and steered N. 70° W. across a large bay in which are successively discharged Chocolate, Dead,* and Presque Isle rivers, all of which lay to the left of our track, and encamped on a point of land, which, from the first appearance of that rock, I shall denominate Granite Point. The distance across this bay, in a direct line, is eighteen miles, but by following the indentations of the shore, which is the usual route, it is fifty-one. The shore of the lake continues rocky from Grand Isle, to near Laughing Fish river, which is bordered by sandy plains. The rocks are red sand stone; on Isle aux Trains they dip towards the northeast. The forest trees are chiefly pine, hemlock, spruce, and birch. On reaching Granite Point a new scene presents itself. Here a bluff of granite rising out of the lake to a height of two hundred feet, is connected to the shore by a neck of land consisting of red and grey sand stone, in horizontal layers. This granite is made up of red feldspar, quartz, and a little mica, and very much mixed with hornblende. It lies in a confused bed, presenting perpendicular fissures, and traversed by regular veins of greenstone trap. These veins of greenstone vary from two to thirty feet in width, and are disposed to break in irregular columnar fragments, resembling, in some degree, the columns of true basalt. The sand stone laps upon the granite, and fits into its irregular indentations in a manner that

* At the mouth of this river, Iron Pyrites of a brass yellow colour, and metalic brilliancy, is found.

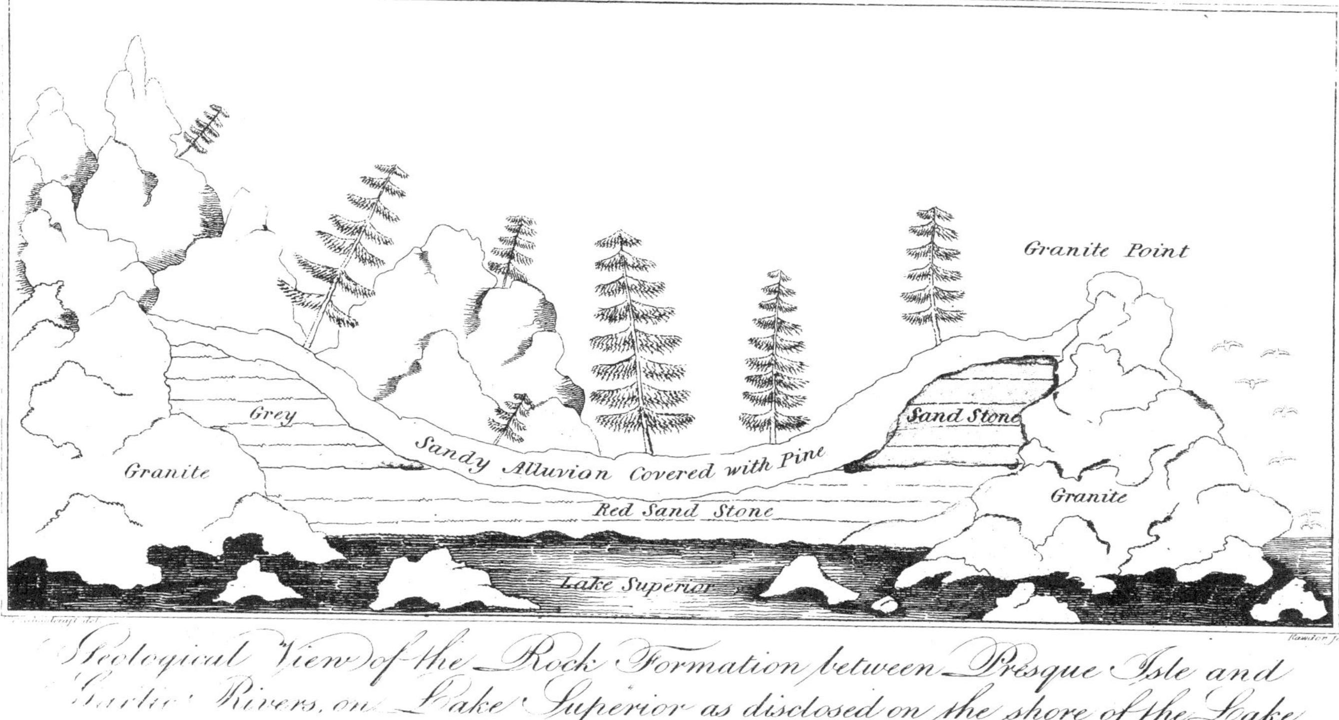

Geological View of the Rock Formation between Presque Isle and Garlic Rivers, on Lake Superior as disclosed on the shore of the Lake

shews it to have assumed that position subsequently to the upheaving of the granite. Its horizontality is perfectly preserved even to the immediate point of contact, which is laid bare to the view. A mutual decomposition for a couple of inches, into each rock has taken place. Dipping under the sand stone, the granite again rises on the contiguous coast in high, rough, and broken hills. All this is handsomely disclosed by a natural transverse section of the country, upon the rocky shore of the lake, and the peninsula, connecting it with Granite Point. This will give to the annexed view, (Plate V.) a value which geological sections, and suppositional charts, it must be conceded, too often lack. The entire width of the point may be estimated at half a mile, and that of the neck of land connecting it with the shore at two hundred yards. A sandy alluvion rests upon the whole, covered with yellow pine, (*pinus resinosa.*) As to the geological age of the sand stone, I possess no means of forming a decisive opinion. It consists of grains of quartz or sand, united by a calcareous cement, and coloured by the red oxyd of iron. Its colour is a brick red, and it possesses the compactness and grain of freestone. In some places it imbeds pebbles of quartz of the size of a pigeon's egg, together with rounded masses of hornblende and other rocks, and it then resembles the pudding stone. It has no imbedded relics of the animal or vegetable kingdom, so far as observed, but this is not always conclusive of the age of a rock viewed at a given point, for it is known that these relics are never uniformly distributed throughout the substance of rocks, even of the newest formations. Its position would indicate a near alliance to the "old red sand stone." Werner has considered this rock in all situations as secondary. Bakewell places it in the class of transition rocks, in which he is followed by McClure and by Eaton. I am not prepared to decide upon a point upon which my opportunities of observation have as yet been limited, and there appears to be something so objectional in the dogmatism with which these things are usually stated, that I shall content myself, in the present instance, with the bare recital of the facts above enumerated.

XXXI. Day.—(*June* 23*d*.)—The morning was cloudy and hazy, but we did not suffer these appearances to deter us from quitting our encampment at an early hour. In a few moments after getting under way, a fair breeze arose, and we proceeded to the next prominent point, a distance of five leagues, in three hours. Here we again saw granite rock overlayed by sand stone. The wind now flagging, we went under oars to the mouth of Huron river, a distance of eleven leagues, where we encamped at four in the afternoon, in consequence of rain. In the course of the day, we have successively passed the Garlic, St. John's, Salmon Trout, and Pine rivers, all streams of secondary magnitude, and originating in highlands at no great distance from the lake. These highlands which have been visible with the naked eye, appear from inspection with a glass, to consist of rugged peaks of granite. Off the Huron river, at the distance of five or six miles in the lake, lie the picturesque cluster of Huron Islands. They appear to be high, rocky, and barren, with some trees. Among the objects surrounding our encampment, an Indian grave, near the mouth of the Huron river, excited our curiosity. It was paled in with pine saplings, sharpened at the top, and regularly inclosing it in the form of a parrallelogram. A covering of bark bent over small poles in the form of a roof, secured the grave from the effects of the weather, and a blazed stake at one end, denoted the head. Between this stake and the grave, a smoothly cut piece of cedar wood with several Indian devices, served the purposes of a monumental record, upon which the figure of a bear denoted either the name of the deceased chief, or the tribe to which he belonged. Seven red marks were interpreted to signify that he had been seven times in battle. Other marks were not understood. It is probable, however, that they were commemorative of some of the most striking events of his life, which we are led to conclude, from these extraordinary marks of respect, had been devoted to the service of his tribe, or distinguished for some extraordinary achievements in hunting. This grave is situated on a sandy plain, which extends for many miles to the west of the Huron, and is covered principally with a growth of yellow pine. Among the shrubs and plants, the pyrola rotundifolia, or common winter green, is very abundant, and we here first noticed a creeping plant called *kinni-kinick* by the Indians, which is used as a substitute for tobacco. This plant appears to have escaped the notice of the indefatigable Pursh, nor do I find any description of it in Micheaux, or Eaton. It is a creeping evergreen with an ovate leaf, of a deep green colour, and velvet-like appearance, and is common to sandy soils. I suspect it to be a new variety of chimaphila.

The Indians prepare it by drying the leaf over a moderate fire, and bruising it between the fingers so that it, in some degree, resembles cut tobacco. In this state it is smoked, and is very mild and pleasant. They, however, prefer mixing it with a portion of the common tobacco, (*nicotiana tabacum*) or perhaps it is done with a view to economy. As the kinnikinick only flourishes on sandy grounds, it is not always to be procured, in which case they employ other substances, the most common of which is the bark scraped off the small red twigs of the acer spicatum, or maple bush. Certain species of willows are also resorted to.

XXXII. Day.—(*June 24th.*)—From Huron river it is eighteen miles to Keweena Point, which extends forty five miles into the lake, and is by far the most striking feature in the topography of the southern shore of Lake Superior. It has sometimes been confounded by geographers and travellers with Point Chegoimegon, which is a hundred and thirty miles further west, and the latter name loosely applied to either Point. Among those who have fallen into this error is Carver, who describes the copper mine, or Ontonagon river, as falling into the lake a hundred miles west of Point Chegoimegon, (Carver's Travels p. 67.) whereas it is found to be a little more than half that distance, west of Keweena. Henry, and McKenzie, have both drawn the proper distinction. In coasting around this point it is estimated to be ninety miles, but canoes shorten the journey by ascending the Portage river, which nearly insulates the point from the main shore, and make a portage of less than a mile into the lake west of the Point. To the east of this point there is a large bay twelve miles wide by twenty in length, called Keweena bay, which it is necessary to cross in order to reach the Portage river. The route from Huron river, is first six miles west to Point Abbaye, which is the eastern cape of Keweena bay, then we coast three leagues up the eastern shore, and make a traverse of twelve miles to the mouth of Portage river. This is often a dangerous passage when the weather is not perfectly settled, and was found so in the present instance. On turning point Abbaye we found a fresh breeze blowing directly ahead, but not apprehending any increase, and anxious to make as little delay as possible, we progressed up the bay the usual distance, and commenced the traverse without hesitation. When, however, only a league from land, the wind had increased to a strong breeze, which raised a considerable swell, and before we were half way across, the bay presented a sheet of foam, and our canoes were tossed about with scarcely the power of controlling them. A perfect gale prevailed, and every moment seemed to add to its violence. The swells broke frequently across our canoes, so that one hand was constantly necessary to bail it out, and we expected them to be broke in two at every succeeding swell. In this dilemma it appeared almost equally hazardous to turn back, or to progress, we were about an equal distance from either shore, with the wind blowing directly ahead; and the conductors of the different canoes were left to use their own discretion. Three, out of five canoes turned back, and reached the shore in safety, with some injury to the canoes. The other two, consisting of the Governor's and that under the command of Lieutenant Mackay, to which I was attached, after an exertion which exhausted the strength of every person on board, reached the mouth of Portage river, and encamped upon the beach before sun down. Distance 30 miles.

XXXIII. Day.—(*June 25th.*)—The canoes which were driven back by the winds yesterday, joined us this morning at seven o'clock, when we commenced the ascent of the Portage river. This is a stream of 50 yards wide, with a good depth of water. At the distance of six miles it expands into a lake which is twelve miles long, and from two to four in width, narrowing to about half a mile towards its head. Here a small stream enters which is just wide enough to admit a canoe to be worked with paddles. It is very serpentine in its course, and overhung with alders and shrubbery, with fallen trees in the channel, so that the ascent is attended with some difficulty. This stream is ascended six miles to its source in a bog meadow, during the latter part of which the canoes are dragged along through mud and water in a channel which is only wide enough for that purpose, and appears to have been partly formed by the voyageurs of former days. From this to the lake, there is a portage of two thousand yards which is passed at two Pauses,* the first of which is swampy, and the

* A Pause (pronounced pôze) is a resting place for the voyageurs, and is computed to be half a mile, but this depends somewhat upon local circumstances. If the country is very swampy or hilly, the pause is much shorter, and over a fine level country it is often three fourths of a mile. These stopping places are, however, regularly marked upon all the travelled portages so that they are always spoken of in the colloquial language of the region, as carrying places of one, two, or more pauses. Miles are wholly out of

other a dry sandy soil covered with tall pines. We reached the lake at an early hour in the afternoon, and formed our encampment upon the gravelly shore. The voyageurs and soldiers were employed in carrying baggage until dark, but did not complete the labour.

XXXIV. Day.—(*June 26th.*)—The forenoon of this day was occupied in carrying the remainder of the baggage and canoes across the portage. In the afternoon a head wind prevented our embarkation. While we were sitting upon a bank of clean pebbles upon the shore, at dinner, and admiring the variety of beautiful water-worn pebbles, I picked up a fragment of beautiful carnelian, and this gave the hint for making a search, in which a great number were afterwards found by different individuals of the party. I also discovered, while loitering along the shore, a mass of native copper, of nearly two pounds weight, attached to a water worn mass of serpentine rock, and a number of smaller pieces. Indeed grains of copper disseminated through pebbles of serpentine rock, are very common at this place, but this metal has not been observed in association with any other species of rock. Radiated zeolite, crystallized quartz, chalcedony, prase, jasper, opal, agate, and sardonyx, are also among the minerals picked up along this part of the shore. Of the specimens of carnelian, I procured several imbedded in rolled pebbles of amygdaloid, and in one instance, observed this mineral imbedded in a large detached mass

the question. Distances are altogether reckoned by leagues or pauses. The pauses are marked upon the carrying paths by little circular greens, where the voyageurs set down their packs.

of hornblende rock. All the rock along this shore, however, which was noticed, *in situ*, is either a red, grey, or variegated sand stone, which appears to be referable to one formation, colour being the only character in which any difference could be perceived. The very interesting character of the mineralogy at this place arrested the attention of several of our party, who had before felt no interest in this study, and from the spirit of imitation, several of the soldiers and voyageurs also turned collectors of specimens. But a greater novelty ensued, the Indians attached to the expedition, on being shewn the substances we were anxious to procure, also undertook the search, and with such good success, that I am indebted to them for some of the finest specimens I have from that locality. This is not the first attention they had manifested to the subject, for on a former occasion they assisted me in chizzeling organic relics from the rock, and seemed to take a delight in being serviceable in that way, although unable to comprehend the object of these collections. It was impossible to find corresponding words in their language to signify the benefit to be derived from geological studies, although they were anxious to be informed, and made repeated enquiries. There is a general impression among the Indians that we possess the skill of turning all minerals either into money or medicine. My attention to this subject had struck them upon the third or fourth day after our departure from Detroit, when they bestowed upon me a name, at least characteristic of my situation in the expedition.*

* *Paw-gwa-be-caw-e-ga.* The destroyer of rocks, or he who employs himself among the rocks. It may be considered as synonymous with the word "Mineralogist."

XXXV. Day.—(*June 27th.*)—We left the head of Keweena Portage at half past four in the morning, and proceeding with a favourable wind, entered the mouth of the river Ontonagon, at half past three in the afternoon. The distance is fifty-one miles, which gives an average rate of travelling of five miles per hour. In the intermediate space, we successively passed the Little Salmon Trout and Graverod's rivers,—La Riviére au Mesiére, and Firesteel river, all streams of secondary size, and not capable of being ascended any considerable distance with canoes. The shore is generally sandy alluvion, upon which pines, spruce, and hemlock predominate. At a distance back a ridge of highlands is visible. The entire distance from the Sault de St. Marie, is one hundred and eight leagues, which we have been ten days occupied in travelling, including a detention of three. We have, therefore, made an average progress of forty-six miles per day, a speed, which our voyageurs tell us, is seldom equalled in passing over the same route. During this time, we have had rain, with violent wind, three days,—clear, with moderate wind, five days,—and variable, (calm, misty, cloudy, windy,) three days. The highest degree of heat during the same period, has been 83°, and the mean temperature, from sun rise to sun set, 66°.* The transitions of temperature have often been sudden, and the heat, during the middle of the day, (from eleven to four) generally severe, and sometimes almost insupportable. Dense fogs have prevailed during the morning, and in one or two instances, mists have been observed during the day.

* See the Meteorological Table on the succeeding page.

Gusts of wind, arising with a momentary warning, have often driven us hastily ashore; and the whole

*METEOROLOGICAL OBSERVATIONS,

ON LAKE SUPERIOR, JUNE, 1820.

1820.	AIR.															WATER.											Mean Temp of Water.	Mean Temp of Air.	WINDS	Weather.
Lake	A. M.								P. M.							A. M.						P. M.								
Superior.	5	6	7	8	9	10	11	12	1	2	3	5	6	7	8	5	6	7	8	10	12	2	3	6	7	9				
June 19		69							76				72															70½	NW.	Rain
20	72							75				68	71				55										55	71½	NW.	Hur. at nt.
21						65					72				50					60				56		56	57	62		Calm.
22		55									63			49			56						54				55	55½	WNW	Clear
23	65							68							70	52					56					64	57	67½	SE.	Clear.
24				58				7[illegible]			60		63				55								51		53	63	NW.	Clear.
25			60				62			76					53			67			66					68	67	62½		
26					69					83					68					56					57		56	73		Rain.
27				68						71			69						57					62			69	69	ENE.	Fair.
																											469	594½		
																											58°	66° mean temp.		

route may be characterized as stormy, and yet we are told this is one of the most favourable months for performing the journey. In the autumn it is seldom attempted. The winds, which generally prevail from the northwest, expose the southern shore to the fury of continual storms. The Canadian shore is more pacific, being sheltered by its elevation, and the voyage on that side is, at all seasons, less liable to accidents and delays. The following table of distances may be found useful to future travellers. It is compiled from the estimates of the voyageurs and traders, as generally agreed upon, but I have reduced their mode of reckoning by French leagues, into miles, and introduced some corrections that appeared necessary.

TABLE

Of the Stationary Distances between Michilimackinac and the River Ontonagon.

	Miles.	Tot. Miles.
From Michilimackinac to Detour, -	40	
Thence to the Sault de St. Marie, -	45	85
Point aux Pins, -	6	91
Point Iroquois, at the entrance into Lake Superior,	9	100
Tonquamenon River, -	15	115
Shelldrake River, -	9	124
White Fish Point, -	9	133
Two-Hearted River, -	24	157
Grande Marráis, and commencement of Grande Sables, -	21	178
La Point la Grande Sables, -	9	187
Pictured Rocks, (La Portaille,) -	12	199
Doric Rock, and Miner's River, -	6	205
Grande Island, -	12	217
River aux Trains, -	9	226
Isle aux Trains, -	3	229
Laughing-Fish River, -	6	235

		Miles.	Tot. Miles.
Chocolate River,	-	15	250
Dead River, (In Presque Isle Bay,)	-	6	256
Granite Point,	-	6	262
Garlic River,	-	9	271
St. John's River,	-	15	286
Salmon-Trout, or Burnt River,	-	12	298
Pine River,	-	6	304
Huron River, (Huron Islands lie off this River,)		9	313
Point Abbaye, (east Cape of Keweena Bay,)	-	6	319
Mouth of Portage River,	-	21	340
Head of Portage River, (through Keweena Lake,)		24	364
Lake Superior, at the head of the Portage,	-	1	365
Little Salmon-Trout River,	-	9	374
Graverod's River, (small, with flat rocks at its mouth,)		6	380
Riviére au Misiére,	-	12	392
Firesteel River,	-	18	410
Ontonagon, or, Copper Mine River,	-	6	416

CHAP. VI.

VISIT TO THE COPPER MINES.

XXXV. Day.—(*June 27th.*)

THE river Ontonagon, (or 'Tenaugon, as it is frequently pronounced,) enters the lake in north latitude 46° 52′ 2″, as determined by Capt. Douglass, and is one of the largest of thirty rivers which are tributary to Lake Superior on its southern shore. It is estimated to be a hundred and twenty miles long, and has a width of two hundred yards, with eight feet depth at its mouth. Indians say they generally walk to its head in three or four days, but on account of numerous rapids, it is only ascended in canoes about thirty-six miles, and a portage then made to its source, which is in a small lake called *Vieux Desert.* This lake has also an outlet into the Menomonie river of Green Bay, and another into the Chippeway river of the Mississippi, by means of which the country is traversed in canoes by the traders and Indians. The lands along this river are generally rough and mountainous, until within three or four leagues of its mouth. Its waters have a reddish colour, like those of the Arkansas, and are moderately turbid; among its forest trees pine and hemlock predominate, but its most remarkable character is the copper, which is found along its banks. This has been known from the earliest times, and is noticed by all the travellers of the region. La Hontan, Charlevoix, Henry, Carver, and McKenzie, have successively published accounts of it, which have served at various periods, to arrest the public attention, and to confer a notoriety upon the country, which it had otherwise certainly lacked. But amid a great many surmises respecting the extent of the mines, very little has been with certainty known. To ascertain how far these accounts are founded in truth, and to examine the mineralogy of the adjacent region, was among the primary objects of the present expedition, and on reaching the mouth of the river, the Governor determined to loose no time in exploring it. It was past three o'clock in the afternoon, when we entered the mouth of the river. The expedition was immediately encamped, and Indian guides procured, at the neighbouring village, and at six o'clock, we proceeded in two light canoes up the river, leaving the greater part of our force encamped at the mouth. Our party in this excursion, consisted of Gov. Cass, Dr. Wolcott, Capt. Douglass, Lieutenant Mackay, Mr. Doty, and myself, with a sufficient number of engagés to conduct our canoes, and four Chippeway guides. A broad river, with a gentle current,---winding course, and heavy wooded banks, with the dark green foliage overshadowing the water, rendered the first part of the tour delightful. At the distance of four miles we reached a Sturgeon fishery, which the Indians have established in the river by means of a wier extending from bank to bank. This wier is constructed of saplings and small trees, sharpened and drove into the clayey bottom of the river, with an inclination down stream, and supported by crotched stakes bracing against the current. Against the sides of these inclined stakes, long poles are placed horizontally, and secured by hickory withes, in such a manner as to afford the Indians a passage from one end to the other, and at the same time allow them to sit and fish upon any part of it. The sturgeon are caught with an iron hook, fixed at the end of a long slender pole, which the Indian, setting on the wier holds to the bottom of the river, and when he feels the fish pressing against the slender pole, jerks it up with a sudden and very dexterous motion, and seldom fails to bring up the sturgeon. On one side of the wier, an opening is left for the fish to pass up, which they do at this season in vast numbers, but in their descent they are hurried by the current against the hooks of the savages, who are thickly planted on every part of the wier. The number of sturgeon caught at this place is astonishing, and the Indians rely almost entirely upon this fishery for a subsistence. What is not wanted for immediate consumption, is cut into thin slices and dried or smoked. Canoes pass up through the opening left for the sturgeon. Five or six Indians were employed in fishing at the time we passed through, and we stopped some time to observe the sport, and had the satisfaction of seeing several brought up, one of which was presented to us. The sturgeon are generally from two feet to four feet in length, and these may be considered as the minimum and maximum size, as they are seldom seen smaller than the former, or larger than the latter. They appear to me to be of the same species as the small sharp-nosed sturgeon of the Hudson; the *acipenser oxyrinchus* of Mitchill. This fishery is of great importance to the

Indians of the region, and appears to have been known to them from the earliest times, and has been constantly resorted to without any apparent diminution in the quantity taken. Henry says in 1765, "that a months subsistence for a regiment, could have been taken in a few hours time." There is a rapid at the spot fixed upon for the fishery, so that the water is not over four feet deep. We encamped two miles above on a sand bar. The musquitoes here gave us great annoyance.

XXXVI. Day.—(*June 28th.*)—We embarked at four o'clock in the morning. The river is bordered with a rich alluvion covered with a heavy forest of maple, elm, and walnut, and with a luxuriant growth of vines and underbrush. At the distance of ten or twelve miles from the lake, a chain of highlands shuts in upon each side of the river, cutting off the bottom lands of the lake, and increasing in altitude as we ascend. Here also the river becomes narrower and has many rapids. At seven o'clock our guides stopped the canoes, and told us that the river above that place, had a great many bad rapids which it would be very difficult to ascend with all the men in the canoes, and that by landing there, we might proceed by a near route through the woods, and reach the mines much sooner than the canoes could by water. Accordingly eight of the party, including myself, determined to proceed that way, while the Governor with the canoes, now lightened of half their burden, went up the river to meet us at the mines. We were accompanied by two Indians as guides, who led us over lofty ridges, gulfs, and ravines, covered with brush or shattered rocks, for a distance of fifteen miles, when we fell into an Indian path leading to the copper. Here our guides sat down to await the arrival of the Governor and party, who were to pass that way. We had thus far followed them with incredible fatigue, owing to the swiftness of their travelling, the roughness of the way, and the extreme heat of the weather.

> " Straining each sinew to ascend,
> " Foot, hand, and knee, their aid must lend ;
> " Now to the oak's warp'd roots we cling,
> " Now trust our weight to the curl'd vine's string,
> " Then like the wild goat must we dare
> " An unsupported leap in air."—SCOTT.

It was one o'clock in the afternoon when we arrived at this path, and the thermometer stood at 90° under the dark shade of the forest. We had not been seated a great while, when the other party approached, and we continued our way to the mines; but the Governor was so much exhausted by clambering up the hills, which skirt the river, that he was compelled to return to the canoes. We found the remainder of the way, (about six miles,) no less sterile, mountainous, or fatiguing; and reached the great mass of copper, the chief object of our excursion, at an early hour in the afternoon. It lies on the edge of the river directly opposite an island, and at the foot a lofty clay bluff, the face of which appears, at a former period, to have slipped into the river, carrying with it detached blocks and rounded masses of granite, hornblende, and other rock, and with them, the mass of copper in question. The first feeling was that of disappointment. It has been greatly overrated by former travellers, both as to size and mineralogical character, but is nevertheless, a remarkable mass of copper, and well worthy a visit from the traveller who is passing through the region. "The copper, which is in a pure and malleable state, lies in connexion with a body of serpentine rock, the face of which it almost completely overlays, and is also disseminated in masses, and grains, throughout the substance of the rock. The surface of the metal, unlike most oxydable metals, which have suffered a long exposure to the atmosphere, presents a metallic brilliancy; which is attributable either to an alloy of the precious metals, or to the action of the river, which during its semi-annual floods, carries down large quantities of sand and other alluvial matter, that may serve to abrade its surface, and keep it bright. The shape of the rock is very irregular—its greatest length is three feet eight inches—its greatest breadth three feet four inches, and it may altogether contain eleven cubic feet. In size, it considerably exceeds the great mass of native iron found some years ago upon the banks of Red River, in Louisiana, and now deposited among the collections of the New-York Historical Society,* but on account of the admixture of rocky matter, is inferior in weight. Henry, who visited it in 1766, estimates its weight at five tons; but after examining it with scrupulous attention, I do not think the weight of *metallic copper* in the rock exceeds *twenty-two hundred pounds.* The quantity may, however, have been much diminished since its first discovery, and the marks of chisels and axes upon it, with the broken tools lying around, prove that portions have been cut off, and carried away. The author just quoted observes, 'that such was its pure and malleable state that with an axe he

* See Bruce's Mineralogical Journal.

PLATE VI.

H. R. Schoolcraft del. Balch sc.

MASS OF NATIVE COPPER ON THE ONTONAGON RIVER

ALBANY, PUBLISHED BY E. & E. HOSFORD 1821.

was able to cut off a portion weighing a hundred pounds." Notwithstanding this reduction it may still be considered one of the largest and most remarkable bodies of native copper upon the globe, and is, so far as my reading extends, only exceeded by a specimen found in a valley in Brazil, weighing 2666 Portuguese pounds.* Viewed merely as a subject for scientific speculation, it presents the most interesting considerations and must be regarded by the geologist as affording illustrative proofs of an important character. Its connexion with a rock which is foreign to the immediate section of country where it lies, indicates a removal from its original bed, while the intimate connexion of the metal and matrix, and the complete envelopement of individual masses of the copper by the rock, point to a common and contemporaneous origin, whether that be referable to the agency of caloric or water. This conclusion admits of an obvious and important application to the extensive strata of serpentine, and other magnesian rocks, found in various parts of the globe!' "†

The accompanying view, (Plate VI,) is taken from a point below the mass of copper, looking up the river On each side appear a lofty range of earthy bluffs, which have caved into the river, throwing down their trees and imbedded rocks into heaps of ruins along the margin of the stream, and exposing their bare surfaces to view. These bluffs may be considered a hundred and fifty feet in perpendicular height, and are capped by a forest of pine, hemlock, cedar, and oak. On the right hand,

* Philips' Mineralogy.

† Extract from my Report to the Secretary at War, on the copper mines of Lake Superior. See the American Journal of Science and the Arts, Edited by Professor Silliman. H. R. S.

partly immersed in water, reposes the copper rock; on the left the little island of cedars divides the river into two channels, and the small depth and rapidity of the water is shewn by the innumerable rocks which project above its surface, from shore to shore. The masses of fallen earth,—the blasted trees, which either lie prostrate at the foot of the bluffs, or hang in a threatening posture above,—the elevation of the banks,—the rapidity and noise of the stream, present such a mixed character of wildness, ruin, and sterility, as to render it one of the most rugged views in nature.

> " It seem'd the mountain, rent and riven,
> " A channel for the stream had given;
> " So high the cliff of sandstone gray,
> " Hung beetling o'er the torrents way,
> " Where he who winds 'twixt rock and wave,
> " May hear the headlong torrent rave;
> " May view her chafe her waves to spray,
> " O'er every rock that bars her way,
> " Till foam globes o'er her eddies glide,
> " Thick as the schemes of human pride
> " That down life's current drive amain,
> " As frail, as frothy, and as vain." SCOTT.

One cannot help fancying that he has gone to the ends of the earth, and beyond the boundaries appointed for the residence of man. Every object tells us that it is a region alike unfavourable to the productions of the animal and vegetable kingdom; and we shudder in casting our eyes over the frightful wreck of trees, and the confused groups of falling-in banks and shattered stones. Yet we have only to ascend these bluffs to behold hills more rugged and elevated; and dark hemlock forests, and yawning gulfs more dreary, and more forbidding to the eye. Such is the frightful region through which, for a distance of twenty miles, we followed our Indian guides to reach this unfrequented spot, in which there is nothing to compensate the toil of the journey but its geological character, and mineral productions. Indeed these are traits which are generally found to increase in interest, in proportion to the increased sterility of the soil, and the impoverished growth of vegetable life. And here also the effect of climate upon the productions of nature, presents a remarkable exception. Trees and plants of particular species, are only found to vegetate in certain latitudes, and to be confined to particular soils, whose chemical constituents are congenial to their growth. Every modification of climate has its peculiar plants and predominating trees. Animals also, particularly the herbiferous species, have, in all countries, more or less confined themselves within the cycle of certain species of vegetable productions,—to the grasses and buds of trees to which they are particularly attached,—or, they are impelled in the search of herbs necessary to their health and vigour. But the inorganic masses of the earth are confined to no particular latitudes, and are uniform in their composition. The granites, the limestones, the spars, and the metals, exhibit the same characters, whether picked up within the arctic circle, or under the torrid zone. The mineralogist discovers the same external signs and appearances, and the chemist finds the same mineral constituents combined in the same proportions. It has, indeed, been asserted, that metals are confined to particular latitudes,—that gold and silver, and precious stones, are productions peculiar to the southern hemisphere; but there is nothing in the theories of the formation of mineral strata, the laws of crystallization, or in the known influence of climates upon mineral bodies, to justify such a conclusion;—there is no reason that can be drawn from philosophical investigations to prove that these substances may not be abundantly found in the climates of the north, even upon the banks of the frozen ocean. The fact that these productions are more abundantly found within the higher latitudes, does not appear capable of explanation, on a supposed effect of climate, but is probably wholly independent of that circumstance. On the contrary, there is reason to presume that the precious metals may be found in the northern regions of the American continent. Nothing appears more improbable than that the veins of silver ore, which are so abundant in Mexico, and the province of Texas, are checked in their progress northward into Arkansaw and Missouri, by the effect of climate. This metal is known to be found in association only with certain limestones, schists, and other rocks, and where these cease, is in vain to be sought. Other metals and minerals have their particular associations, serving as a geognostic matrix, and hence rock strata may be considered as indexes to particular metals, minerals, and ores; and the geologist is thus enabled to predict, with considerable certainty, from the examination of the exterior of a country, whether it is metalliferous, or not. Until such examinations are made, we must be permitted to say, that there does not appear any thing to forbid the hope of finding the precious metals in the regions of the northwest, while there are several facts to prove that it is highly probable. It is here that the stinted growth of vegetation, and the rocky and elevated nature of the country. leads us to look for those treasures in the mineral kingdom which nature has denied in soil and climate. In various places have lead, iron, and copper already been discovered, and the beauty of the carnelian, the agates, and the chalcedonies, picked up along the shores of Lake Superior, prove that the hardy regions of the north are not unfavourable to the production of mineral gems. But it is chiefly, so far as actually known, in the abundance of copper that the mineralogy of this region claims particular attention, and the more so, as it is found in the native form. Pieces of this metal have been discovered in various parts of the region, from the banks of Muddy river, in Illinois, to the mouth of the Copper-Mine river, which enters the Frozen ocean. At the latter place, Mr. Hearne found it in his visit to the Copper-Mine river, in 1771, and represents it as in common use for knives, trinkets, &c. among the Esquimaux, the Dog-ribbed, and the Copper-Mine tribes, who inhabit that inclement region.* It has also been found in various parts of Illinois, as at Harrison, and old Piora,—at Dubuques mines,—Winnebago lake,—on the St. Peter's,—St. Croix,—Sauteur, and other rivers,—but most abundantly upon Lake Superior, and particularly upon the river Ontonagon, where the large mass which is the object of our present visit, has long attracted attention. It is, indeed, notwithstanding the exaggerated accounts, a wonderful mass, and viewed in connexion with the mineral appearances of the surrounding country, leaves little doubt that extensive mines of this metal exist in the vicinity. But to explore it with

* See Hearne's Journey to the Northern Ocean, p. 172.

any degree of satisfaction, a week or a fortnight affords a very inadequate period, while the extent of the route to be performed, and the danger of so large a party's getting out of provisions in a country almost wholly destitute of game, forbids even the devotion of a few days to that object. Having, therefore, examined appearances, and taken such notes, and specimens of the metal, as time and circumstances would permit, we returned to our canoes, which had been left at the distance of six miles below. On reaching the canoes, we were alarmed on finding that Gov. Cass, from whom we had parted at the Indian path, at two o'clock, had not yet reached the camp, nor any of the attendants who were with him,—among whom was one of the Indian guides. Some idea of the rugged nature of the country may be formed when it is stated, that they had lost their way in attempting to reach the river, notwithstanding that they were only distant three miles, and led by an Indian acquainted with those parts generally. Night was rapidly closing around us, and after firing repeated signal guns, and sending out in all directions, nothing could be heard of them. The feelings of the party may be imagined upon this occasion, seated, as we were, in the midst of one of the most awful solitudes, and in a region which had impressed every individual with an indescribable feeling, that was manifested in a general anxiety to depart from it. I was perhaps alone in the wish to continue our examinations. At length the lost party were discovered by a canoe sent up the river, setting upon the shore, and exhausted with fatigue, and their arrival restored tranquillity to our camp.

XXXVII. Day.—(*June 29th.*)—At five o'clock in the morning we commenced our return. On descending eight or ten miles, our Indian guides stopped on the east bank of the river, to examine a bear-fall that had been previously set, and were overjoyed to find a large bear entrapped. As it was no great distance from the river, we all landed to enjoy the sight. The animal sat up on his fore paws facing us, the hinder paws being pressed to the ground by a heavy weight of logs which had been arranged in such a manner as to allow the bear to creep under, and then by seizing the bait, had sprung the trap, and he could not extricate himself, although, with his fore paws, he had demolished a part of the works. After viewing him for some time, a ball was fired through his head, but it did not kill him, the bear kept his position, and seemed to growl in defiance. A second ball was aimed at the heart, and took effect, but he did not resign the contest immediately, and was at last despatched with an axe. As soon as the bear fell, one of the Indians walked up, and addressing him by the name of *Muck-wah*, shook him by the paw, with a smiling countenance, as if he had met with an old acquaintance, saying, in the Indian language, he was sorry they had been under the necessity of killing him, and hoped the offence would be forgiven, particularly as *Che-mo-que-mon** had fired one of the balls. This animal measures five feet in length, and would probably weigh three hundred pounds. The head is small and narrow, with a long pointednose, and covered with glossy black

* This is a general name among the Chippeways for the Americans. It signifies the "Long Knife." Sag-a-nosh is the term for the British.

hair all over the body, except some spots of brownish yellow upon the cheeks and throat. It appears to be the common black bear of naturalists, (*ursus niger*,) which is frequent in the United States. By the joy which was evident upon the countenances of the savages upon this occasion, it is a rare occurrence among them to kill a bear. But perhaps this animal is never killed without exultation, as it is universally considered the noblest object of the chase. Some difficulty has arisen among naturalists as to the character of this animal, which, although provided with canine teeth, is supposed to subsist principally upon vegetable food. It is, however, certain that it is also carniverous, and will prey upon hogs and other animals when pressed for food. The Indians say that it is very fond of all sorts of nuts, esculent roots, and wild honey, and frequently attacks their corn fields. It will travel a great way from its den into the pine ridges to feed upon whortle berries, and is also very fond of mulberries, blackberries, and all sweet flavoured and spicy fruits. They add, that it is only in the utmost extremity that it takes hold of animal food, and in a region where its favourite fruits are plenty, will pass by the carcass of a deer without touching it. On the same account it never attacks men, unless wounded, and too hotly pressed, when it turns upon its pursuers with the fury of a lion. On such occasions one stroke of the paw is sufficient to kill their stoutest dogs The Indians hold this animal in the highest estimation, not only on account of their great fondness of its flesh, but because there is no part of it which is useless. The carcass, the skin, the claws and head, and even the intestines, are all turned to account. The fleshy part of the claws is considered a very great delicacy,—the claws themselves are cut out, strung together upon a deer's sinew, and worn as an ornament about the neck. The oil, is, however, considered the most valuable part, whether kept for use, or for the purpose of selling to the traders. They rub their bodies with it to protect themselves from the bite of the musquitoe. It has the singular property of destroying lice in the hair, and if occasionally used, of preventing their appearance altogether. They also rub their joints with it, believing with the Romans, that it renders them supple. A singular fact is mentioned by Pennant, that the female bear is never killed with young, and it is explained on the supposition, (for the fact admits of doubt,) that the male possesses such an unnatural dislike to its offspring, as to kill and devour the cubs. On this account, the female retires before the period of parturition, into remote woods and clefts of rocks, and does not return until the cubs have attained a certain growth.

In passing down the river one of the Indians had promised to discover another mass of copper near the river, but after landing and hunting sometime, pretended he could not find it. An Indian afterwards brought us a lump of copper weighing between eight and nine pounds, which he said was picked up upon the banks of the Ontonagon. This specimen was covered with a green crust, and not in so pure a state as the great mass above. On reaching the lake we found the wind directly ahead, and were detained the remainder of the day. In the afternoon a council was held with the Indians, and presents distributed among them, and one of the number, who appeared to merit it, constituted a chief, by being invested with a flag and silver medal. In the evening, they danced upon the sand for our amusement. I have already spoken of Indian dancing and music. It is perhaps all we could expect from untutored savages, but there is nothing about it which has ever struck me as either interesting or amusing, and after having seen these performances once or twice, they become particularly tedious, and it is a severe tax upon one's patience to sit and be compelled, in order to keep their good opinions, to appear pleased with it.

XXXVIII. Day.—(*June* 30*th.*)—Detained by head winds. There is very little in the appearances of the country in the vicinity of our encampment, to compensate for our delay. A sandy plain stretches along the shore of the lake as far as the eye can reach. The highlands of the Ontonagon are visible towards the south, and the Porcupine mountains at the distance of thirty miles west, appear to rise out of the lake, and imprint their lofty and rugged outlines upon the distant clouds. Towards the north there is an interminable expanse of water, without a solitary island to variegate the view. Letting the eye fall upon the immediate vicinity of our camp, the Indian village appears on the opposite side of the river, and we are surrounded on all sides by a bed of loose sand, which the wind is continually drifting into heaps. There is not a pebble upon the shore, nor a stratum of rock within a dozen miles. Occasional strata of iron sand, very pure and black, are found. An Indian brought me a number of specimens of iron ore, procured at Point Keweena, near the portage, where he represents it to exist in large quantity. The specimens consist of red *hematite* and *iron pyrites*. Both these substances are said to occur in quantity on Iron river, which enters the lake fifteen miles west of the Ontonagon. While encamped here, pigeons have been very plenty, and vast numbers have been killed, some with sticks and stones. The Indians have also supplied us with sturgeon from the fishery, both fresh and dried, and with a part of the bear which they entrapped, but the latter, being in poor order, and a male, has not possessed that flavour for which young bear's meat killed in the proper season, is generally relished.

The weather since our arrival upon the banks of this river, has been clear and warm, and during the middle of the day, oppressively sultry. The wind which blew fair from the E. N. E. on our arrival, shifted to the north west on the following day, and has blown steadily from that point without change. The thermometer stood at 91° on the 28th, at 94° on the 29th, and at 89° on the 30th, and the mean heat as deduced from three daily observations has been 80°. During the same time the mean temperature of the water of Lake Superior has been 66°, and of the water of the Ontonagon river 73°. The following thermometrical memoranda made at irregular intervals, as circumstances would permit, may here be added.

Temperature of the Air.

June 28th, at 8 A. M. 74°—at 1 P. M. 91°—at 6 P. M. 74° av. 79°
" 29th, at 8 A. M. 79°—at 1 P. M. 94°—at 7 P. M. 86° av. 86°
" 30th, at 9 A. M. 76°—at 2 P. M. 89°—at 8 P. M. 60° av. 75°

3)240

Mean temp. for three days 80°

Water of the Ontonagon River.

June 28th, at 8 A. M. 69°—at 3 P. M. 73°—at 6 P. M. 71° av. 71°
" 29th, at 8 A. M. 68°—at 1 P. M. 76°—at 7 P. M. 75° av. 76°
" 30th, at 8 A. M. 74°—at 3 P. M. 71° av. 72°

3)219

Average temperature 73°

Water of Lake Superior.

June 28th, at 8 A. M. 26°—at 6 P. M. 72° ———— av. 67°
" 29th, at 8 A. M. 61°—at 7 P. M. 68° ———— av. 74°
" 30th, at 8 A. M. 60°—at 9 P. M. 58° ———— av. 59°

3)200

Mean temperature 66½

CHAP. VII.

JOURNEY,

FROM THE ONTONAGON RIVER TO THE FOND DU LAC.

XXXIX. Day.—(*July* 1*st.*)

THE wind ceased during the night, and the morning was calm, with a dense fog, which rendered it impossible to discern objects at the distance of two or three hundred yards. We left the mouth of the Ontonagon at half past four in the morning. In going eight or ten miles a favourable wind arose which enabled us to proceed under sail for a couple of hours. Fifteen miles beyond the Ontonagon, we passed the mouth of Iron river, which is very rapid, and interlocks with some of the tributaries of the Ousconsing. Iron ore and pyrites are said to abound upon its banks. Five leagues beyond, we passed the Carp river, which originates in the Porcupine mountains, and has a perpendicular fall of forty feet, three miles from its mouth. Presque Isle river is six miles further. It is also very rapid and not much navigated in canoes. Black river is next passed, at the distance of two leagues. It is also rapid, and originates in the broken lands south of the Porcupine mountains.

Eight miles beyond this, we encamped, having proceeded fifty miles. The shore of the lake from the Ontonagon river, until we arrive off the Porcupine mountains, is sandy, with the exception of a ledge of sand rock which appears a few feet above the water at the mouth of Iron river, and is inclined towards the N. E. at an angle of six or eight degrees. On passing by the Porcupine mountains, the same rock, (red sand stone) is visible along the shore, but in a position so highly inclined, as to appear nearly vertical. It dips under the lake towards the north, and appearances seem to indicate that it has been thrown into this position by the upheaving of the granitic masses of the Porcupine mountains, which rise at a very short distance from the lake. These mountains have a very rugged and commanding appearance, and rise to a surprising height. We saw them under the influence of great atmospheric refraction, from Keweena Portage, a distance of eighty miles. Captain Douglass has estimated their altitude at from one thousand eight hundred to two thousand feet above Lake Superior. His data are the distances at which they are visible with the naked eye, under different degrees of refraction. Mr. Darby says "any object capable of being seen upon the curve of the earth's surface forty miles, must be within a trifle of one thousand one hundred feet high."—*Tour to Detroit*, p. 175.

Charlevoix observes, "when a storm is about to rise on Lake Superior, you are advertised of it, two or three days previous. At first, you perceive a gentle murmuring on the surface of the water, which lasts the whole day without increasing in any sensible manner; the day after the lake is covered with pretty large waves, but without breaking all that day, so that you may proceed without fear, and even make good way if the wind is favourable ; but on the third day when you are the least thinking of it, the lake becomes all on fire, the ocean in its greatest rage is not more tost, in which case you must take care to be near shelter, to save yourself. This you are always sure to find on the north shore, whereas on the *south* you are obliged to secure yourself the second day at a considerable distance from the water side."* Although we are not prepared to corroborate this remark, yet something of the kind has this day been witnessed, for notwithstanding the prevalence of a calm during the whole day, with the exception of about two hours in the morning, when the wind was however light, the lake towards evening has been in a perfect rage, and we effected a landing with greater hazard than has yet been encountered. At the same time scarce a breath of air was stirring, and the atmosphere was beautifully clear.

XL. Day.—(*July 2d.*)—Thirteen miles from our encampment, we reached the mouth of the Montreal river, which we entered, and landed upon its banks. This is a long and rapid river, and is connected with the head waters of the Chippeway and Ousconsing. About eight hundred yards above its mouth it has a fall of eighty or ninety feet, where the river is precipitated over a rugged barrier of vertical rocks, by several successive leaps, the last of which is about forty feet perpendicular. This brings the stream on a level with Lake Superior, which it joins in a broad

* Charlevoix, p. 44. vol. 2.

deep stream, with reddish coloured water. This view is highly picturesque as presented from the point of land formed by the junction of the river with the lake. Notwithstanding its rapidity, and falls, it is frequently ascended by the traders, and a portage of one hundred and twenty pauses commences at its mouth. The southwest company have an establishment on Lac du Flambeau, which is near the head of this river. Between the foot of the falls and the lake, the Indians have a wier similar to that on the Ontonagon, for catching sturgeon, and there is an Indian village a few miles west of it. During a short stay here, we found pigeons very abundant, and several were killed with clubs.

Twelve miles beyond the Montreal river, is the Mauváis which is navigable a hundred miles in canoes, and takes its rise in the Ottaway Lake. From this a portage is made into branches of the St. Croix and Chippeway rivers, through a series of small lakes, the principal of which are Spear, Clam, Summer, Pacquayahwan, and Lac du Coutére, On the latter the southwest company have a trading establishment. On the banks of the Ottaway lake the Indians procure a sort of red steatite, similar to that of St. Peter's, of which they manufacture pipes. Six miles beyond the Mauváise, is Point Che-goi-megon, once the grand rendezvous of the Chippeway tribe, but now reduced to a few lodges. Three miles further west is the island of St. Michael, which lies in the traverse across Chegoimegon Bay, where M. Cadotte has an establishment. This was formerly an important trading post but is now dwindled to nothing. There is a dwelling of logs, stockaded in the usual manner of trading houses, besides several out buildings, and some land in cultivation. We here also found several cows and horses, which have been transported with great labour. On this island two pieces of native copper were found some years ago, one of which was a foot long, and weighed twenty-eight pounds. It is also stated that a silver mine exists on the main shore southwest of the island, but during the short time of our stay, we could procure no satisfactory information on the subject. The Indians appear very jealous of every attempt to explore the mineralogy of their territories, and are loth to communicate any information that would lead to a discovery. We encamped seven miles west of this island, on the main shore.

The shore of the lake during this day's journey has exhibited some diversity. Red sand stone, in a vertical position, continues for a few miles beyond Montreal river. It generally rises out of the water abruptly, and in some places, as between Black and Montreal rivers, to a height of eighty or a hundred feet. In the interstices of the rock, the water has driven up pebbles of granite, hornblende, quartz, &c. A bank of red clay, of twenty or thirty feet in depth, overlays the rock, covered with a young growth of birch and poplar. There are no large, or apparently old trees, seen along this part of the coast. About four miles beyond Montreal river, the rock ceases, and a sandy shore succeeds, which continues to Point Chegoimegon, or Sandy Point. The Mauvaise river enters through this plain of sand. On reaching the main shore west of Chegoimegon Bay, we perceive a rough, high, and broken region of hills, consisting chiefly of hornblende rock. There is a sandy beach on the lake shore, and at the distance of from one to five miles in the lake, lie a cluster of wooded islands, which Carver called the Twelve Apostles. There appears to be fifteen or twenty in number, and they present a very beautiful and picturesque groupe.

XLI. Day.—(*July 3d.*)—We had rain during the night and it continued until six o'clock in the morning, when we embarked, and proceeded northwest eight miles to Raspberry river,—then southwest six miles to Sandy river, where a head wind and an approaching storm compelled us to land. Before we could unload our canoes, or pitch a tent, rain commenced, and it poured down in torrents for an hour or more, during which there was no alternative but to stand patiently upon the sand. If we had lain at the bottom of the lake, we could not have been more completely drenched. When the rain ceased, the wind arose from the southwest, and confined us to that spot during the remainder of the day.

XLII. Day.—(*July 4th.*)—We passed the forty-fifth Anniversary of American Independance until two o'clock, at the mouth of Sandy river. The wind continued to blow unfavourably a great part of the day. In the afternoon it changed so that we were able to put out, although the lake was still agitated: on going three miles we turned a prominent point of land called De Tour, which lies at the foot of the great Fond du Lac, or West Bay. Here we changed our course from N. W. to S. S. W. and continued it, with little variation, to the mouth of Cranberry river, where we encamped at eight o'clock, having progressed thirty-three miles. The evening was clear and calm and twilight was observable all night. In the latitude of 67° 47', Mackenzie saw the sun above the horizon at 12 o'clock, P. M. This was on the 11th July, 1789. In 42°, (the meridian of Albany and Detroit,) the light of the sun is wholly invisible at this season after eight o'clock.

XLIII. Day.—(*July 5th.*)—We were upon the lake this morning before three o'clock. The sun rose above the horizon at ten minutes before four, giving us day light nearly an hour sooner than it will reach our friends on the shores of the Atlantic. The morning was clear and calm, and the prospect of reaching the head of the lake, before the sun would again set, put our party in the finest spirits, and the voyageurs worked with renewed vigour. At the distance of five leagues from Cranberry river, we passed the mouth of the Bois Brulé, which enters the lake at the foot of a small bay. This river is navigated 80 miles, and a portage of two pauses then made into a small lake, which is the source of St. Croix river. The latter enters the Mississippi between St. Peter's and lake Pepin, and is navigable at all seasons. The South West Company have an establishment one hundred leagues from its mouth, and about twenty-five leagues south of the Fond du Lac. Three miles beyond Bois Brulé we landed on the sandy shore a few moments, and here found an immense body of iron sand, very pure and black. It lay in a stratum of a foot in thickness along the shore, and extending either way, as far as we examined. At eleven o'clock a northeast wind arose which enabled us to hoist sail, and an hour afterwards we entered the mouth of the river St. Louis, which enters the lake at the head of the Fond du Lac. Thus have we completed the passage of Lake Superior on the eighteenth day after our departure from Point aux Pins, including the excursion up the Ontonagon and the delay at the mouth of that river. The entire distance from Point Iroquois is four hundred and ninety miles, and this is the greatest length of the lake, in a direct course from east to west. In traversing around the Canadian shore it is estimated at twelve hundred miles, and its extreme breadth from the bottom of Keweena Bay, to the mouth of Nipegon river, is a hundred and ninety miles. Its circumference may be estimated at seventeen hundred miles. Mr. Darby has calculated its medium depth at 900 feet, and its superficial area at 836,352,000,000 feet.* It has a number of large and well wooded islands, the principal of which are Maurepas, Phillipoux, the Island of Yellow Sands, and Isle Royal. The latter is represented by Carver as being "an hundred miles long, and in many places, forty broad." The island of Maurepas is reputed to abound in minerals, and was formerly explored by the copper mine company. "I found it," says the agent, "one solid rock, thinly covered with soil, except in the valleys; but generally well wooded. Its circumference is twelve leagues. On examining the surface, I saw nothing remarkable, except large veins of transparent spar, and a mass of rock, at the south

* The following comparative estimate of the volume of water in the chain of northwestern Lakes is given by Mr. Darby in his Tour to Detroit p. 117.

LAKES.	Medium depth.	Sup. area in feet.	Solid contents in feet.
Superior,	900	836,352,000,000	752,716,800,000,000
Huron,	900	557,568,000.000	501,811,200,000,000
Michigan,	900	376,898,400,000	339,208,560.000,000
Erie,	120	418,176,000,000	50.181,120,000,000
Ontario,	492	200,724,480,000	98,756,444,160,000

end of the island, which appeared to be composed of iron ore." The Island of Yellow Sands derives its chief interest from the traditions and fanciful tales which the Indians relate concerning its mineral treasures, and their supernatural guardians. They pretend that its shores are covered with a heavy shining yellow sand, which they would persuade us is gold, but that the guardian spirit of the island, will not permit any of it to be carried away. To enforce his commands he has drawn together upon it, myriads of eagles, hawks, and other birds of prey, who by their cries warn him of any intrusions upon the domain, and assist with their claws and beaks to expel the enemy He has also called from the depths of the lake, large serpents of the most hideous forms, who lie thickly coiled upon the golden sands, and hiss defiance to the steps of the invader. A great many years ago, it is pretended, that some people of their nation were driven by stress of weather, to take shelter upon the enchanted island, and being struck with the beautiful and glittering appearance of the treasure, they put a large quantity of it in their canoes, and attempted to carry it off, but a gigantic spirit strode into the water, and in a voice of thunder, commanded them to bring it back. Terrified with his amazing size, and threatening aspect, they obeyed, and were afterwards suffered to depart without molestation, but they have never since attempted to land upon it.

"Listen white man—go not there,
"Unseen spirits stalk the air;
"Ravenous birds their influence lend,
"Snakes defy—and kites defend.
"There the star-eyed panther prowls,
"And the wolf in hunger howls;

"There the speckled adder breeds,
"And the famished eagle feeds,
"Spirits keep them—fiends incite,
"They are eager for the fight,
"And are thirsting night and day,
"On the human heart to prey,
"Touch not then the guarded lands
"Of the isle of yellow sands."—MSS.

Carver represents "the country on the north and east parts of Lake Superior as very mountainous and barren," and Mackenzie adds, that "it is a continued mountainous embankment of rock, from three hundred to one thousand five hundred feet in height." The principal rivers on that shore are the Pic, Nipegon, and Michepicoten. The climate is described as very unfavourable and the vegetation slow and scanty. We can only speak with certainty of the southern coast, on which it receives thirty tributary rivers, but none of them exceed a hundred and fifty miles in length. Of these the Ontonagon, Montreal, Mauvaise, Bois Brulé, and St. Louis are the largest, and communicate with the waters of the Mississippi. The coast is sandy from Point Iroquois to the Pictured Rocks; then rocky to the foot of the Fond du Lac, with occasional plains of sand, as at the Ontonagon, and Point Chegoimegon, and from that to the head of the lake, sandy and without hills. The forest trees are white and yellow pine, hemlock, spruce, birch, poplar, and oak, with a mixture of elm, maple, and ash, upon the banks of the rivers. The coast is very elevated,—in some places mountainous,—generally sterile,—and dangerous to navigate. It is subject to storms and sudden transitions of temperature, and to fogs and mists, which are often so dense as to obscure objects at a short distance, and prove disastrous to canoe travellers, by separating the party and driving them upon rocks and sand banks. It appears to enjoy a warm atmosphere during the summer season, the result of our observations indicating a mean heat of 66° for June, and 64° for July. We found strawberries ripe at Keweena Portage on the 25th, and at the Ontonagon on the 27th of June. But it has a long and frightful winter. The Indians living upon its shores are divided into small bands, and rely more upon the fish of the lake, than upon the chace. There are two kinds of trout, some of which weigh fifty pounds. White fish, sturgeon, pickerel, pike, carp, black bass, and herring, are also abundant. Although we have occasionally met ducks along the shore, it is not a favourite resort of water fowl. The waters are too pure and deep, and the coast too rocky for the growth of the wild rice, and those aquatic plants which draw such myriads of these birds into the northwestern regions. Its mineralogy and geology have been detailed in the progress of the voyage. No part of the union presents a more attractive field for geological investigation or mineral discoveries. Its copper, iron, and lead, promise to become important items in the future commerce of the country. The beds of iron sand along the shore exceed every thing of the kind found in the United States. It presents two harbours for vessels which are rarely equalled :—These are Grand Isle, and Chegoimegon Bay. The former is perhaps the most capacious, deep, and completely land-locked of any in America. Such are the leading traits of the southern shore of Superior. The French it appears bestowed unsuccessfully upon this lake the names of Condé, and Tracy. The former had previously been applied to Erie, but neither were ever fully adopted. I was anxious from the time of our entrance upon it, to learn the Indian name; it is *Missisawgaiegon*, signifying simply "great lake." According to the estimates which I have made, this lake has an elevation of fifty-one feet above Lake Huron.—eighty-one, above Lake Erie,—and six hundred and forty-one, above the Atlantic ocean at high tide.*

On turning Point de Tour, a few miles beyond Sandy river, we have the first glimpse of the mountains on the north side of the lake, which are distant probably forty miles. These become more distinct, and continue to increase in apparent altitude as we ascend the Fond du Lac, while on the south shore the highlands either recede so widely from the lake as to become invisible, or entirely cease. On reaching the mouth of St. Louis, or Fond du Lac river, the Cabotian† mountains present a lofty barrier towards the north, and have an apparent altitude of a thousand feet above the lake. The chain runs from

* *ELEVATION OF THE AMERICAN LAKES.*

	Feet.		Tot. Feet.
Level of Lake Erie above the tide waters of the Hudson, (as surveyed by the N. Y. Canal Commissioners,	560		
Lake St. Clair. (see estimate in chapter 2.)	10		570
Lake Huron, (see estimate in chapter 2.)	19		589
Mean fall of the river St. Mary, between De Tour and Point Iroquois, sixty miles, at three inches per mile, (rapids not included)	15		
Nibish rapid,	9		
Sugar Island rapid	6		
Sault de St. Marie, (according to Col. Gratiot,)	22	10	
Lake Superior,	52	10	641

† Col. Bouchette, in his Topographical Description of the Canadas, has applied the name Cabotia, (in allusion to Christian Cabot, the discoverer,) to all that part of North America lying north of the Great Lakes.

east to west, and as far as the eye can reach stretches off in a lofty line towards the Mississippi. It is this barrier which we have to cross with our baggage and canoes in ascending the St. Louis river, for this precipitous stream has worn its rugged channel through these mountains, and throws itself into Lake Superior at its extreme head. The mouth of this river is not more than a hundred and fifty yards wide, but immediately on entering, it expands to a mile, and continues this width for five or six miles, and this part of it resembles a lake more than a river, having little or no current,—shallow in many places, and filled with aquatic plants. We here first saw in plenty the folle avoine, or wild rice, which is so common throughout the northwestern regions, and serves the Indians as a substitute for corn. We had previously noticed this plant in small patches, in passing through the river St. Mary, and along the shores of a few of the tributary rivers of Lake Superior,—but it is in no place seen along the shore of the lake itself. Neither does that lake afford any of the water grasses, rushes, or liliaceous plants common to most of the lakes and ponds of the north. Naturalists do not seem agreed as to the character of this plant, and a discrepancy appears in the botanical nomenclature. Linnæus has arranged it as a variety of the species plantarum, under the name of *Zezania Aquatica.* Micheaux and Eaton denominate it *Zezania Clavulosa.* The Linnæan name is the most characteristic. Other names have been given by different botanists, but few in fact have enjoyed the opportunity of examining the plant in its natural situation, and it is not even settled whether the fruit is annually produced from new seed, or the same root continues to germinate for many years. There can be no doubt, as Pursh has suggested, that it is a perennial plant. It ripens about the first of September, when the Indians gather it by pushing their canoes into the thickest fields of it,—breaking down the tops of the stalks, and beating out the grain with their paddles, which falls upon a spread blanket in their canoes. This is a labour which is performed by the squaws. A great deal of chaff falls in with the grain, which is afterwards partially fanned out upon a blanket, but it is never got entirely clean. The grain has a long cylindrical shape, and becomes dark coloured and hard as it dries. It contains more gluten than common rice, and is very nourishing. It is simply boiled in water until it assumes a pasty consistence, and it has an agreeable flavour. The Indians have no salt, but make use of maple sugar, when in season. They have no method of reducing it into meal, but the squaws sometimes, in cases of sickness, pound small quantities in a deer-skin bag, and thus procure a kind of flour of which panada is made.

Three miles above the mouth of the St. Louis river, there is a village of Chippeway Indians, of fourteen lodges, and containing a population of about sixty souls. Among these we noticed a negro who has been long in the service of the fur company, and who married a squaw, by whom he has four children. It is worthy of remark, that the children are as black as the father, and have the curled hair and glossy skin of the native African. It does not appear that *climate* has had any more influence here, than it has along the borders of the Atlantic, in ameliorating the colour of this race. But this evidence is certainly not wanted in the present state of physical and philosophical science, to establish the fact that the radical colours of the different species of the human family, are independent of the influence of climate.

A short distance above this village, on the opposite side of the river, are the ruins of one of the old forts and trading houses of the northwest company, which was abandoned about six years ago. The site is elevated and pleasant, but the American company have not thought proper to re-occupy it, and have fixed their establishment for the Fond du Lac department, eighteen miles above, where the first portage commences. By this change of site, they save the labour of loading and unloading their canoes at the mouth of the river. We arrived at the company's house at seven o'clock in the evening. The establishment consists of a range of log buildings, inclosing three sides of a square, open toward the river, and containing the ware-house, canoe, and boat yard, dwelling house of the resident clerk, and accommodations for the voyageurs. There are about four acres of ground under cultivation, upon which potatoes are raised. No species of grain has been tried. The department is supplied with wild rice by the Indians. The buildings are situated upon an alluvial plain elevated a few feet above the river, and the site is healthy and pleasant. We here see pines and sugar maple growing beside each other, —which is, I believe, a rare occurrence. The company have recently sent up a number of agricultural implements, with a view of experimenting upon the soil and climate, together with three horses, two oxen, three cows, and four bulls. These animals have been transported with great difficulty.

The weather, since leaving the Ontonagon, has been variable. We have had rain a part of two days, and it has been misty, cloudy or stormy, the balance of the time, with the exception of a part of the second of July, and the morning of this day. The highest atmospheric heat during this time has been 80°, and the average heat 64°. The wind has blown successively N. N. W.—W. S. W.—S. S. W. and N. E. The mean temperature of the water of Lake Superior has been 61°* The following are the stationary distances of the route.

	Miles.	Tot. Miles.
From the Ontonagon to Iron River,	15	
Carp River, and the Porcupine Mountains,	15	30
Presque Isle River,	6	36
Black River,	6	42
Montreal River,	21	63
La Mauváise Riviére, (Bad River,)	12	75
Point Chegoimegon,	6	81
Cadotte's House, (Island of St. Michael,)	3	84
Fromboise, (Raspberry,) River,	15	99
Sandy River,	6	105
De Tour (foot of Fond du Lac,)	3	108
Cranberry Creek,	30	138
Bois Brulé (Burntwood) River,	15	153
Mouth of St. Louis River, or (Fond du Lac,)	21	174
Chippeway village,	3	177
American Fur Company's Establishment,	18	195

* *Meteorological Observations on the journey from the Ontonagon to the Fond du Lac.*

	AIR.										WATER.							Meantemp of water.	Meantemp of Air.	Prevailing Winds.	Weather.
	A. M.					P. M.					A. M.			P. M.							
July	4	6	7	8	10	2	3	4	6	9	4	6	8	2	3	6	9				
1	54			61		75		80	68				61	65		66		64	67	NNW	Misty.
2	60			70	75	76		65		65	63		64	68			62	64	68	WSW	Clear.
3		70					66		62	67		62			60		58	60	65	SSW	Rain.
4			57		61			58					58					58	58	SSW	Misty.
5				63	75	68				54			63	64				63	65	NE	Calm.
																		5|309	5|323		
																		Water 61°	64° Air.		

CHAPTER VIII.

JOURNEY,

FROM THE FOND DU LAC TO SANDY LAKE.

XLIV. Day.—(*July* 6th.)

WE left the establishment at ten o'clock in the morning. The river is ascended two miles further, to the foot of the Grand Portage. Here the goods are all landed, and the carrying commences, but the canoes, without load, ascend two miles higher to the *Galley*, where they are also taken out and carried across. The first part of the portage is excessively rough, and the fatigue was rendered almost insupportable by the heat of the day, the thermometer standing at 82° at noon. With the assistance of the Indians, (sixteen of whom were brought up from the mouth of the river for that purpose,) we proceeded however, with all our baggage, five pauses, and encamped at twilight.

XLV. Day.—(*July 7th.*)—A storm of rain commenced during the night, and continued until noon, when the sun appeared for half an hour, but the afternoon continued dark and cloudy, with showers. We commenced carrying at six o'clock, notwithstanding the rain, and with great exertions, went ten pauses and encamped on the banks of a small brook. The difficulties of the portage have been very much increased by the rain, which has filled the carrying path with mud and water. We are advancing into a dreary region.—Every thing around us wears a wild and sterile aspect, and the extreme ruggedness of the country—the succession of swampy grounds, and rocky precipices—the dark forest of hemlock and pines which overshadow the soil—and the distant roaring of the river, would render it a gloomy and dismal scene, without the toil of transporting baggage, and the saddening influence of one of the most dreary days.

XLVI. Day.—(*July 8th.*)—We progressed four pauses, and reached the river at the head of the portage, in season to air our baggage—repair the canoes—and make the necessary dispositions for an early departure on the following day. The entire distance of this portage is nine miles, which is passed at nineteen pauses, divided according to the unevenness of the ground, and the facilities of travelling. I have already mentioned that a pause is reckoned at half a mile, but when the country is rough and the way bad, it is much shorter, while on a level road, it often exceeds that distance. The labour, however, of travelling across a short pause is as great as that of the longest, and about the same time is required in crossing it, so that this term is rather expressive of a division of the labour of making a portage, than of the geographical distance. The fall of the St. Louis river, between the extremes of this portage is very great, being one continued chain of rapids and falls. and at one place there is a perpendicular pitch of thirty feet. Altogether, the descent may be estimated at two hundred and twenty feet. It is here that the river forces a passage through a chain of mountains consisting of short broken ridges, which give the country a very rugged appearance, and render the travelling excessively toilsome. Where we leave the river at the foot of the portage, these ridges consist of red sand stone rocks in horizontal layers, but on reaching the head of the portage, we find the banks of the river composed of slate, (*argillite,*) in a vertical position, traversed by veins of greenstone and milky quartz. The change in the rock strata takes place at some intermediate point, which was not precisely noticed. At the foot of the portage I picked up among the loose stones along the shore, a specimen of the micaceous oxide of iron, and some pyrites were also found at that place. While examining the argillite above, I discovered a vein of graphite (plumbago or blacklead) between the vertical layers of that rock, but of an indifferent quality for economical purposes. Probably the interior of the vein would yield this mineral in a more perfect form. Large detached blocks of black crystallized hornblende rock are found scattered along the shore of the river, but this rock is not observed in situ. A stratum of alluvial soil, of two or three feet in depth rests upon the slate. It also contains imbedded masses of hornblende, together with granite, quartz, and argillite, and a thin sub-stratum of vegetable mould overlays all. The growth of trees is pine, hemlock, spruce, birch, oak, and maple, the former predominating. In clambering among the rocks along the river, I found the red raspberry ripe. This appears to be the common rubus strigosus, with a thornless stem,—berries a scarlet red, very sweet,—acines slightly adhering. Where depressions exist in the surface of the soil, so that it remains wet and marshy, the tamarack is found, and the white cedar is seen overhanging the cliffs on the banks of the river, and adds very much to the picturesque appearance of the St. Louis at this place.

XLVII. Day.—(*July 9th.*)—On reaching the foot of the Grand Portage, we exchanged two of our largest canoes with the American Fur Company, for four of smaller size adapted to the navigation of the river above the portage, and now proceeded on our voyage in seven small canoes. The river is ascended six miles to the Portage aux Coteaux, which consists of three pauses, and is a mile and a half across. The carrying path lies over an elevated tract of rough country consisting of slate in a vertical position, which is in many places naked, and some idea may be formed of the singular appearance of the rock, by comparing it to the leaves of a book standing edgewise. The effect of this arrangement of the strata, upon the mockasins and feet of the voyageurs, who cross this portage has led to its name—*the portage of knives.* At the lower end of it, this slate forms a lone standing pile, or pyramid, in the centre of the river, of eighty or ninety feet in height, and supporting in its crevices a few stunted cedars and pines. The banks on either side are comparatively low at the water's edge, but preserve the same geological character and position, and at a short distance back, rise to a corresponding elevation. It appears evident that the river has here rent and worn a passage through the rock, as it must have done at innumerable other places, in its rapid and rugged course. The growth of trees here is almost exclusively cedar, pine, and spruce. We encamped at the head of the portage at an early hour in the afternoon. Here the river has a perpendicular fall of fourteen feet. At the foot of it there is a vein of chlorite slate, about two hundred yards below the fall on the west shore. At this place we also found the red raspberry. A tall elm which overshadows the little green which has been formed on the bank of the river, at the head of the portage, in connexion with the fall and surrounding woods and rocks, throws an air of rural beauty over this scene—

> " So wond'rous wild, the whole might seem
> " The scenery of a fairy dream."

XLVIII. Day.—(*July* 10*th.*)—The difficulties attending our ascent of the St. Louis river, induced the Governor to determine on detaching a part of the expedition across the country by land, to Sandy Lake, whenever we should arrive at an eligible spot. For this purpose two Chippeway guides, of the Fond du Lac band, had been brought along from the head of the Grand Portage, and this was the place chosen for the separation. The party thus detached, consisted of eight soldiers under the command of Lieut. Mackay, accompanied by Mr. Doty, Mr. Trowbridge, Mr. Chase, and myself, together with an interpreter of the Chippeway language, and the two Indian guides—sixteen in all. The route was represented as capable of being performed in two day's journey, if no accident occurred. We left the camp at the head of the portage at 6 o'clock in the morning, each carrying a pack containing five day's provisions, a knife, a musquitoe bar, and a cloak or blanket. Several were armed, but others left their guns, as it was thought we should see little game, and they would be cumbersome in travelling. Our guides taking their course by the sun, immediately struck into a close matted forest of pine and hemlock, through which we urged our way with some difficulty. On travelling two miles we fell into an Indian path, leading in the required direction, which we followed until it became lost in swamps. After pursuing it two miles, we passed through a succession of ponds and marshes, where the mud and water were in some places half leg deep. These marshes continued four miles, and were succeeded by a strip of three miles of open dry sandy barren, covered with shrubbery, and occasionally clumps of pitch pines. This terminated in a thick forest of hemlock and spruce, of a young growth, which continued two miles and brought us to the banks of a small lake, with clear water and a pebbly shore. Having no canoe to cross, we took a circuitous route around its southern shore, through thick woods and swamps, where the difficulty of travelling was very much increased, by fallen trees and brush. In order to avoid these difficulties, on approaching the head of this lake, we walked along the shore of it and occasionally in the water, and here we picked up several beautiful specimens of agate and carnelian. We now again fell into the Indian path which led us to two small lakes, similar in size to the Carnelian lake, but with marshy shores, and reddish water, and filled with pond flowers, rushes, and folle avoine. At the second lake the path ceased at the water's edge, and our guides could not afterwards find it. Here they found a large green tortoise, which they killed in a very ingenious and effectual way, by a blow with a hatchet upon the neck, at the point where the under part of the shell serves as a sheath to it. I had never before seen the tortoise killed in so expeditious a manner: it was carried along to be eaten at night. They here appeared to be in doubt about the way. We now entered the great tamarack swamp, in which we progressed about eight miles, and encamped at 5 o'clock near the shore of the third lake, having travelled eleven hours. and passed a distance of about twenty miles. The weather in the morning was cloudy, and rain commenced about seven o'clock, and continued at intervals all day. The thermometer at 6 A. M. stood at 53°,—at 12 A. M. at 72°, and at 6 P. M. 51°. The sun was not visible during the day. The principal forest trees are tamarack (*pinus pendula*,) yellow pine, cedar, spruce, and birch. The winter green has been common on the pine barrens, the sarsaparilla (*aralia nundicaulis*) in the forests.

XLIX. Day.—(*July* 11*th*.)—On quitting our encampment this morning, the Indians left a memorial of our journey inscribed upon bark, for the information of such of their tribe as should happen to fall upon our track. This we find to be a common custom among them. It is done by tracing, either with paint or with their knives upon birch bark, (*betula papyracea*) a number of figures and hieroglyphics which are understood by their nation. This sheet of bark is afterwards inserted in the end of a pole, blazed, and drove into the ground, with an inclination towards the course of travelling. In the present instance the whole party were represented in a manner that was perfectly intelligible, with the aid of our interpreter, each one being characterized by something emblematic of his situation or employment. They distinguish the Indian from the white man, by the particular manner of drawing the figure, the former being without a hat, &c. Other distinctive symbols are employed, thus—Lieut. Mackay was figured with a sword to signify that he was an officer, —Mr. Doty, with a book, the Indians having understood that he was an attorney,—myself, with a hammer, in allusion to the mineral hammer I carried in my belt, &c. The figure of a tortoise and prairy hen, denoted that these had been killed,—three smokes —that our encampment consisted of three fires,— eight muskets,—that this was the number armed,— three hacks upon the pole, leaning N. W. that we were going three days N. W.—the figure of a white man with a tongue near his mouth, (like the Azteek hieroglyphics) that he was an interpreter, &c. Should an Indian hereafter visit this spot, he would therefore read upon this memorial of bark,—that fourteen white men and two Indians encamped at that place,—that five of the white men were chiefs or officers,—one an interpreter,—and eight common soldiers,—that they were going to Sandy Lake, (knowing three days journey N. W. must carry us there)— that we were armed with eight guns, and a sword,— that we had killed a tortoise, a prairy hen, &c. I had no previous idea of the existence of such a medium of intelligence among the northern Indians. All the travellers of the region, are silent on the subject. I had before witnessed the facility with which one of the lake Indians had drawn a map of certain parts of the southern coast of Lake Superior, but here was a historical record of passing events, as permanent certainly as any written record among us, and full as intelligible to those for whom it was intended. We left our encampment at seven o'clock, and after travelling nine hours in the Tamarack swamp, encamped, having progressed by estimation, 14 miles. This has been the most fatiguing days journey onthe tour, and several of our party lay down at night in a complète state of exhaustion. Even our Indian guides demanded a halt. All that could render travelling tiresome and perplexing, has been encountered—swamps--mud--bog—windfalls--stagnant water—the want of spots sufficiently dry to sit down upon—and of water that could be drank, have successively opposed our progress, and enhanced the labour of the journey. To increase these perplexities, our guides seemed uncertain of their way, and we wandered about among bogs and morasses, without the satisfaction of knowing that we approached nearer to the place we were in search of. While toiling our way through this dreary and inhospitable region, the remark of the Baron La Hontan, respecting the northwestern region of Canada, that it is "the fag end of the world," came forcibly to mind. It was probably by reverting, under similar circumstances to the smiling regions of the south of France, his native country, that the Baron was induced to throw out this geographical anathema. Without applying the remark to the whole region of the northwest, or presuming to say, that this particular section of it is indicated by the lowest degree in the scale of countries geologically cursed, it may be remarked, that it is subject to the influence of a winter atmosphere for nine months in the year, and that it can never be rendered subservient to the purposes of agriculture, or traversed by roads. Even the Indians never visit it except during the winter season upon the ice, for the purpose of taking the marten, beaver, and muskrat. The dreadful storms which prevail here at certain seasons, are indicated by the prostration of entire forests, and the up-rooting of the firmest trees. These lie invariably pointing towards the southeast, indicating the strongest winds to prevail from the opposite point. It is one of the most fatiguing labours of the route, to cross these immense windfalls,—the trees are chiefly tamarack, spruce, cedar, ash, white birch, and hemlock. In the course of the day we have crossed a turbid stream running towards the south, called *Akeek Seebe* (kettle river,) which is tributary to the Missisawgaiegon which enters the Mississippi, a short distance above the falls of St. Anthony, after having passed in the intermediate distance through the Great Spirit Lake.

L. Day.—(*July* 12*th.*)--The dampness of the ground upon which we lay, and the torment of the musquitoes, gave us little rest. We commenced our march at five o'clock, and after travelling twelve hours passed out of the great swamp, and encamped upon the banks of a small stream called Buffaloe creek, which is tributary to Sandy Lake. Here our guides came to a country which they recognised, and by their reiterated shouts convinced us that they were no less overjoyed than ourselves upon this discovery. In a short time they pointed out to us hacked trees and bushes where they had formerly passed, which entirely restored our lost confidence, and before night we fell into an Indian trail which they followed with as much apparent facility and confidence as an American traveller would a turnpike road, although we could seldom distinguish the marks and signs by which they were guided. We compute this day's journey at 20 miles. In crossing the swamp we found the cranberry (*oxycoccus macrocarpus*) in great abundance. Upon the same bog were to be seen the fruit of last year's growth, the green berries of the present season, and flowers that were just expanding. The agreeable taste of this berry was a grateful treat, at a time when we were much fatigued, by travelling for many miles over an elastic open bog where no drink-water could be procured.

LI. Day.—(*July* 13*th.*)—We were aroused between four and five o'clock by a shower of rain, and after taking our customary breakfast of dried beef and biscuit, pursued the Indian trail towards Sandy Lake, which we reached after travelling fourteen miles, at 12 o'clock. Our path after leaving the swamps lay across a succession of sandy ridges, covered with white and yellow pine, with some poplar and thickets of underbrush in the valleys, and altogether, of a barren appearance. In crossing these I noticed among the shrubbery the witch hazel, sarsaparilla, wild cherry, kinnikinick, and the Labrador tea plant, (*ledum latifolium* of Pursh.) Imbedded in the sandy alluvion of these ridges are found scattered masses of hornblende, granite, argillite, sand stone, milky and red ferruginous quartz, jasper, and carnelian. The largest masses consist of granite and hornblende. The carnelian is in small fragments of a red colour, sometimes clouded or striped with white, or pale yellow. The blue jay, and brown thresher, the pigeon and turtle dove occasionally appeared in the forest, to enliven this part of the journey. On approaching the lake we ascended a lofty pine ridge, which forms its southern barrier, and commands one of the most charming views of this romantic little lake, which suddenly rose to our impatient sight like a "burnished sheet of living gold" that gleaming with the declining sun—

" In all her length far winding lay
" With promontory, creek, and bay ;
" And islands that empurpled bright
" Floated amid the livelier light ;
" And mountains that like giants stand
" To sentinel enchanted land."—Scott.

The Indian name for this lake is Kom-tong-gog-o-mog,—the Canadians call it Lac du Sable : both are significant of its sandy shores. It is about five miles long, by four in breadth, and twelve in circumference,—of a very irregular shape, with innumerable islands,--bays,--and points, some of which project into it half its width. Strewed along its shores, we find detached fragments of granite, and other rocks, together with carnelian, agate, jasper, and hornstone. The adjoining lands are hilly and covered with pine. The islands are characterized by oak. It has an outlet by which, at the distance of two miles, it communicates with the Mississippi river. On this lake the American Fur Company have an establishment, which we in vain endeavoured to descry on first reaching the eminence that overlooked it. We carried a letter to the clerks from the agent of the establishment, Mr. Morrison, whom we met, on our passage through Lake Superior, on his annual return to Michilimackinac, and were informed that a gun fired upon any part of it could be heard at the fort, (as it is called.) Our first care, therefore, on reaching the shore, was to fire a volley of musketry, to advertise them of our approach, and procure a boat to take us across. As it seemed to produce no effect the signal was reiterated, and at last two men were descried in a canoe, cautiously approaching. They appeared to be in doubt whether we were white men or Indians,—friends or foes,—but we soon convinced them by parading our soldiers upon the beach, and by signals, that we were Americans and friends. On reaching us they proved to be the two clerks of the company's establishment, to whom ve carried an introductory letter. They were not less surprised at our appearance, than we overjoyed at theirs, and while passing across the lake, they related the singular effect which our firing had produced at their establishment, and in the contiguous Indian village. The Indians of this region being at war with the Sioux, had mistaken the firing for an attack of that nation upon some part of their tribe, and were thrown into the utmost consternation. Some of the women pretended to have heard the war whoop, and all were unprepared, totally, for such an encounter. The possibility of its being a straggling party of hunters, had occurred to them, but they did not venture to reconnoitre us until they had driven off their cattle and secured them in the woods, and made some other dispositions suggested on the emergency.

We reached the fort a short time before sunset. It is situated on a sandy point, on the south shore of the lake, near its outlet, and consists of a stockade one hundred feet square, with bastions at the south-east, and northwest angles, pierced for musketry. The pickets are of pitch pine, thirteen feet above the ground, and a foot square, and pinned together with stout plates of the same wood. There are three gates, the principal one facing the north, which are shut whenever liquor is dealt out to the Indians. The stockade incloses two ranges of buildings containing the provision store, workshop, ware house, rooms for the clerks, and accommodations for the men. On the west and northwest angles of the fort there are four acres of ground inclosed with pickets, devoted to the culture of potatoes. No garden vegetables, or grain are attempted to be raised. This is one of the posts visited by Lieut. Pike, in 1806, and there are still several people here who remember that visit. It was then occupied by the North-west Company, by whom it was first erected in 1794.

LII. Day.—(*July* 14*th.*)—This morning we embarked, accompanied by one of the clerks of the company's establishment, and sixteen Indians of the Sandy Lake band, to meet the expedition on the Savannah Portage, and assist in carrying the baggage across. On going a league we landed in a bay on the northeast shore of the lake, and proceeded along an old trail, leading to the west end of the portage, where we arrived about twelve o'clock, at noon, and to our surprise found a part of the baggage already there. Governor Cass, and some of the gentlemen who accompanied him from the Portage aux

Coteaux, had also arrived, and in the course of an hour, we had the pleasure of seeing the whole party there, but it was five o'clock in the evening before the last baggage and canoes were carried over, and it was then concluded to encamp. The expedition after our departure from the Portage aux Coteaux, on the tenth, proceeded up the St. Louis about twenty miles against a strong current, in the course of which they ascended the Grand Rapids, where the river was estimated to have a fall of 90 feet, in six miles.—On the eleventh they proceeded thirty-three miles, and encamped at the mouth of the Savannah river.—On the twelfth, they ascended that river to within two miles of its source, and there left two of the canoes which had been procured of the American Fur Company.—On the thirteenth, they proceeded three pauses upon the portage.—These three pauses were a perfect quagmire, in which the men often sank half-thigh deep into the mud.—On the fourteenth, they moved ten pauses to the west end of the portage, where we rejoined them after a separation of five days. The geological character of the country in the intermediate distance, is considerably diversified. Having requested Dr. Wolcott, on leaving the Portage aux Coteaux, to note the geological appearances of the country, he obligingly furnished me with the following observations:

"*July* 10*th*.—We left the vertical strata of slate, about two miles above the head of the Portage aux Coteaux. They were succeeded by rocks of hornblende, which continued the whole distance to the head of the Grand Rapid. These rocks were only to be observed in the bed of the r ver, and appeared to be much water-worn, and manifestly out of place. Soon after we left the Portage aux Coteaux, the hills receded from the river, and its banks for the rest of the way were generally low,—often alluvial,—and always covered with a thick growth of birch, elm, sugar tree, (*acer saccharinum,*) and the whole tribe of pines, with an almost impenetrable thicket of underbrush.

"*July* 11*th.*—The appearances of this day have been similar to those of yesterday, except that the country bordering the river, became entirely alluvial, and the poplar became the predominating growth while the evergreen almost entirely disappeared. The rocks were seldom visible except upon the rapids, and then only in the bed of the river, and were entirely composed of hornblende all out of place, and exhibiting no signs of stratification, but evidently thrown confusedly together by the force of the current.

"*July* 12*th.*—The Savannah river is about twenty yards broad at its junction with the St. Louis, but soon narrows to about half the breadth, which it retains until it forks at the distance of twelve miles from its mouth. Its whole course runs through a low marshy meadow the timbered land occasionally reaching to the banks of the river, but generally keeping a distance of about twenty rods on either side. The meadow is for the most part covered with tufts of willow and other shrubs, common to marshes. The woods, which skirt it, are of the same kinds observed on the preceding days, except that a species of small oak, frequently appears among it. The river becomes so narrow towards its head, that it is with great difficulty canoes can make their way through its windings; and the portage commences a mile or two from its source, which is in a tamarack swamp."

The descent of the St. Louis river in the same distance, according to the estimate kept by Dr. Wolcott,* is two hundred and thirty feet. The length of the Savannah portage is six miles, and is passed at thirteen pauses. The first three pauses are shockingly bad. It is not only a bed of mire, but the difficulty of passing it is greatly increased by fallen trees, limbs, and sharp knots of the pitch pine, in some places on the surface, in others imbedded one or two feet below. Where there are hollows or depressions in the ground, tall coarse grass, brush, and pools of stagnant water are encountered. Old voyageurs say. that this part of the portage was formerly covered with a heavy bog, or a kind of peat, upon which the walking was very good, but that during a dry season, it accidentally caught fire and burnt over the surface of the earth so as to lower its level two or three feet when it became mirey, and subject to

	Miles.	Feet.
* From the head of the Portage aux Coteaux, to the Isle aux Plaie, distance	3	15
To the Isle aux Pins,	6	6
To the head of said Isle,	$\frac{1}{8}$	6
To the foot of the Grand Rapidé,	2	2
To the head of the Grand Rapidé,	6	90
To Glukié Rapidé,	6	4
To the head of ditto.	$\frac{1}{4}$	5
To Grosse Roché,	21	12 6
To Savannah river,	12	72
To the Portage,	24	18
Total fall in	80 $\frac{3}{8}$	230 6

inundation from the Savannah river. The country, after passing the third pause, changes in a short distance, from a marsh to a region of sand hills covered mostly with white and yellow pine, intermixed with aspen. The hills are short and conical, with a moderate elevation. In some places they are drawn out into ridges, but these ridges cannot be observed to run in any uniform course; on the contrary they are confused in their arrangement. The country has a general rise from the East to the West Savannah, which may be estimated at thirty feet. This is the dividing ridge between the waters of Lake Superior, and the Mississippi river. Where the portage path approaches the sources of the West Savannah there is a descent into a small valley covered with rank grass—without forest trees—and here and there clumps of willows, similar to those on the East Savannah. This valley is skirted with a thick and brushy growth of alder, aspen, hazel, &c. The adjoining hills are sandy, covered with pine. The stream here is just large enough to swim a canoe, and the navigation commences within a mile of its source. It pursues a very serpentine course to Sandy Lake, in a general direction northwest, and has several rapids. The thermometer this day stood at 80° at noon.

LIII. Day.—(*July* 15*th.*)—At five o'clock in the morning we commenced our descent. The water being very shallow, only two men were allowed to embark in each canoe; the remainder of the party proceeded on foot by the path we yesterday came up. On descending four miles, there is a portage of six hundred yards where half the baggage is carried across, but the canoes go over the rapids with half-loads. Here the men were halted to assist. Eight miles lower there is another portage of four or five hundred yards, where the same labour is performed. The river here receives a tributary from the south, called Ox creek, and from the point of its junction the navigation is good at all seasons, to Sandy Lake, a distance of six miles. It is one league from the mouth of the West Savannah to the company's fort, where the expedition arrived at four o'clock in the afternoon. We were received with a salute from the Indians *á la mode de savâge*, with balls. The custom of firing salutes was introduced into this region by the North West Company, who were in the habit of receiving their agents and clerks, on their annual return from Montreal, with this mark of respect. But the Indians never use blank cartridges on these occasions, the precise reason for which I did not learn. The balls dropped in the water all around us, and it would seem as if they were apparantly trying how near they could strike to the canoes without endangering our lives. The Sandy Lake band of Indians consists at present of one hundred and twenty souls, but it appears to have been much larger, at a former period. Pike states the numerical force of this band in 1805, at three hundred and forty-eight, forty-five of whom were warriors, seventy-nine women, and two hundred and twenty-four children. The principal chief is Bookoo-sainge-gon, or Broken Arm. It is also the residence of De Breche, who exercises something like an imperial sway among the Chippeway bands, inhabiting the sources of the Mississippi. This band subsists by hunting the beaver, otter, muskrat, moose, marten, wolverine, and black and silver fox. They have neither the deer, buffaloe, or elk. In the fall they gather large quantities of the wild rice, which is the only bread stuff of the region. No corn is ever raised. Their hunting grounds extend east to the Fond du Lac band at the head of Lake Superior, north to the Rainy Lakes, west to the Leech Lake tribe, and south to the Mississippi prairies of the Sioux countries. Like all the erratic bands of Chippeways, they speak the Algonquin language, and are at war with the Sioux. The remarks that are applicable to one of these bands, are equally so to all, for they exhibit little diversity as to their mode of living, dress, habits, and opinions. Notwithstanding the advantages of a long intercourse with Europeans, they may still be represented as exhibiting human society in one of its rudest possible forms, and remain essentially without agriculture, without arts, and without religion. Their physical constitution is generally excellent. Inhabiting a hardy climate, where the influence of winter is experienced eight months in the year, they have acquired a hardihood of body,—a patience under hunger and long suffering,—and a contempt for the inclemencies of the weather, which is peculiar to the savage tribes of the north; and we are tempted to apply to them the remark which Polibius makes concerning the Arcadians, "that the cold and gloomy climate of Arcadia, gives the inhabitants a harsh and austere aspect; for it is natural that men, in their manners, figure, complexion, and institutions, should resemble their climate." They appear also, since the Six Nations have dropped their ancient character, to possess in a higher degree, than any other tribe, that heroic contempt of death, and manly fortitude under the pressure of misfortune, which is so finely described by one of our colonial poets,—

> " Begin ye tormentors, your threats are in vain,
> " For the sons of Alknomook shall never complain."
>
> FRENAU.

" A man," says the Baron La Hontan, " is not a man with us, any further than riches will make him so ; but among them the true qualifications of a man are, to run well,—to hunt,—to bend the bow, and manage the fusee,—to work a canoe,—to understand war,—to know forests,—to subsist upon a little, —to build cottages,—to fell trees, and to be able to travel an hundred leagues in a wood, without any guide, or other provision than his bow and arrows."*

Pike states the collective strength of the Chippeway tribes at eleven thousand one hundred and seventy-seven, two thousand and forty-nine of whom are warriors, three thousand one hundred and eighty-five women, and five thousand nine hundred and forty-four children.† They consist of innumerable petty bands, scattered over the immense region from Detroit to the sources of the Mississippi, and the Red River of Hudson's Bay. In no place is there any large body permanently located, the internal bands generally consist of from thirty to sixty warriors. It is owing to this great distribution of force, that they have been enabled to maintain so long and successful a war with their more powerful neighbours, the Sioux, for it has been a defensive

* La Hontan's Voyages, Vol. 2. p. 9.

† See Pike's Expeditions.

war on their part; and by living in small detached bands, they have rendered the superior power of the Sioux in a great measure useless, and have been enabled to evade their attacks, and often to fall upon them to great advantage. They have relied chiefly upon their cunning and dexterity, while the Sioux have placed too much confidence in their superior numbers. "This nation," says Lieut. Pike, "is more mild and docile than the Sioux; and if we may judge from unprejudiced observers, more cool and deliberate in action; but the latter possess a much higher sense of the honour of their nation: the Chippeways plan for self-preservation. The Sioux attack with impetuosity; the others defend with every necessary precaution. But the superior number of the Sioux, would have enabled them to have annihilated the Chippeways long since, had it not been for the nature of their country, which entirely precludes the possibility of an attack on horseback. Also, gives them a decided advantage over an enemy, who, being half armed with arrows, the least twig of a bush turns the shaft of death out of its direction. Whereas, the whizzing bullet holds its course, nor spends its force short of its destined victim. Thus, we generally have found, that when engaged in a prairie, the Sioux came off victorious; but if in the woods, even, if not obliged to retreat, the carcasses of their slaughtered brethren shew how dearly they purchase the victory." Very few of the Chippeway bands have fixed habitations, and their erratic disposition appears to be attributable, in a great measure, to the poverty of the regions they inhabit, and the inclemency of their climate. Throughout a great proportion of the region no corn can be cultivated, and when their game, or fish, or wild rice fails them, they are compelled to change their residence in quest of food. All the bands are subject to their own chiefs, who are elected for their superior acquirements as hunters, warriors, or orators. The same climate, however, which renders them a scanty subsistence, exempts them from other evils, with which their southern neighbours are afflicted. Sickness and disease are almost unknown in their territories. They are wholly exempted from the bilious complaints of the southern latitudes of our continent. Their mode of life also favours a healthful constitution of body,—open air,—free exercise,—without exhausting fatigue, and a simple diet, exempt them from a train of diseases incident to refined society. It has been said that their wandering mode of life, and the rapidity of their marches through the woods, generally proves fatal to such as are stricken by age or infirmity; and that ill-formed children are destroyed by their mothers in infancy. Nothing has, however, been observed to strengthen this opinion. It is probable individual cases of such barbarity, (and those of extreme deformity,) have occurred, but there does not appear to prevail any general custom in regard to it. On the contrary, several naturally deformed savages which we have seen, appear to disprove the prevalence of such a custom, or may, at least, be looked upon as instances of the humanity and attachment of their mothers.

There are no bands of the northern Indians who go entirely without clothes, even in the hottest summer weather; and like all other savages they possess a great fondness for grotesque ornaments of feathers, skins, bones, and claws of animals. They have also an unconquerable passion for silver bands, beads, rings, and all light, showy, and fantastic articles of European manufacture. When silver cannot be procured they use copper, which is a native product of the region, and is beaten out by them in a rude way with a hatchet upon a stone, and afterwards rubbed smooth. The women being compelled to do the work and drudgery of savage life, have less opportunity and time for dress, but their taste, in this respect, remains the same, and whenever they can procure them, dress themselves with the most gaudy articles. They do not, however, use feathers, an ornament which appears exclusively appropriated to the men and warriors. The great occasions which draw them out in all their finery, are war and feasting. War and feasting, form, however, the great employments of savage society, when it has not been ameliorated by European intercourse. The northern savages play several games at cards, and have an inordinate passion for gambling, which carries them to such excesses, that they will stake their arm-bands, rings, and other articles of ornament, or dress. This practice which was probably first introduced by the French Couriers du Bois is attended by all the bad consequences, without any of the advantages resulting from it, in civilized society—for they never play for amusement. Hence many of their quarrels and murders are attributable to gambling disputes.

It has been remarked that the North American Indians have tamed no wild animals, so as to render them subservient to the purposes of domestic economy. To this remark their dogs are an exception, for they appear to be nothing more than the tamed wolf, and tamed fox, in some instances a mixed breed, and in all possessing the essential characters of these two animals. They have a long pointed head, sharp ears, and long coarse grey hair, and cannot bark in the manner of the European dog. This has given Buffon occasion to say, that dogs which have been transported from Europe to America, suffer so much under the deteriorating influence of our climate, that they completely loose the power of barking. The domesticated wolf, or Indian dog, has a sullen growl, and where there is no intermixture, retains its primitive howl, which it is easy to distinguish from that of the true dog.

Notwithstanding the abundance of wild rice in this region, there is a great part of the year that they subsist without this article, owing to their want of industry and foresight in gathering a sufficient quantity before it is destroyed by the myriads of aquatic fowl, which it attracts; and also to their improvidence in living riotously upon it in the harvest season, without thinking of the coming winter. The bands of Chippeways and Ottaways inhabiting the peninsula of Michigan, plant corn. Northwest of the Sault de St. Marie, the Indians may be represented as wholly without agriculture. When their wild rice is gone, they rely chiefly upon the fish which are abundant in all the northern lakes. Hunting is less an object to procure meat, than to procure furs, the animals being mostly of the small and well-furred kind. In times of great scarcity, they resort to several roots, of an alimentary character, afforded by the region, and which like the manioc of the native Brizilians, supplies the place of bread. The principal of these is the Indian potatoe, a production that remains unnoticed in American Botany. What analogy it bears, if any, to the tuckaho of the southern states, of which a description has lately been read before the New-York Lyceum, by Dr. John Torrey, I am unable to say. When caught without this resource, and game failing, they are often known to gather up the bleached bones in the woods, and by long boiling in water, extract some nutritive matter, which is drank in the form of a soup. In desperate cases, they also collect the river and lake muscles, which are eaten, after having been previously boiled. These are considered by the Indians the most insipid food which they are ever driven by necessity to make use of. There is a species of lichen, in some parts of the country, which is also sometimes eaten. It is called *waac* by the Indians, and *Tripe de Roché* by the French, and is eaten, after being boiled down to the consistence of a mucilage. They are the only tribes of American Indians who live *without salt*, their country affording no brine-springs, and being either unable to buy from the traders, or wanting the opportunity. Such is the miserable life which these people live, owing to the dreariness of the climate, the want of agriculture, and their own improvidence.

The custom of painting their bodies is characteristic of all savage tribes. The native Britons formerly practised it. Those of the island of St. Salvador, when Columbus first landed in the new world, were found to paint grotesque figures and ornaments upon their bodies. The native Brazilians,—the inhabitants of New-Holland, and Van Dieman's Land, and all the tribes of North America, are more or less in the practice of employing paint upon their faces, and other parts of their bodies, either with a view of rendering themselves more attractive to their friends, or more terrible to their enemies. The northern tribes use it upon all occasions. The substances employed are ochres, clays, native oxyds of iron, bole, and some other minerals, the production of their country. The Sioux procure a fine green coloured clay, on the banks of the St. Peter's, which is highly esteemed. They have also a white and red clay, and a fine red oxide of iron, which are much employed, and by their admixture, they are enabled to paint themselves of almost any colour. Red is the colour with which they decorate themselves on going to war, and for this purpose vermilion is sold them by the traders at the rate of eight dollars per pound. Black, is used when they mourn the loss of relatives, and for this purpose lampblack, or soot, mixed with bears oil, is employed.

Of the state of female society among the northern Indians, I shall say little, because on a review of it, I find very little to admire, either in their collective morality, or personal endowments. The savage state is universally found to display itself in the most striking degree in the situation, dress, personal accomplishments, and employments of females, and these evidences may be looked upon as unerring indexes to the degree of civilization,—to the mental powers, and to the moral refinements of the other sex. Doomed to drudgery and hardship from infancy,—without the elegance of dress,—without either mental resources, or personal beauty,—what can be said in favour of the Indian women! The custom of binding the feet of female infants in such a manner as to make the toes point inwards, gives them in after life a very awkward appearance in walking; and in regard to the absence of female beauty, I am not able, from my own observations, to make a single exception.

That exceptions exist, however, among some of the northern tribes, we have the authority of M'Kenzie, for asserting. "Of all the nations," he remarks, "which I have seen on this continent, the Knistenaux women are the most comely. Their figure is generally well proportioned, and the regularity of their features would be acknowledged by the more civilized people of Europe. Their complexion has less of that dark tinge, which is common to those savages who have less cleanly habits.

"It does not appear, however," he continues, "that chastity is considered by them as a virtue; or that fidelity is believed to be essential to the happiness of wedded life. Though it sometimes happens, that the infidelity of a wife is punished by the husband, with the loss of her hair, nose, and perhaps life; such severity proceeds from its having been practised without his permission: for a temporary interchange of wives is not uncommon; and the offer of their persons, is considered as a necessary part of the hospitality due to strangers.

"When a man looses his wife, it is considered as a duty to marry her sister, if she has one; or he may, if he pleases, have them both at the same time."*

We here first observed a custom which is prevalent among the northern bands, of inclosing their dead in coffins bound around with bark, and expos-

* M'Kenzie's Voyages to the Frozen, and Pacific Oceans, p. 66.

ing them on scaffolds ten or fifteen feet in the air. This custom is said to have been borrowed by them from the Sioux, who have practised it from the earliest times. It is not now universal among the Chippeways, and they frequently bury their dead in the European manner. In this case, however, a roof is built over the grave, which is closed all around, except at the head, where a hole is cut through the bark large enough to put in a wooden dish, with meats for the use of the dead. If a warrior dies, his war club and other weapons and ornaments, are buried with him, as it is supposed, he will require them in another world. If it is a woman that dies, a paddle and carrying strap are buried with her, that she may perform the same drudgery in a future state she is required to do in this. This certainly implies some notion of immortality, but they do not appear to have any distinct conceptions of the body and soul. It is difficult indeed to reduce their opinions to any settled points. It is only certain that they expect to live hereafter in a country far more beautiful and delightful than the present,—where there will be perpetual spring,—where game will be plenty,—and where all the implements they have made use of in this life, will be required as the means of ensuring them a support. This idea has been seized upon, in one of the most happy moments of the poet of Twickenham.

"Lo, the poor Indian, whose untutored mind
"Sees God in clouds, or hears him in the wind;
"His soul proud science never taught to stray
"Far as the solar walk, or milky way;
"Yet simple nature to his hope has giv'n,
"Behind the cloud-topt hill, an humbler heav'n;

"Some safer world in depth of woods embrac'd,
"Some happier island in the watery waste,
"Where slaves once more their native land behold,
"No fiends torment,—no Christians thirst for gold.
"To be,—contents his natural desire,
"He asks no angel's wing, no seraph's fire;
"But thinks, admitted to that equal sky,
"His faithful dog shall bear him company." Pope.

LIV. Day.—(*July* 16*th.*)—A council was held this morning with the Sandy-Lake Indians, at their own solicitation, and several speeches presented to Gov. Cass, as the representative of the president of the United States, who is addressed by the title of "Great Father." These speeches, as they have been interpreted to us, do not possess the characteristic eloquence of Indian oratory, although apparently delivered by the Indians in a very impassioned and animated manner. But it appears, at least in these instances, that they do not "suit the action to the word and the word to the action," as what we have supposed to be the most impassioned eloquence when heard in the Indian tongue, has turned out, when translated, to be a tissue of common place ideas, without passion, eloquence, or figures. As one of the best specimens of the speeches which have generally been addressed to the Governor, during our progress through this region, the following is presented.

"Father,—We are glad you have come among us, to see how we live, and what kind of a country we inhabit, and to tell these things to our Great Father, the President.

"Father, you see us here,—we are poor,—we want every thing,—we have neither knives or blankets,—guns or powder,—lead or cloth,—kettles or tomahawks,—tobacco or whiskey.—We hope you will give us these things.

"Father, we are glad that the President has thought proper to send you among us,—we are glad to see his flag wave upon this lake,—we are his children,—he is our Father,—we smoke the same pipe,—we take hold of the same tomahawk,—we are inseparable friends. It shall never be said that the Chippeways are ungrateful. Father, depend upon this, and take this pipe of peace as a pledge of our sincerity.

"Father, we are of the race of strong men,—of good warriors, and good hunters, but we cannot always kill game, or catch fish.—We can live a great while upon a little, but we cannot live upon nothing.

"Father, our wild rice is all eaten up,—the buffaloes live in the land of our enemies, the Sioux,—we are hungry, and naked,—we are dry and needy.—We hope you will relieve us.

"Father, the President of the United States is a very great man, even like a lofty pine upon the mountain's top.—You are also a great man,—and the Americans are a great people. Can it be possible they will allow us to suffer!"

Governor Cass proposed to negociate a peace between them and the Sioux. They readily assented, and are to send some of their old men as embassadors to accompany us to the Falls of St. Anthony, on our return from the sources of the Mississippi.

The following tables present a view of the state of the weather,—the stationary distances,—and the elevation of the country between the Fond du Lac and Sandy Lake.

TABLE I.

METEOROLOGICAL OBSERVATIONS.

	Atmospheric Temperature.										Mean heat.	WINDS	WEATHER.
	A. M.				P. M.								
	6	7	8	12	1	5	6	7	8	9			
July 6th	68			78	–			54			64	NE.	Clear.
7th			66	71			65				67	NE.	Rain.
8th			63	80					64		69	ENE.	Clear & warm.
9th	57			75					53		61	ENE.	Clear.
10th	53			72			51				58	NE.	Rainy.
11th	51			68			49				56	WNW.	Cloudy & cool.
12th	53			71			50				58	NW.	Showery & cloud.
13th		42			74	58					58	NW.	Clear.
14th		67		80			64				70	NW.	Clear.
15th			64		78				53		65	NW.	Cloudy with rain.
16th		50			71					50	57	NNW.	Fair.

11|683

67° mean daily temp.

TABLE II.

STATIONARY DISTANCES.

	Miles.	Tot. Miles.
From the South-West Company's House, to the foot of the Grand Portage,	2	
To the Galley, - - - - -	2	4
To the head of Grand Portage, - -	7	11
To the foot of the Portage aux Coteaux, -	6	17
To the head of do. - .	1½	18½
To the mouth of Savannah river, as detailed in Day LII. - - - - -	56½	75
To the commencement of the Savannah Portage,	24	99
Length of Savannah Portage, - -	6	105
To Sandy Lake, at the discharge of the West Savannah, - - - - -	18	123
South-West Company's Fort, on Sandy Lake,	3	126

TABLE III.

ELEVATION OF THE COUNTRY.

	Feet.	Total Feet.
Estimated fall of the St. Louis River, from the head of Lake Superior to the South-West Company's House, 24 miles, at 2 inches per mile,	4	
Thence to the Galley, 4 miles, - -	8	12
To the head of the Grand Portage, -	220	232
To the foot of the Portage aux Coteaux, 2 leagues, at 3 feet per mile, - - - -	18	250
To the head of the Portage aux Coteaux, (falls not included,) - - - -	28	278
Coteaux Falls, - - - -	14	292
Thence to the mouth of the Savannah River, as estimated by Dr. Wolcott, see DAY LII.	212.6	504.6
Thence to the Savannah Portage, -	18	522.6
Thence to the head of the West Savannah,	30	550.6
DESCENT OF THE WEST SAVANNAH.		
From the place of embarkation to the first Rapid, 4 miles, at 6 inches per mile, - .	2	
Descent of the first Rapid, - -	5	7
To the head of the second Rapid, 8 miles, at 6 inches per mile, - - - -	4	11
Descent of the second Rapid, - -	8	19
Thence to the level of Sandy Lake, -	4.6	23.6
Elevation of Sandy Lake above Lake Superior,	Feet	527

CHAPTER IX.

JOURNEY,

FROM SANDY LAKE TO THE SOURCES OF THE MISSISSIPPI.

LV. DAY.—(*July* 17*th.*)

WE left the fort at half past nine in the morning, in three canoes, manned by nineteen voyageurs and Indians, and provisioned for twelve days. Our party now, exclusive of the working men, consisted of Governor Cass, Dr. Wolcott, Capt. Douglass, Lieut. Mackay, Maj. Forsyth, and myself. The balance of the expedition,—men, baggage, and canoes, was left at the Company's establishment. A mile from the fort we entered the mouth of Sandy Lake River, which discharges into the Mississippi, two miles below. Its course is winding, and near its junction with the Mississippi, it has a rapid where the water descends three feet in sixty yards. On entering the Mississippi, we found a strong current,—reddish water, a little turbid,—some snags and drifts,—and alluvial banks, elevated from four to eight feet, bearing a forest of elm, maple, oak, poplar, pine, and ash. The elm predominates; maple and oak are common,—pine, ash, and poplar, sparing. The river has a width of sixty yards, and the shores are skirted with bull rushes, foille avoine, and tufts of willow. In the course of the day we passed the following rapids, numbered and estimated from the mouth of Sandy Lake River.

1st Rapid,	3 miles,	descent	2 feet in	50 yards	
2d	- 4	-	5	- 200	-
3d	- 3	-	6	- 100	-
4th	- 1	-	1 foot in	50	-
5th	- 5	-	7 feet in	100	-
6th	- 11	-	8	- 200	-

We encamped twenty miles above the sixth rapid at eight o'clock in the evening, having been eleven hours in our canoes, and progressed forty-six miles. The weather has been variable.—At day light there was a violent wind, attended with rain, which ceased at nine o'clock.—Cloudy all day,—sun shone out hot at one o'clock,—then a shower; cloudy and cool in the evening. The river has received no tributary streams; no islands have been encountered, nor have any hills been seen, but the country is low, and swampy at a short distance from the river. Detached stones of hornblende, sand stone, and granite, appear upon the rapids. The musquitoes have been very troublesome.

LVI. Day.—(*July* 18*th*.)—There was a shower of rain during the night,—it ceased at four o'clock. We embarked at five,—the weather remained cloudy and misty. On ascending one mile, we passed Swan River, which enters, by a mouth of twenty yards wide, on the right shore. Loose rocks appear in the water at its mouth. This stream is sixty miles long, and originates in Swan Lake, in which trout are caught. It is rapid for a distance, but expands to a great width towards its source, where it has a still current, and abounds in wild rice. Thirteen leagues above we passed Rapid No. 7, where the water falls three feet in a hundred and fifty yards. Trout river enters six miles higher, on the right side. It is about thirty feet wide at its mouth, but deep, and widens above. It originates in Trout Lake, and is connected with Swan River near its source. Prairie River is four miles above, and enters on the same side. It is ninety feet wide at its mouth,—has a considerable rapid three miles above, but may be ascended with canoes, through an open prairie country, ninety miles. It communicates, by short portages, with one of the western tributaries of St. Louis river, and with Swan river. We encamped on a sand bank, five hundred yards above its entrance, having progressed fifty-one miles. The current of the Mississippi river, this day, has been strong, and a number of snags and drifts have been encountered. The velocity is computed, by Captain Douglass, at $2\frac{2}{5}$ miles per hour. The timber has been much the same as yesterday,—elm and maple predominate. In the afternoon we passed several ridges of pine land elevated twenty or thirty feet above the water,—and a few miles below Trout river, came through a forest of burnt dead pines, which continue about three miles on either shore. The general course of the river is west of north; it is very serpentine, and the curves short, seldom exceeding a mile,—the width of the river has been less than yesterday, and may be computed to average forty yards. Tufts of willow, grass, and wild rice, skirt the water's edge. No islands or rock strata are seen,—detached stones, such as were yesterday noticed, appear in the bed of the stream at the rapids, and occasionally along the shore. The banks are the most recent kind of alluvion, in which very minute shining particles of mica are seen. The common fresh water muscle is very abundant along the shore, and some of an extraordinary size. Ducks and plover have been continually in sight.—The robin, (*turdus migratorius*) brown thrush, blackbird, crow, and water loon, have also been noticed. It is not a region favourable to serpents, and the Indians say that the common garter, (*coluber æstivus*,) and water snake, are the only species known. The weather continued cloudy and cool during the day, and very chilly at night. The musquitoes have been less annoying in consequence.

LVII. Day.—(*July* 19*th.*)—The night was so cold that water froze upon the bottoms of our canoes, and they were encrusted with a scale of ice of the thickness of a knife blade. The thermometer stood at 36° at sun-rise. There was a very heavy dew during the night, and a dense fog in the morning. The forenoon remained cloudy and chilly. Six miles above our encampment we passed the eighth Rapid, where the water falls two feet in a hundred yards; and half a mile above, the ninth Rapid, which consists of a series of small rapids, extending a thousand yards, in the course of which, there is an aggregate fall of sixteen feet. Four miles above the termination of the ninth Rapid, we landed at the foot of the falls of Peckagama, where the river has a descent of twenty feet in three hundred yards. This forms an interruption to the navigation, and there is a portage around the falls of two hundred and seventy-five yards. The Mississippi, at this fall is compressed to a eighty feet in width, and precipitated over a rugged bed of sand stone, highly inclined towards the northeast. There is no perpendicular pitch, but the river rushes down a rocky channel, inclined at an angle of from 35° to 40°. The view is wild and picturesque. Immediately at the head of the falls is the first island noticed in the river. It is small, rocky,—covered with spruce and cedar,—and divides the channel nearly in its centre, at the point where the fall commences. In crossing this portage, I observed the small bush-whortleberry, (*vaccinium dumosum.*) A portion of the berries were already ripe. After passing the falls of Peckagama, a striking change is witnessed in the character of the country. We appear to have attained the summit level of waters. The forests of maple, elm, and oak, cease, and the river winds in the most devious manner through an extensive prairie, covered with tall grass, wild rice, and rushes. This prairie has a mean width of three miles, and is bounded by ridges of dry sand, of moderate elevation, and covered sparingly with yellow pine. Sometimes the river washes close against one of these sand ridges,—then turns into the centre of the prairie, or crosses to the opposite side; but nothing can equal its sinuosities,—we move towards all points of the compass in the same hour,—and we appear to be winding about in an endless labyrinth, without approaching nearer to the object in view. In one instance, we rowed nine miles by the windings of the stream, and advanced but one mile in a direct line. While sitting in our canoes, in the centre of this prairie.

the rank growth of grass, rushes, &c. completely hid the adjoining forests from view, and it appeared as if we were lost in a boundless field of waving grass. Nothing was to be seen but the sky above, and the lofty fields of nodding grass, oats, and reeds upon each side of the stream. The monotony of the view can only be conceived by those who have been at sea,—and we turned away with the same kind of interest to admire the birds, and water fowl, who have chosen this region, for their abode. The current of the river is gentle, its velocity not exceeding one mile per hour:—its width is about eighty feet. It receives a tributary from the left at the distance of forty miles above the falls of Peckagama, called Vermilion river, and three miles above, another called Chevréuil, or Deer river, from the right, bank. We encamped upon the prairie, six miles above Chevréuil river, at a late hour, having ascended sixty miles. Ducks have been abundant throughout the day. We saw no plover in the prairies, although they were common below. The blackbird has been constantly in sight, and the small white gull, such as is common upon the lakes, has been so abundant as to annoy our progress, particularly by its scream, which is harsh and unpleasant. These birds had their nests all along the banks, and were constantly alarmed for their young. The loon, the wild goose, and the heron, have also been observed. The weather has been cloudy, with occasional gleams of sunshine, and chilly towards evening. At the place of our encampment we found a very delicious species of red raspberry, growing upon a small bush of the size of a strawberry vine. Here also, as night approached, we first noticed the fire-fly, which has not before been seen upon the Mississippi.

LVIII. Day.—(*July* 20*th.*)—We had rain during the night,—the morning was cloudy, with a heavy fog. We embarked at half past five; our route lay through a prairie country, similar in every respect to that yesterday passed. At the distance of ten miles we passed the mouth of Leech river, entering on the left. This is the main southwestern fork of the Mississippi, and is ascended about fifty miles, to its source, in Leech lake, where the American fur company have an establishment. This lake is twelve miles across, and was considered, by Lieut. Pike, as the main source of the Mississippi. "The fort," he observes, "is situated on the west side of the lake, in 47° 16′ 13″ north latitude. It is built near the shore, on the declivity of a rising ground, having an inclosed garden, of about five acres, on the north-west. It is a square stockade, of one hundred and fifty feet,—the pickets being sixteen feet in length, three feet under ground, and thirteen feet above, —and are bound together by horizontal bars, each ten feet long. Pickets of ten feet are likewise drove into the ground, on the inside of the work, opposite the apertures between the large pickets. At the west and east angles are bastions pierced for fire arms."* The Leech lake band of Chippeways are located in the vicinity of the fort. It consists of one thousand one hundred and twenty souls, one hundred and fifty of whom are warriors. The principal chiefs are *Eskibugeckoga*, or, Flat-Mouth,

* Pike's Expeditions.

Obiguette, or the chief of the Land, and *Oole*, or the Burnt. They hunt the beaver, marten, muskrat, otter, and black fox. The moose is sometimes killed. They subsist chiefly upon the flesh of these animals, and obtain European and American fabrics in exchange for their furs. Their neighbours are the Assenniboins, (a revolted band of the Sioux,) on the west,—the Upper Red Cedar, and Red Lake tribes of Chippeways, on the north,—and the Sandy Lake Indians on the east and south. Leech-lake river runs its whole length through a savannah,—is very serpentine,—and in many places not more than ten or fifteen yards wide, although it has a depth of twelve or fifteen feet. The current of the Mississippi river, above its junction, is perceptibly stronger, and the water quite clear. The bends are also more abrupt, and the width of the stream a little more than half what it maintains below. It may be estimated above the Leech-lake branch, at sixty feet, but still preserves a good depth. From Sandy lake river, to the falls of Peckagama, the mean fall of the river may be estimated at six inches per mile, exclusive of the rapids;—from thence to the confluence of the Leech-lake branch, at two inches per mile, and thence to Lake Winnipec, at four inches per mile.

At the distance of thirty-five miles above Leech river, we entered Little lake Winnipec, which is about five miles long, and three in width. The water is clear. Its shores are low and marshy, covered with rushes, spear grass, and wild rice, which in some places extend quite across the lake, giving it rather the appearance of a marsh. On passing through this, the river again assumes the size and general appearance it had below, for a distance of ten miles, when it opens into a spacious bay, which is the northeastern extremity of the Upper lake Winnipec. We proceeded through this, and encamped on the north shore of the lake, at the mouth of Turtle Portage river. Lake Winnipec is about fourteen miles long by nine in width, and its waters are deep and transparent. Its shores are generally low and covered, at the water's edge, with rushes, and wild oats. Upon its banks we find oak, maple, poplar, birch, and white pine. It receives four tributaries, Turtle Portage river, Round Lake river, Thornberry river, and an inlet from the southwest, which being somewhat larger than the others, preserves the name of the Mississippi. Turtle Portage river, communicates through several intermediate little lakes, with the Rainy lakes, and the Lake of the Woods. The journey to the Upper Rainy Lake is performed in eight days, and from thence to the Lake of the Woods in ten days.

Round Lake river is the outlet of a lake which is connected by its higher tributaries, with the waters of Turtle Portage river, and the Rainy Lakes. Thornberry river, or La rivière des Epinettes, is smaller than the two former, and is not ascended any considerable distance in canoes. Its origin is also in lakes. The Mississippi branch is navigable fifty miles to its source in the Upper Red Cedar Lake.

On passing through Little Lake Winnipec, we met a couple of Indian women in a canoe, being the first natives seen on the river, of whom our interpreter made enquiry as to the course of the river, and the nature of the country above. They manifested no alarm on our approach, and communicated what they knew frankly and without reserve. They had come down the river for the purpose of observing the state of the wild rice, and at what places it could be most advantageously gathered. None, however, was yet sufficiently ripe to admit of harvesting, but this precaution evinces a degree of care and foresight, which is not always found among savages.

In the course of this day we have observed, either upon the river, or its banks, the wild goose, duck, turkey-buzzard, raven, eagle, king-fisher, (*alcedo alcyon*,) and blackbird.

LIX. Day. (*July* 21*st.*)—We continued our journey at half past four o'clock in the morning. Passing around the northern shore of Lake Winnipec, we observed at a distance a rocky island of such snowy whiteness, as to give it an appearance of singular novelty, and to baffle every conjecture as to the substance of which it was composed. On reaching its shores, we found it to be a confused pile of water-worn fragments of granite, hornblende, quartz, &c. covered with a thick limey incrustation, produced from the excrescence of the myriads of water-fowl who resort to it. These birds were driven away in flocks by our approach, and we particularly noticed the wild goose, black duck, pelican, cormorant, brant, and plover. On landing a dead pelican (*pelecanus onocratolus*,) was found upon the rocks, having apparently been killed that morning, either in a strife among its own species or through disease.—No marks of violence, or external disease could however be observed. This is one of the largest of web-footed water fowl, often exceeding in size the swan.. It has been known to weigh twenty-five pounds, and to measure eleven feet between the tips of the wings. Its most remarkable character, and one which distinguishes it from all other birds, is a large membranaceous pouch extending from the mandible nine or ten inches down the front of the neck. This serves as a repository for its food, and when empty, the bird has the power of wrinkling it up. It has the colour and consistence of a wetted bladder and is naked to appearance, but on examination is found to be partially covered with a very fine downy substance. These pouches are fashioned by the Indians into caps for summer wear, being very light and airy. Notwithstanding the great bulk of this bird, it is said to be very expert upon the wing, and soars to a great height, which is in some measure attributable to the extreme lightness of its bones, which do not altogether exceed a pound and a half in weight.

Disregarding artificial arrangements, all water fowl may be considered under these great natural divisions, namely, those of the penguin kind, with short blunt wings, round bills, and legs hid in the abdomen, which dive in quest of food;—those of the gull kind, with long slender legs, sharp pointed wings, and round bills, which fly along the water to seize their prey;—and those of the goose kind, with broad flat bills, and heavy-quilled wings, which generally lead harmless lives, and subsist mostly upon vegetables and insects. The pelican, from its singular conformation, will not, strictly speaking, fall under any of these denominations, although it seems more nearly allied to the family of the goose. Its feathers are white all over the body, and its wings, which are strong and heavy, clothed with a thick plumage of quills and downy feathers. Its legs are red, and its bill of a greenish tinge at the base, but changing to a reddish blue towards its extremity, which is slightly hooked downward. The eyes are small, compared with the magnitude of the head, and altogether the bird has a heavy and demure look. Like the heron and the cormorant, the pelican is an inordinate eater, and is represented to be indolent and stupid to the last degree.

"This species," says Pennant, "extends over most parts of the torrid zone, and many parts of the warmer temperate. It is found in Europe, on the lower parts of the Danube, and in all parts of the Mediterranean Sea, almost all Africa, and Asia Minor. Are seen in incredible numbers about the Black and Caspian Seas; and come far up the rivers, and into the inland lakes of the Asiatic Russian empire; but grow scarcer eastward, and are seldom met with so far north as the Siberian lakes; yet are not unknown about that of Baikal. They are common on the coast of New Holland, where they grow to an enormous size. They feed upon fish, which they take sometimes by plunging from a great height in the air, and seizing, like the gannet: at other times they fish in concert, swimming in flocks, and forming a large circle in the great rivers, which they gradually contract, beating the water with their wings and feet, in order to drive the fish into the centre; which when they approach, they open their vast mouths, and fill their pouches with their prey, then incline their bills to empty the bag of the water; after which they swim to shore and eat their booty in quiet. As the pouch is capable of holding a dozen quarts of water, a guess may be made of the quantity of fishes it can contain. The French very properly call them *Grande Gosiers*, or *Great Throats*. It is said that when they make their nests in the dry deserts, they carry the water to their young in their vast pouches, and that the lions and beasts of prey come there to quench their thirst, sparing the young, the cause of this salutary provision. Possibly, on this account, the Egyptians style this bird the *camel of the river*:—the Persians *taeub*, or water-carrier.*" The popular fable that this bird feeds its young with blood from its own breast, owes its origin to the circumstance of its permitting them to eat from its pouch the food which it collects for that purpose.

On quitting Pelican Island, we steered northwest across the bay, and entered the mouth of the Mississippi inlet, which we pursued up fifty miles to its origin, in Upper Red Cedar or Cassina† Lake, where we arrived at three o'clock in the afternoon. This may be considered the true source of the Mississippi River, although the greatest body of water is said to come down the Leech Lake Branch. The river between Lake Winnipec and Cassina Lake winds through a prairie-valley, a mile in width, which is bounded by ridges of sandy land covered with yellow and white pine. The river pursues the same devious course, and its banks are overgrown with wild oats, rushes, and grass. Cassina Lake is about

* Arctic Zoology.

† I have proposed to the Topographical Engineer of the Expedition, to designate the lake by this term, in order to prevent its being confounded with Red Cedar Lake, which is situated about 250 miles below. It is in allusion to Governor Cass.

eight miles long by six in width, and presents to the eye a beautiful sheet of transparent water. (*See the perspective view upon the Map.*) Its banks are overshadowed by elm, maple, and pine. Along its margin there are some fields of Indian rice, rushes and reeds: in other places, there is an open beach of clean pebbles, driven up by the waves, but no rock strata appear. The pike, carp, trout, and catfish are caught in its waters. It has an island towards its western extremity covered with trees, from which it derives its local name, but no red cedar is found around its shores. This lake is supplied by two inlets called Turtle and La Beesh rivers, both tributary on the northwestern margin. The former originates in Turtle Lake, near the banks of the Rainy Lakes, and after pursuing a southerly course for forty miles, in which distance it opens into several small lakes, enters Red Cedar or Cassina Lake by a mouth of fifteen yards in width. This branch is ascended with canoes passing to the Lake of the Woods, and has three short portages.

La Beesh river is the outlet of Lake La Beesh, which lies six days journey, with a canoe, west-northwest of Cassina Lake, and has no inlets. A short distance from its shores, the waters run north into the Red River of Hudson's Bay. Its outlet has several rapids, and expands into a number of intermediate lakes, the largest of which are lakes Traversé, Oganga, and Kiskahoo. It also receives several tributaries, all of which originate in small lakes. It is only capable of being ascended in canoes, during the spring and autumnal freshets, and then there are several portages. This branch is considered the largest inlet, and preserves, in the language of the voyageurs, the name of the Mississippi.

On the north shore of this lake, on a cleared eminence, is a village of Chippeways, of ten lodges and sixty souls, under *Wiscoup*, or the Sweet. They received the party with every mark of friendship, and presented us an abundance of the most delicious red raspberries, and a quantity of pemican, or pounded moose meat. Here we also found two Frenchmen, who have been in the employ of the American Fur Company, and located themselves at this spot, for the purpose of trading with the Indians. In the person of one of these, Mons. D———, we witnessed one of the most striking objects of human misery. It appears, that in the prosecution of the fur trade, he had, according to the custom of the country, taken an Indian wife, and spent several winters in that inclement region. During the last, he was, however, caught in a severe snow storm, and froze both his feet in such a manner, that they dropped off shortly after his return to his wigwam. In this helpless situation, he was supported some time by his wife, who caught fish in the lake; but she at last deserted him; and on our arrival, he had subsisted several months upon the pig weed which grew around his cabin. As he was unable to walk, this had been thrown in by his countryman, or by the Indians, and appeared to have been the extent of their benevolence. We found him seated in a small bark cabin, on a rush mat, with the stumps of his legs tied up with deerskins, and wholly destitute of covering. He was poor and emaciated to the last degree—his beard was long—cheeks fallen in—eyes sunk, but darting a look of despair—and every bone in his body visible through the skin. He could speak no English, but was continually uttering curses in his mother tongue, upon his own existence, and apparently, upon all that surrounded him. We could only endure the painful sight for a moment, and hastened from this abode of human wretchedness; but before leaving the village, Governor Cass sent him a present of Indian goods, groceries, and ammunition, and engaged a person to convey him to the American Fur Company's Fort at Sandy Lake, where he could still receive the attention due to suffering humanity. These donations were swelled by every individual of the party, each one taking a pleasure in being able to contribute something, with a view either to clothe and lodge him with decency and comfort, or to enable him to purchase provisions, for his subsistence, from the Indians.

The latitude of this lake as determined by Lieut. Pike, in 1806, is 47° 42′ 40.″ Owing to cloudy weather, no opportunity of testing the correctness of this observation, was presented to us; but Capt. Douglass had an observation fifty eight miles below, and calculated the latitude of that place to be 47° 38′. The distance from Sandy Lake, by the windings of the river is two hundred and seventy one miles, and from the Fond du Lac, at the head of Lake Superior, 429. It is but thirty miles by land south to Leech Lake, and is walked in the winter season, when the swamps are frozen over, in one day. It is about one hundred miles west-northwest, to Red Lake, where there is a band of Chippeways of one hundred and sixty warriors; and a hundred and twenty miles northwest to the Lake of the Woods, via Turtle Portage, and the Rainy Lakes; but in a direct line about half that distance. Cassina Lake, the source of the Mississippi, is situated seventeen degrees north of the Balize on the Gulph of Mexico, and two thousand nine hundred and seventy-eight miles, pursuing the course of the river. Estimating the distance to Lake La Beesh, its extreme northwestern inlet at sixty miles, which I conclude to be within bounds, we have a result of three thousand and thirty-eight miles, as the entire length of this wonderful river, which extends over the surface of the earth in a direct line, more than half the distance from the Arctic Circle to the Equator. It is also deserving of remark, that its sources lie in a region of almost continual winter, while it enters the Ocean under the latitude of perpetual verdure; and at last, as if disdaining to terminate its career at the usual point of embouchure of other large rivers, has protruded its banks into the Gulf of Mexico, more than a hundred miles beyond any other part of the main. To have visited both the sources and the mouth of this celebrated stream, falls to the lot of few, *and I believe there is no person living, beside myself, of whom the remark can now be made.* On the 10th of July, 1819, I passed out of the mouth of the Mississippi in a brig bound for New-York, after descending it in a steam-boat from St. Louis, and little thinking I should soon revisit its waters; yet, on the 21st of July of the following year, I found myself seated in an Indian canoe, upon its source.

In deciding upon the physical character of the Mississippi, it may be advantageously considered under four natural divisions, as indicated by the permanent differences in the colour of its waters,—the geological character of its bed and banks,—its forest trees and other vegetable productions,—its velocity,—the difficulties it opposes to navigation,—and other natural appearances and circumstances.

Originating in a region of lakes, upon the table lands, which throw their waters north into Hudson's Bay,—south into the Gulph of Mexico,—and east into the Gulf of St. Lawrence--it pursues its course to the falls of Peckagama, a distance of two hundred and thirty miles, through a low prairie, covered with wild rice, rushes, sword grass, and other aquatic plants. During this distance, it is extremely devious as to course and width, sometimes expanding into small lakes, at others, narrowing into a channel of about eighty feet. It is about sixty feet wide on its exit from Red Cedar or Cassina Lake, with an average depth of two feet; but from the junction of the Leech Lake fork, increases to a hundred feet in width, with a corresponding increase of depth. Its current, during this distance, is still and gentle; and its mean velocity may be estimated at a mile and a half per hour, with a descent of three inches per mile. This is the favourite resort of water-fowl, and amphibious quadrupeds.

At the falls of Peckagama, the first rock stratum, and the first wooded island, is seen. Here the river has a fall of twenty feet; and from this to the falls of St. Anthony, a distance of six hundred and eighty-five miles, exhibits its second characteristic division. At the head of the falls of Peckagama, the prairies entirely cease; and below, a forest of elm, maple, birch, oak, and ash, overshadows the stream. The black walnut (*juglans nigra*) is first seen below Sandy Lake river, and the sycamore below the river De Corbeau. The river, in this distance, has innumerable well wooded islands, and receives a number of tributaries, the largest of which is the river De Corbeau, its great southwestern fork. The Pine, Elk, Sac, and Crow rivers, also enter on the west, and the St. Francis and Missisawgaiegon, on the east. The course of the river, although serpentine, is less so, than above the falls of Peckagama, and its bends are not so short and abrupt. Its mean width may be estimated at three hundred feet until the junction of the De Corbeau, and below that at two hundred and fifty yards. Its navigation is impeded, agreeably to a memorandum which I have kept, by thirty-five rapids, nineteen ripples, and two minor falls, called the Little and the Big Falls, in all of which the river has an aggregate descent of two hundred and twenty four feet in fourteen thousand six hundred and forty yards, or about eight miles. The mean fall of the current, exclusive of the rapids, may be computed at six inches per mile, and its velocity at three miles per hour. In the course of this distance it receives several small turbid streams, and acquires a brownish hue, but still preserves its transparency, and is palatable drink-water. A few miles above the river De Corbeau, on the east side, we observe the first dry prairies, or natural meadows, and they continue to the falls of St. Anthony. These prairies are the great resort of the buffalo, elk, and deer, and are the only part of the banks of the Mississippi where the buffalo is now to be found. Granite rocks appear at several of the rapids, in rolled pieces, and in beds; and in some places attain an elevation of one or two hundred feet above the level of the water, but the banks of the river are generally alluvial.

At the Falls of St. Anthony, the river has a perpendicular pitch of forty feet, and from this to its junction with the Missouri, a distance of eight hundred and forty three miles, it is bounded by limestone bluffs, which attain various elevations from one to four hundred feet, and present a succession of the most sublime and picturesque views. This forms the third characteristic change of the Mississippi. The river prairies cease, and the rocky bluffs commence precisely at the falls of St. Anthony. Nine miles below it receives the St. Peter's from the west, and is successively swelled on that side by the Ocano, Iowa, Turkey, Desmoines, and Salt rivers, and on the east by the St. Croix, Chippeway, Black, Ousconsing, Rock, and Illinois. One hundred miles below the Falls of St. Anthony, the river expands into a lake, called Pepin, which is twenty-four miles long and four in width. It is, on issuing from this lake, that the river first exhibits, in a striking manner, those extensive and moving sand bars, innumerable islands and channels, and drifts and snags, which continue to characterize it to the ocean. Its bends from this point onward are larger, and its course more direct; and although its waters are adulterated by several dark coloured and turbid streams, it may still be considered transparent. The principal impediments to navigation in this distance are the Desmoine, and Rock river rapids. The latter extends six miles, and opposes an effectual barrier to steam-boat navigation, although keel boats and barges of the largest class, may ascend. This rapid is three hundred and ninety miles above St. Louis.

The fourth change in the physical aspect of this river is at the junction of the Missouri, and this is a total and complete one, the character of the Mississippi being entirely lost in that of the Missouri.

The latter is, in fact, much the largest stream of the two, and carries its characteristic appearances to the ocean. It should also have carried the name, but its exploration took place too long after the course of the Mississippi had been perpetuated in the written geography of the country, to render an alteration in this respect, either practicable or expedient. The waters of the Mississippi at its confluence with the Missouri, are moderately clear, and of a greenish hue.—The Missouri is turbid and opake, of a greyish-white colour, and during its floods, which happen twice a year, communicates, almost instantaneously, to the combined stream its predominating qualities, but towards the close of the summer season, when it is at its lowest stage of water, the streams do not fully incorporate for twenty or thirty miles, but preserve opposite sides of the river; and I have observed this phenomenon at the town of Herculaneum, which is forty-eight miles below the junction. The water in this part of the river cannot be drank until it has been set aside to allow the mud to settle. The distance from the mouth of the Missouri to the Gulf of Mexico is one thousand two hundred and twenty miles, in the course of which it receives from the west, the Merrimack, St. Francis, White, Arkansas, and Red rivers; and from the east, the Kaskaskia, Great Muddy, Ohio, Wolf, and Yazoo. This part of the river is more particularly characterized by snags and sawyers,—falling-in banks and islands;—sand bars and mud banks;—and a channel which is shifting by every flood, and of such extreme velocity, that it was formerly thought it could not be navigated by vessels propelled with sails. Subsequent experience has shown this conjecture to be unfounded, although a strong wind is required for its ascent. It is daily navigated in ships of from four hundred to eight hundred tons burden, from the Balize to New Orleans, a distance of one hundred miles, and could be ascended higher were it necessary; but the commerce of the river above New Orleans is now carried on, in a great measure, by steamboats. The width of the river opposite St. Louis is one mile; it is somewhat less at New Orleans, and still less at its disembochure. A bar at its mouth prevents ships drawing more than eighteen feet water from entering. This river is occupied by different bands of the Chippeway Indians from its sources, to the Buffalo Plains in the vicinity of the upper St. Francis, the precise limit being a matter of dispute, and the cause of the long war between them and the Sioux. The Sioux bands claim from thence to the Prarie du Chein, and the Foxes and Sacs to the river Desmoines. From this vicinity to the Gulf of Mexico the Indian title has been extinguished by the United States Government either through purchase, treaty, or conquest, and we have now the complete control of this river and all its tributary streams, with the exception of the upper part of Red River. The wild rice, (*zezania aquatica*,) is not found on the waters of the Mississippi south of the forty-first degree of north latitude, nor the Indian reed, or cane, north of the thirty-eighth. These two productions characterize the extremes of this river. It has been observed by McKenzie, that the former is hardly known, or at least, does not come to maturity, north of the fiftieth degree of north latitude. The alligator is first seen below the junction of the Arkansas. The paroquet is found as far north as the mouth of the Illinois, and flocks have occasionally been seen as high as Chicago. The name of this river is derived from the Algonquin language, one of the original tongues of our continent, which is now spoken nearly in its primeval purity by the different bands of Chippeways ;—less so by the Knistineaux and Ottaways ;—with great corruptions by the Foxes, Sacs, and Pottowatomies, and some other tribes ;—and in various dialects by the five bands of Iroquois of New-York. It is a compound of the word *Missi*, signifying *great*, and *Sepe*, a *river*. The former is variously pronounced *missil* or *michil*, as in Michilimackinac ;—*michi* as in Michigan ;—*Missu*—as in Missouri ;—and *missi*, as in Mississineway, and Mississippi. The variation does not appear greater than we should expect in an unwritten language. They have no other word to express the highest degree of magnitude either in a moral or physical sense, and it may be considered as synonymous not only with our word great, but also, magnificent,—supreme,—stupendous,—sublime,—enormous,—extensive,—prodigious,—ample, &c.—words which are certainly not synonymous, in our language, but have only one term by which they can be translated into theirs. The word *Sippi*, may be considered as the English pronunciation, (derived through the medium of the French) of *Sepe*, and affords an instance of an Indian term, of much melody, being corrupted by Europeans, into one that has a harsh and hissing sound.

No attempt has heretofore been made to determine the elevation of that part of the American continent which gives origin to the Mississippi, the St. Lawrence, and the Red River of the North ;—

and from the immense distance of this summit level from the ocean, and the difficulties that must attend the survey, it is probable that many years may elapse before this point will be determined by actual observation. With a view, however, of approaching the probable altitude, I have estimated from the best data I could command, the descent of the different rapids,—streams, and falls in the whole route, with the elevation of the highlands which separate the waters of Lake Superior from those of the Mississippi, and the descent of the streams flowing into the latter; and I shall here present the results of these observations. The estimates have always been made upon the spot, and noted in a particular book kept for that purpose, and I have made it a constant practice to avail myself of the judgment of the members of the expedition, in deciding upon the mean velocity of streams,—the heights of falls and rapids, and the elevation of highlands; and feel particularly indebted to the observations of Gov. Cass, and Doct. Wolcott. Taking the elevation of Lake Erie as determined by the actual survey of the New-York Canal Commissioners for a basis, we find the surface of Lake Superior to be six hundred and forty-one feet above the Atlantic ocean. From the head of this lake, following up the St. Louis river to the Savannah portage, and from thence across the dividing ground, to the spot where we first strike the waters of the Mississippi, at the head of the west Savannah, the aggregate elevation, (as detailed in Chap. 8,) may be estimated at five hundred and fifty feet. The descent of this stream into Sandy Lake, and from thence into the Mississippi river, as given at page 235, will reduce this estimate by the sum of sixty feet. From the junction of Sandy Lake river, to the principal source of the Mississippi in Cassina lake, we attain an elevation agreeably to the annexed schedule* of one hundred and sixty-two feet, which superadded to the former estimates, shews the Mississippi river to originate at an altitude of *thirteen hundred and thirty feet above the Atlantic.* This is thirty feet higher than the Alleghany mountains in Pennsylvania, but less by two hundred and fifty feet, than the highest peak (New Beacon) of the Highlands of the Hudson. What the descent of the river La Beesh, the principal inlet of Cassina lake, may be, we cannot determine, as we have not explored that stream, but the Indians represent it to have many rapids. Taking the length of the Mississippi, however, from Cassina lake, to the ocean, this result will give it a mean descent of two feet, 2 $\frac{1156}{1330}$ inches per mile, the falls of St. Anthony and Lake Pepin, inclusive,—for what the estimate would loose by the perpendicular pitch of the former, is compensated by the dead level of twenty-four miles in the latter.

**DESCENT OF THE MISSISSIPPI:*

	Feet.	Total Feet.
Rapids above the junction of Sandy Lake river numbered from 1 to 6, see Day LIV.	29	
Rapid No. 7,	3	31
Rapid No. 8,	2	33
Rapid No. 9,	16	49
Falls of Peckagama,	20	69
Mean descent of the Mississippi from Cassina lake to the falls of Peckagama, 170 miles, at 3 inches per mile,	42-9	111-6
Mean fall of the Mississippi from the falls of Peckagama to the junction of Sandy Lake river, 102 miles, at 6 inches per mile,	51	162

To those who are conversant with the hydrography of rivers, this result will communicate a better notion of the rapidity of the Mississippi, than the most laboured description of the difficulties of its ascent.— I am not aware of any fallacies in these calculations, but think they have generally been made within bounds, and that whenever the altitude is determined by scientific measurement it will be found to exceed the present result.

There is no part of the Mississippi river which originates in the territories of British America. The northern boundary line of the United States will probably run a hundred miles north of its extreme source; but this is a point which still remains unsettled between the two governments, and some difficulties, it is apprehended, may prevent a ready adjustment of this line. The treaty of 1783 which designates the limits of the United States, fixes the northern boundary as a line drawn through the great chain of lakes to the head of Lake Superior, thence by the most practicable water communication to the Lake of the Woods, and from its most northwestern extremity *due west* to the Mississippi. It is well ascertained that a line drawn due west from the northwestern extremity of the Lake of the Woods, would not strike the sources of the Mississippi. McKenzie states the northwestern point of the Lake of the Woods to lie in north latitude 49° 37′, and west longitude from Greenwich, 94° 31′.

Mr. Thompson, the Astronomer to the Northwest Company, determined the latitude of Red Cedar or Cassina lake to be 47° 38′; which is not, however, presumed to be entirely correct. The great northern bend of the Missouri is laid down by Lewis and

Clark in north latitude 47° 32′, and the river above that point is described as running *south of west*, so that a line drawn in the manner directed, from the Lake of the Woods, would not strike either of these streams. This was anticipated at the conclusion of Jay's treaty in 1794, but nothing further was agreed upon in this respect, than that the line should be established by a negociation, according to the spirit of the former treaty, to the principles of justice, and the mutual convenience of the parties. No provision is made for it in the treaty of Ghent.

Some difficulty appears also to exist as to the true construction of that part of the treaty which requires a line to be drawn from the head of Lake Superior by the most practicable water communication to the lake of the woods. There are two grand routes of communication pursued by the north west traders. namely;—1. By way of the Grande Portage, commencing on the north shore of lake Superior, four hundred and eighty miles from the Sault de St. Marie, which leads through a succession of small lakes to the Rainy lakes, and thence to the Lake of the Woods:—2. By the St. Louis river and Savannah Portage into Sandy Lake and the Mississippi, and thence through lake Winnipec and across the Turtle Portage into the Rainy lakes, or,—by following up the St. Louis to its source which is near the borders of the little Rainy lake. The first route has long been the thoroughfare of the northwest company, and although less travelled now than formerly, is the most direct, expeditious, and practicable route; and was the only one in use at the conclusion of the treaty.—The United States claim this as the northern boundary, and it has accordingly obtained upon all our maps.

In the maps of the north west company, however, the line is drawn through the St. Louis river. The territory in dispute is equal in extent to any of the original states of the confederation, Virginia, Pennsylvania, and New-York excepted. This part of the boundary will come under the cognizance of the commissioners appointed under the treaty of Ghent.

Finding it impracticable to proceed at this season of the year, in canoes to lake La Beesh, an immediate return was here determined upon, and we embarked at five o'clock in the afternoon on our descent. Crossing the lake we passed down the Mississippi eighteen miles and encamped on the right bank of the river at twilight.

LX. Day. (*July 22d.*)—Quitting our encampment before day light, we reached lake Winnipec at eight o'clock, and performed the traverse against a strong head wind. This occupied two hours, during which our canoes were violently tossed upon the waves, and the voyageurs manifested some apprehensions for our safety. Entering the outlet of this lake which is the Mississippi, we left our encampment of the 20th on our right, and successively passing little Winnipec or Rush lake, and the confluence of Leech lake river, we descended to within ten miles of the spot of our encampment on the 19th, having progressed altogether a distance of ninety-eight miles. In the course of the day we passed nine Indian canoes on their ascent. They were freighted with rolls of birch bark, of the kind employed for canoes, and with bundles of rushes of which they manufacture matts for bedding and for covering their wigwams. The weather continued cloudy, with wind, and occasional showers of rain.

LXI. Day.—(*July* 23*d.*)—Between our sufferings from the stings of the musquitoes, and our anxiety to rejoin our friends at Sandy lake, we obtained little rest, and decamped at a quarter past four in the morning. We reached the falls of Peckagama at one o'clock, and spent forty minutes in crossing the portage with our baggage and canoes. We now successively passed the Prairie and Trout rivers, and proceeded twenty-eight miles below our encampment of the 18th, distance ninety-eight miles.—Weather cloudy, with rain. During the forenoon we met a canoe of Chippeways on their ascent, and passing with rapidity, merely exchanged the common salutation of *bon jour*, a term they have borrowed from the French. Towards evening, an animal of singular appearance, supposed to be the Wolverine, was seen swimming across the river, but our efforts to take it proved unavailing. Such are the incidents of a voyage in this remote region.

LXII. Day.—(*July* 24*th,*)—A change of wind took place during the night, and we were favoured with the most delightful weather. Proceeding under the double influence of a strong current and the force of our paddles, we progressed with surprising rapidity, and at two o'clock in the afternoon landed at the Southwest Company's Fort on Sandy lake, a distance of seventy-two miles, having performed on our return, the same distance in three days, which we were occupied four and a half in ascending. We were rejoiced to find our friends in perfect health.

and that no attempts had been made by the savages, during our absence, to molest them. A pleasure, scarcely less satisfactory in its nature, arose from the termination of a part of our voyage, which had appeared to us to present greater difficulties in its accomplishment, and less in its character and productions to reward exploration, than any other section of the tour; and in fact, we have neither found the labour less, nor the reward greater, than was anticipated. Barren in its geological character and physical productions, the incidents of the tour have offered little to compensate the want of zoological interest, picturesque views, and populous Indian settlements:—and a number of circumstances have concurred to render our situation on this visit, one of peculiar privation, fatigue, and physical suffering. Not the least among these, have been the calls of an unsatisfied appetite, the stings of the musquito, and the almost incessant motion of travelling, depriving us of due rest at night. By this vigilance, however—by this constant hurry onvard—by dismissing the greatest part of our baggage, and the few conveniences we had thus far carried—by stinting ourselves as to provisions,and by leaving the weight of the expedition at Sandy lake, we have performed the voyage in less than half the time it would otherwise have required, and in less time than it has ever, as we are told by the voyageurs, been before performed.

The state of the weather during our absence has presented several striking transitions, in regard to the distribution of heat, as well as the transparency of the atmosphere, winds, rain, &c. Having left my thermometer with Mr. Doty, during the time of our journey to the sources of the Mississippi, he favoured me with the following observations, made at the Company's Fort.

Meteorological Register kept at Sandy Lake.

SANDY LAKE. 1820.	Atm. Temp. A. M. 8	12	P. M. 2	8	9	Mean temp.	WEATHER.
July 17		76	80	79	78	78	Morning rain—then fair.
- 18	51	64	66	53	50	57	Fair.
- 19	46	63	70	55		58	Night rain—morning cloudy—then clear.
- 20	60	80	84	75		74	
- 21	68	86	88	85	74	80	
- 22	73	88	90	77		82	Clear—some thunder.
- 23	70	82	88	78		79	Night and morn. rain—afternoon thunder.
- 24	74	87	89	78		81	Fair. (Broke thermometer.)
						8)589	
						$73\frac{5}{8}$	mean daily temperature.

CHAPTER X.

JOURNEY,

FROM SANDY LAKE TO THE AMERICAN GARRISON AT ST. PETER'S.

LXIII. Day.—(*July 25th.*)

THE expedition embarked at the Fort at twelve o'clock, in three canoes and a barge on its descent to the falls of St. Anthony, accompanied by embassadors of peace from the Chippeway tribes to the Sioux of St. Peter's. These occupied a separate canoe. It is three miles from the Fort to the Mississippi. The current of the river below the outlet of Sandy lake, and the natural appearances, are similar to what it exhibits for a hundred miles above. The banks are alluvial, elevated from six to ten feet; trees—elm, maple, pine. and birch. We descended twenty-eight miles and encamped on a high sandy bank on the west shore. The river has several rapids in that distance, and some small islands covered entirely with grass, and small tufts of willows, with piles of driftwood collected at their heads. No rock strata appear, but loose stones of granite, hornblende, and red ferruginous quartz, are seen in the bed of the stream in passing over the rapids, and in some places, along the margin of the river. Among the forest trees, pine appears to predominate on the lands which lie a distance off the river, but elm is most abundant along the shore: maple and birch less so, and black walnut and oak sparing. The colour of the water on looking into the river resembles that of chocolate, but on dipping up a cup full, it appears colourless and clear. The weather remained fair and pleasant during the day, but clouded up towards evening.

LXIV. Day.—(*July 26th.*)—It commenced raining during the night, and as we had neglected to have our tents pitched, we were first awoke by the falling rain, and during the intervals of the showers, the musquitoes assailed us in such numbers, as to forbid the hope of rest. In this situation we passed the remainder of the night, around our fires, endeavouring to divert our reflections, by the interchange of anecdote, and absolutely prevented from falling asleep by the labour of brushing away the voracious hordes of musquitoes, which unceasingly beset us with their stings, and poured forth their hateful and incessant buzzing upon our ears. It certainly requires a different species of philosophy to withstand, undisturbed, the attacks of this ravenous insect, from that which we are called upon to exercise upon the sudden occurrence of any of the great calamities and misfortunes of life. He who is afflicted, without complaining, by an unexpected change of fortune, or the death of a friend, may be thrown into a fit of restless impatience by the stings of the musquito; and the traveller who is prepared to withstand the savage scalping knife, and the enraged bear, has nothing to oppose to the attacks of an enemy, which is too minute to be dreaded, and too numerous to be destroyed.

We embarked a few moments before five o'clock in the morning, the atmosphere being misty and dark, and the weather cloudy, which eventuated in rain before six o'clock. It ceased again as the sun approached the meridian, and the weather was clear and delightful at noon. A few minutes before eight o'clock we passed the mouth of the *River au Solé* (Alder river) a stream of twenty yards wide entering on the right shore. In the afternoon we passed four streams of considerable size, entering on the left shore, at short distances from each other—names unknown; and at half past seven in the evening passed the mouth of Pine river, a stream of sixty yards wide, flowing from the west. This river is a hundred and forty miles in length, expanding in that distance into several small lakes, which communicate with the waters of Leech lake. In ascending it the Indians pursue the following route. It is one day's journey into White Fish lake, which is six miles long and two in width—then five miles to lake Poppenosh, which is three miles long by one in width—then three miles to a third lake, which is seven miles long and two in width. From this it is a short distance to Caspetawgan, or Tobacco-pouch Lake, which is five miles in circumference, and nearly circular, from which it is one day's journey into a fifth lake—thence two day's to a portage, which conveys you to the sixth lake, from which there are several short portages from lake to lake until you arrive at Leech Lake. The whole of this distance is a succession of pine ridges and swamps, and the Indians affirm that one half of the land is covered with lakes. There is an island in the mouth of Pine river, well timbered with pine, elm, and maple, and a rapid in the Mississippi river a short distance below, at the foot of which we encamped, on a high bank on the east shore, having descended one hundred miles. In the course of this day's journey, the river has presented several rapids, islands, and ripples. The fall at none of the rapids will exceed six feet in a distance of three hundred yards. The islands are small and not well wooded, and are encumbered with piles of drifted trees, limbs, and leaves, which give them a novel appearance, and at the same time serve to convey an idea of the rise of the river, and of the force of its current, during its semi-annual floods. Snags become more frequent in this part of the channel; and the river in several places undermines its banks, which are elevated from ten to twenty feet, and bear a forest of elm, birch, pine, maple, black walnut, and oak (*quercus nigra.*) Loose stones are found at all the rapids; they are chiefly referable to the different varieties of granite, hornblende, slate, and sand stone. Ducks, the teal, and the plover, have been observed;—also, the bald eagle, kingfisher, mock bird, robin, and pigeon. As night approached, we heard, for the first time in the region, the whipporwill, which is called by the Indians *Muck-a-wiss*, being the sounds, according to their notions, which it utters. Among the plants, at the spot of our encampment, we noticed the wild rose (*rosa parviflora*) and a flower, resembling in some of its characters the ipomaea nil, but with a short floriferous stem, and lance-oblong leaves: peduncle one-flowered, bell-shaped, white, downy. It appears to have escaped the notice of Pursh, in his botanical researches in the northwest. We also, during this day's journey, first noticed the common red barking squirrel, which, invited from its nest, by the beauty of the weather during the afternoon, has been frequently observed playing among the branches of the black walnut, and other favourite trees. This sprightly little animal is equally entitled to our admiration from the beauty of its form and the agility of its movements; and there is no person who has visited an American forest during the summer season, either as a sportsman or an admirer of nature, who is not ready to acknowledge how much this pretty and playful little quadruped contributes to enliven and beautify the scene. There are several species of this animal in the forests of the Mississippi, and other parts of the United States. They are all referable to the natural genus sciurus, in the Linnæan system, the generic characters of which are two fore teeth in each jaw, the upper ones wedge-shaped and cutters like those of the beaver; the inferior ones sharp-pointed, like those of the dog and wolf. Some of the species of this genus, however, have their fore and hind legs connected by a thin membrane covered with hair by means of which they are enabled to support themselves in the air while leaping from one tree to another. Naturalists have seized upon this character to separate the genus into two divisions; distinguishing those which possess the membrane petauri, or flying-squirrels, and those without it *sciuri scadentes*, or climbing squirrels. The specific name of the common red squirrel is sciurus vulgaris.

LXV. Day.—(*July* 27*th.*)—There was a heavy fall of dew during the night, and a foggy atmosphere at early day light, but the sun arose clear, and the day continued pleasant, with the exception of the oppressive heat at noon. We quit our encampment at five o'clock. The pine lands which commenced yesterday at the junction of Pine river with the Mississipi, continued to within a short distance of the mouth of the river De Corbeau. They are elevated from sixty to a hundred feet, and lie in ridges. The principal timber is the yellow pine.—Mixed with the sand which is in some places naked, and destitute of vegetation, are fragments of granite, hornblende, quartz, jasper, and carnelian. This strip of sandy country was denominated the *Dead Pines* by Pike. At twelve o'clock we passed the mouth of the river De Corbeau, the largest stream which has yet entered the Mississippi, and by which a communication is maintained with the Red river. It is ascended by the traders a hundred and eighty miles to the mouth of the Pemmisco, or *Go-by-water* river, which flows in from the north west. This is also ascended a like distance, and a portage of two pauses then made into Otter Tail Lake, which has a navigable outlet into Red River, of which it is indeed, one of the principal sources. The south fork of the De Corbeau originates near the sources of the St. Peter's, and the Indians are in the practice of passing that way in canoes. The river De Corbeau joins the Mississippi in north latitude 45° 49′ 50″ and is the largest tributary which it receives above the falls of St. Anthony, being nearly of equal magnitude.— The lands upon its banks are rich, and covered with a heavy growth of hard wood, chiefly elm, sugar tree, black walnut, and oak. At the point of junction there is a large and well wooded island called the Isle De Corbeau, by which the river is hid from the view until you have nearly passed it, when by turning the eye towards the south, you have a fine view of its broad and beautiful surface, and the luxuriant foliage which overshadows its banks. The Mississippi assumes an increased width below, and is particularly characterized by numerous and heavy timbered islands, all of which present immense drifts of floodwood at their heads, and by dividing the river into a number of channels, serve to increase its width, and the difficulties of its navigation. Here also, the Buffalo Plains commence, and continue downward, on both banks of the river, to the falls of St. Anthony. These plains are elevated about sixty feet above the summer-level of the water, and consist of a sandy alluvion covered with rank grass, and occasional clumps of the dwarf black oak. They generally present steep, naked, and falling-in banks towards the river, and disclose innumerable small fragments of carnelian, agate, and jasper, along with masses of coarser rock, such as granite, hornblende, &c.

We descended the river a distance of ninety miles, having been eleven hours in our canoes, and encamped on the prairie on the left bank. Here our Indians killed an elk and a buffalo, a number of which were seen upon the contiguous plain. A short distance above, we passed a hunting camp of Chippeways, consisting of probably one hundred and fifty souls. On landing, we were received with a salute in the Indian method, and exchanged some corn, of which they were much in need, for pemmican, and dried buffalo beef.

LXVI. Day. (*July 28th.*)—Embarked at half past four. Two miles below we passed the mouth of Elk river, entering on the right shore. This is a stream of forty yards wide, and has a rapid near its mouth which is visible from the Mississippi. It is, however, ascended a great distance in canoes, and communicates with the St. Peter's, by two short portages.

The little Falls are four miles below the mouth of Elk river, where the Mississippi forces its way through a narrow defile of rocks which appear in rugged masses in the bed of the stream, and attain an elevation of from twenty to forty feet upon its banks. Passing with great velocity over the schute of the falls, it was difficult to ascertain the geological character of the rock, but it appeared to be granite very much mixed and darkened with hornblende. The river at this place is narrowed to half its usual width. The descent of water may be estimated at ten feet, in one hundred and fifty yards. Between Elk river and the little Falls, we pass the Painted Rock standing upon the west bank of the river. It consists of a mass of granite and hornblende, upon which the Indians have drawn a number of hieroglyphics, and rude designs.

Being now in the region of buffalo, we concluded to land, in the course of the day, at some convenient place for hunting them. This we were soon invited to do by seeing one of those animals along the shore of the river, and on ascending the bank, we observed, upon a boundless prairie, two droves of them, feeding upon the grass. All who had guns adapted for the purpose, sallied forth in separate parties upon the prairie, while those who felt less ambition to signalize themselves upon the occasion, or were more illy accoutred for the activities of the chase, remained upon an eminence which overlooked the plain, to observe the movements of this animal while under an attack of musketry, and to enjoy the novel spectacle of a buffalo-hunt. The grass was so tall as to allow an unobserved approach towards the spot where they remained feeding, but the first fire proved unsuccessful, at the same time that it scattered the herd, which were now seen running in all directions across the prairie, and an incessant fire of random shots was kept up for about two hours; during which three buffaloes were killed, and a great number wounded, which made their escape. While thus harassed, they often passed within a few yards of us, and we enjoyed a fine opportunity of witnessing their form, size, colour, and speed. The buffalo has a clumsy gait, like the domestic ox, which it also resembles in size and general appearance. Unlike the ox, however, this animal exhibits no diversity of colour, being a uniform dark brown inclining to dun. It is never spotted, with black, red, or white. It has short black horns growing nearly straight from the head, and set at a considerable distance apart. The male has a hunch upon its shoulders, covered with long flocks of shaggy hair, extending to the top of the head from which it falls over the eyes and horns, giving the animal a very formidable appearance. The hoofs are cloven like those of the cow, but the legs are much stouter, and altogether, it is more clumsy and ill-proportioned. The tail is naked till towards the end, where it is tufted, in the manner of the lion. The general weight of this animal is from eight hundred to a thousand pounds; but they sometimes attain an enormous size, and have been killed upon the Mississippi prairies weighing two thousand pounds.—The skin of a buffalo-bull when first taken off, is three fourths of an inch in thickness, and cannot be lifted by the strongest man. A hundred and fifty pounds of tallow have been taken from one animal, and it is highly esteemed by the Indians in preparing their hommony. Instances of excessive fatness are, however, rare, and such over-fed animals become so unweildy that they often fall a prey to wolves; particularly if they happen to stray a distance from the herd. The buffalo is a timid animal, and flies at the approach of man. It is however asserted by the hunters, that when painfully wounded, it becomes furious, and will turn upon its pursuers. There is a particular art in killing the buffalo with a rifle, only known to experienced hunters, and when they do not drop down, which is often the case, it requires a person intimately acquainted with their habits, to pursue them with success. This has been fully instanced in the futile exertions of our party, upon the present occasion, for out of a great number of shots few have reached the object, and very few proved effectual, and the little success we met with is chiefly attributable to the superior skill of the Indians who accompanied us.—Unless a vital part is touched, the shot proves useless. It also requires a larger ball than the deer and elk. Lieutenant Pike thinks that in the open prairies, the bow and arrow could be used to better advantage than the gun, particularly on horseback, for you might ride immediately along side the animal and strike it where you pleased.* The Indians employ both the rifle, and arrow, and in the prairies of Missouri and Arkansas, pursue the herds on horseback; but on the upper Mississippi, where they are destitute of horses, they make amends for this deficiency by several ingenious stratagems. One of the most common of these is the method of hunting with fire. For this purpose a great number of hunters disperse themselves around a large prairie where herds of buffalo happen to be feeding, and setting fire to the grass encompass them on all sides. The buffalo, having a great dread of fire, retire towards the centre of the prairie as they see it approach, and here being pressed together in great numbers, many are trampled under foot, and the Indians rushing in with their arrows and musketry, slaughter immense numbers in a short period. It is asserted that a thousand animals have been killed by this stratagem in one day. They have another method of hunting by driving them over precipices, which is chiefly practised by the bands inhabiting the Missouri. To decoy the herds, several Indians disguise themselves in the skins of the buffalo, taken off entire, and by counterfeiting the lowing of this animal in distress, they attract the herds in a certain direction, and when they are at full speed, suddenly disappear behind a cleft in the top of a precipice when those animals which are in front on reaching the brink, are pushed over by those pressing behind, and in this

* Pike's Expeditions, page 46.

manner great numbers are crushed to death. These practices are less common now than formerly, the introduction of fire arms among most of the tribes, putting it into the power of almost every individual to kill sufficient for the support of his family. By a very bad policy, however, they prefer the flesh of the cows, which will in time destroy the species.—Few of the native animals of the American forest contribute more to the comforts of savage society than the buffalo. Its skin when dressed, by a process peculiar to them, forms one of the principal articles of clothing. The Sioux tribes particularly excel in the method of dressing it, and are very much in the habit of ornamenting their dresses with porcupine quills, and paints. The skin dressed with the hair on, supplies them with blankets, and constitutes those durable and often beautiful sleigh-robes which are now in such universal use in the United States and the Canadas. The tallow of this animal, as well as the beef, has also become an article of commerce, particularly in the south western states and territories, and its horns are exported for the manufacture of powder-flasks. The tongue is considered superior in flavour to that of the domestic cow, and the animal is often hunted for no other purpose. I have seen stockings and hats manufactured from its wool with a little addition of common wool, or of cotton. This practice is very common among the white hunters of Missouri and Arkansas. The flesh of the buffalo is not equal, in its fresh state, to that of the cow or ox, but is superior when *dried*, which is the Indian mode of preserving it.

The attempts which have been made to domesticate this animal, have not been attended with success. Calves which have been taken in the woods and brought up with the tame breed, have afterwards discovered a wild and ungovernable temper, and manifested their savage nature by breaking down the strongest enclosures, and enticing the tame cattle into the woods. The mixed breed is said to be barren, like the mule. The period of gesticulation is ascertained to be twelve months, whereas that of the cow is nine. A remarkable proof of the little affinity existing between it, and the domestic breed of cattle, was exhibited a few years ago in Canada, where the connexion resulted in the death of the cows submitted to the experiment.

Naturalists have generally considered the American buffalo (*Bos Bubalus*) of the same species with the *Bison* and *Aurochs* of Europe and Asia, the difference consisting in the former being less shaggy, the hair partaking less of the character of wool, and the conformation of the hind parts of the animal being stouter and more like that of the common ox. Several varieties of this species are found; as the anoa, seminudus, bos cafer, wild grunting ox, guavera, musk buffalo, urus, and zebu, or Barbary cow.

The bison is at present found throughout the southern parts of Asia and Africa, and is said to attain its greatest size at Malabar, Abyssinia and Madagascar, where the extensive savannahs are clothed with the most luxuriant herbage. The only parts of Europe where this animal is now found, are the province of Lithuania, the Carpathian mountains, and the great Hercynian forest.

In America the buffalo is confined to the regions

situated between the 31st and 49th degrees of north latitude, and west of the Mississippi river. The only part of the country *east* of this river, where the buffalo now remains, is that included between the falls of St. Anthony and Sandy Lake, a range of about six hundred miles. South of the 31st degree of north latitude the buffalo is not found, but its place is supplied in Mexico by the wild ox, without a bunch, which is considered of European origin.

Having spent several hours in the chase of this animal, and driven the herds off to a great distance, we embarked, and proceeded down the river until three o'clock, when we again landed on a high prairie bank on the west shore, at the site of an old Indian encampment of sixteen lodges. Here we spent the remainder of the afternoon in hunting buffalo, many of which were seen on the contiguous plain, and encamped at night, having descended the river fifty-four miles. The first object which attracted our attention on landing was an Indian sign, or letter of birch bark, affixed to a long pole in the centre of the deserted encampment. This had been left for the information of the Chippeways by a large party of Sioux, on the termination of an excursion up the river, for the purpose of meeting with the former. As we carried embassadors of peace from the Chippeway nation, they approached the hieroglyphical sign with great eagerness, and learned its import with equal satisfaction. By it, they were informed, that at the solicitation of the commandant of the American garrison at St. Peter's, a large party of the Sioux had proceeded thus far up the river on a mission of peace, but not meeting with any of the Chippeways, had returned; and that they were equally disposed for peace or war. The number of the party,—the chiefs who headed them,—their route,—the situation of their villages on the St. Peter's,—the American garrison, and other particulars were accurately delineated, or represented by symbols and characters in common use, so that they experienced no difficulty in the perusal, and explained to us with great facility the import of the message. I have already adverted to this method of communication between the Indian tribes of the north, and can now add, that the information given in this instance, was strictly corroborated on our arrival at St. Peter's.

The Mississippi below the junction of the river De Corbeau, pursues a more direct course towards the southwest. This has been particularly observable to-day. The current continues strong, and presents a great many islands and rapids. Piles of drift-wood appear upon the heads of islands, and loose granitic stones at the rapids. Snags become more frequent. Several rivers and creeks join the river on either shore, but none of any considerable magnitude. The soil continues alluvial on both banks—Ducks, geese, pelican, swan, and snipe, have been frequently seen;—also, the eagle, hawk, buzzard, heron, pigeon, and red squirrel. We passed Pike's Block House about ten o'clock in the morning. Opposite our present encampment, on the east side of the river, there is a bed of granite, two hundred and fifty feet in height. It is considerably mixed with hornblende. On ascending it I found the most charming prospects in every direction. It commands a view of the prairies on both banks of the Mississippi, with the windings of the stream, and its islands and rapids for many miles above and below, and the interest of the scene was greatly enhanced at the moment, by the herds of buffalo and deer which were seen in various groupes upon the prairies, and the delightful influence of a mild and transparent summer atmosphere.

The Indians of this region subsist wholly without the use of salt with their provisions.

LXVII. Day.—(*July* 29*th.*)—There is a heavy fall of dew upon the banks of the Mississippi during the summer nights which is in some measure proportioned to the heat of the preceding day; and increases in a direct ratio from its sources to its mouth. An exposure to this is considered particularly injurious to health, and is thought to be among the predisposing causes of malignant fevers. Any article capable of imbibing moisture, which is left out of the tent during the night, becomes as completely saturated with water, as if it had been exposed to a shower of rain.

In the course of the night a pack of wolves were heard on the opposite side of the river. There is something doleful as well as terrific in the howling of this animal, particularly when we start from a sound sleep during the stillness of night. It is, however, little to be dreaded, and I have never heard of an instance of its making an attack upon man, in the wilderness, although such instances have frequently occurred on the frontiers of our settlements. The cause of this apparently reversed order of nature is obvious. In the wilderness the wolf finds no difficulty in preying upon deer, buffalo, and elk, and is thus supplied with food; but such animals as linger upon the borders of society, where the deer has long been driven off, are compelled to resort to sheep and young cattle, and in cases of extreme hunger, are excited to acts of the most daring ferocity, and will attack men and horses, and whatever happens to fall in their way. There are two species of the wolf upon the banks of the Mississippi,—the common grey wolf (*Canis Lupus*) and the prairie wolf, which is unknown in Europe. The latter consists of two varieties, the *yellow* and *black* wolf. Both are much smaller than the canis lupus, and hunt together in larger packs. They possess in a superior degree the cunning, ferocity, and activity of the species, and are characterized by a fierce, sparkling yellow eye, and very sharp pointed ears. The yellow kind exceeds the terrier dog in size, which it also very much resembles in the shape of its head, and the general conformation of its body. The black wolf is larger, and I have seen an animal of this kind killed on the Missouri prairies, measuring three feet nine inches, from the tip of the nose to the insertion of the tail, being covered in every part with long black hair, but so coarse and bristly that no value is set upon it by the traders. The sagacity of the black and yellow prairie wolf, is such that when in a gang in the pursuit of deer, or buffalo, they will divide themselves into separate parties, and surrounding their prey, in a valley or open prairie, seldom fail to take a number, particularly such as are disabled by hunters, accidents, or age, or become unwieldly from over-feeding.

There is another sound which will frequently disturb the nightly rest of the traveller in the region of the Mississippi. It is the half-human cry of the Strix Nyctea, or great white owl, which inhabits the coldest regions of our continent, and is seldom found south of the falls of St. Anthony. This animal utters its most hideous cry, a few moments before the first glimpse of day light, and is thus the unerring herald of day. At this time it betakes itself to those recesses where it spends the day in seclusion. With this warning cry we were called to embark, and quit our encampment at half past four, the weather fair, and the thermometer standing at 50°. On descending six miles, we passed the mouth of Sac river, a stream of a hundred yards in width, entering on the west shore. This is one of the principal hunting grounds of the Minow Kantong band of Sioux. It is represented as a gentle river, and bordered in its whole course with the most luxuriant prairies, interspersed with copses of woods, the favorite resort of buffalo, elk, and deer.

At ten o'clock we encountered a formidable rapid, called the Big Falls, which consists of a series of breaks and schutes extending about eight hundred yards, in which distance the river may be estimated to have an aggregate fall of sixteen feet. The bed of the river at this fall is beset with sharp fragments of granitic and hornblende rock, which also appear in rolled masses upon the shores. The next remarkable trait in the river is Prairie rapids, which are six in number, and have a mean descent of about twenty feet in five miles.

At half past four in the afternoon, we passed the mouth of the river St. Francis, a large stream falling in on the east shore. For a great distance above its mouth it runs parallel with the Mississippi, which is the cause that so few tributaries enter the latter on the east shore after passing the mouth of the river De Corbeau. Its principal fork is Muddy river.—Here Carver terminated his travels up the Mississippi in the year 1765; and Father Hennepin in 1681. An island in the river opposite its mouth hides the view of it from those who descend by the west channel.

At six o'clock we passed Crow river, which is tributary on the western bank. It is a long stream and has a width of forty yards at its mouth, which it preserves a great distance up. It is ascended in canoes to within a few miles of its source, which is six days journey west of the Mississippi. Its principal fork is Tawtonga or Buffalo creek, which originates in Dog lake, in the centre of a boundless prairie. This is one of the best hunting grounds of the Sioux.

We encamped five miles below Crow river on the east bank of the Mississippi, having been thirteen hours in our canoes, and descended ninety miles. The current of the river this day has been unusually strong, with many rapids and ripples.—Very few snags have been observed.—A great many islands were passed in the afternoon, and some small sand bars, being the first noticed.—Prairies continue on both banks, with occasional clumps of trees, and forests of two or three miles in extent. The growth of wood upon the islands is elm, black and white walnut, maple, oak, and ash:—upon the prairies, dwarf black oak. Along the banks of the river, pebbles of quartz, granite, hornblende, carnelian, and agate are seen. In one instance, I picked up a fine specimen of agatized wood, such as is common upon the lower Mississippi, and along the shores of the

Missouri. The colour of the water continues a light chocolate brown in the stream, but appears clear in small quantities. Pebblesat the bottom of the river can be plainly discerned through it at four or five feet depth. The quality of the soil of the prairies improves as we descend, and during the last twenty miles may be considered of the richest kind. The prairies are in fact covered with a stratum of the most recently deposited, black, marly alluvion, which appears to be composed, in a great degree, of vegetable mould. It is entirely destitute of those rounded pebbles and stones which generally characterize upland soils, although bottomed upon a stratum of alluvion in which they are abundantly disseminated. The whole, apparently, rests immediately upon granitic and hornblende rock, which occasionally rises through it, in rugged peaks, and beds.

LXVIII. Day.—(*July* 30*th.*)—It was five o'clock in the morning when we left our encampment. On descending six miles we reached the mouth of the Mississawgaigon or Rum river, a large and long stream coming in upon the east bank. It originates in Spirit Lake, which is ten days journey north of its mouth. This lake is twelve miles long and four in width, of an irregular shape and beautified with several islands. It is only two days journey southwest of Sandy Lake. Its waters are very transparent, and afford a variety of fish, and the Indians say that its shores are strewed with an infinite variety of clear and shining stones, some of which are as large as a man's fist. These, from their descriptions, are presumed to be carnelians, agates, chalcedonies, and other silicious gems, which are known

PLATE VII.

H. R. Schoolcraft del.

Balch, sc.

FALLS OF S^{T.} ANTHONY

to be the product of the contiguous regions. Spirit Lake has two inlets, one of which called Akeek Seeba, originates a few miles west of the banks of St. Louis river near the Grand Rapids; the other is ascended in canoes within a day's walk of Lower Red Cedar Lake.

The falls of St. Anthony are fourteen miles below the confluence of the Mississawgaeigon. We reached the upper end of the portage at half past eight in the morning, and while the voyageurs were busied in the transportation of our baggage, hastened to take a view of this celebrated cataract. The river has a perpendicular pitch of forty feet, with a formidable rapid above and below. An island at the brink of the falls, divides the current into two sheets, the largest of which passes on the west of the island. The rapid below the schute is filled with large fragments of rock, in the interstices of which some alluvial soil has accumulated, which nourishes a stinted growth of cedars. This rapid extends half a mile, in which distance the river may be estimated to have a descent of fifteen feet. The rapid preceding the falls, has a descent of about ten feet in the distance of three hundred yards, where the river runs with a swift but unruffled current over a smooth stratum of rock a little inclined towards the brink. The entire fall therefore in a little less than three fourths of a mile, is sixty-five feet. The rock is a white sand stone overlayed by secondary lime stone. This formation is first seen half a mile above the falls, where it breaks out abruptly on the banks of the river. The perspective view (Plate VII.) is taken from a point about two hundred yards below the schute of the falls on the east shore, and a short distance west of the portage path. The scene presents nothing of that majesty and awe which is experienced in the gulf below the cataract of Niagara. We do not hear that deep and appalling tone in the roar of water, nor do we feel that tremulous motion of the rocks under our feet, which impresses the visitor at Niagara with an idea of *greatness*, that its magnificent outline of rock and water, would not, independently, create. The falls of St. Anthony, however, present attractions of a different nature, and have a simplicity of character which is very pleasing. We see nothing in the view which may not be considered either rude or picturesque, and perhaps there are few scenes in the natural topography of our country, where these features are blended with more harmony and effect. It is in fact the precise point of transition, where the beautiful prairies of the upper Mississippi, are merged in the rugged lime stone bluffs which skirt the banks of the river from that point downward.—With this change of geological character, we perceive a corresponding one, in the vegetable productions, and the eye embraces at one view, the copses of oak upon the prairies, and the cedars and pines which characterize the calcareous bluffs. Nothing can exceed the beauty of the prairies which skirt both banks of the river above the falls. They do not, however, consist of an unbroken plain, but are diversified with gentle ascents and small ravines covered with the most luxuriant growth of grass and heath-flowers, interspersed with groves of oak, which throw an air of the most picturesque beauty over the scene.

It is probable, too, that during the high floods of the Mississippi in the spring and fall, this cataract attains a character of sublimity, from the increased volume and tumult of the water, and the inundation of the accumulated debris, which presents, at this season, so rugged an aspect. It is said, also, that this accession of water produces a cloud of spray which must take away a certain nakedness in the appearance of the falls, that will strike every visitor who has previously enjoyed the sight of the Niagara.

The European name of these falls is due to father Lewis Hennepin, a French missionary of the order of Recollects, who first visited them in 1680. The Indian name in the Narcotah, or Sioux language, is *Owah-Menah*, or the falling water.

At the east side of the river, close under the sheet of the principal column of water, the Indians procure a kind of clay of a brownish red colour with which they paint their canoes and baskets. It appears to be an aluminous substance very much mixed with iron pyrites in a state of decomposition, and penetrated with vegetable juices. It is found in a crevice about ten feet below the water, and they pretend that it is renewed when taken away.

The length of the portage around the falls, as measured by Lieutenant Pike in 1805, is two hundred and sixty poles, but in high water is somewhat less. The width of the river on the brink of the fall is stated at two hundred and twenty-seven yards, but narrows to two hundred and nine yards a short distance below, where the river is compressed between opposing ledges of rock.

We completed the portage of our canoes and baggage at half past one, and descending the river nine miles, reached the American garrison at St. Peter's at three, and were received with a national salute.— The spot which it is proposed to fortify is a high bluff at the junction of the river St. Peter's with the Mississippi—a spot which commands the navigation of both rivers, and appears capable of being rendered impregnable with little expense. It is in fact the same point of land which first suggested to Lieutenant Pike the idea of its being an eligible situation for a fort, and led to its subsequent purchase from the Sioux Indians. This purchase was effected at a treaty* held by Lieut. Pike in September, 1805, by which they cede to the United States the district of country from the junction of the St. Peter's with the Mississippi, to the falls of St. Anthony inclusive, and extending nine miles on each side of the river. The consideration for this grant was two thousand

* *The following is the Treaty alluded to:*

At a conference held between the United States of America and the Sioux nation of Indians: lieutenant Z. M. Pike, of the army of the United States, and the chiefs and the warriors of said tribe, have agreed to the following articles, which, when ratified and approved of by the proper authority, shall be binding on both parties.

Art. 1. That the Sioux nation grant unto the United States, for the purpose of establishment of military posts, nine miles square at the mouth of the St. Croix,* also from below the confluence of the Mississippi and St. Peter's up the Mississippi to include the falls of St. Anthony, extending nine miles on each side of the river, that the Sioux nation grants to the United States the full sovereignty and power over said district for ever.

Art. 2. That, in consideration of the above grants, the United States shall pay (filled up by the senate with 2000 dollars.)

Art. 3. The United States promise, on their part, to permit

* My demand was one league below: their reply was "from below."— I imagine (without iniquity) they may be made to agree.

dollars. It could hardly have been anticipated at that time, when there were probably not more than a hundred American families in the extensive region now composing the states of Indiana, Illinois, and Missouri, that in the short space of thirteen years the progress of our settlements would have demanded the occupancy of a post in so remote a section of the union. Yet it was loudly called for even within that time, as a protection to the defenceless settlers on our northwestern and southwestern frontiers—and as a check to the undue influence which the British traders have too long exercised over the Indian tribes inhabiting the territories of the United States. Yielding to this expression of the public voice, the government determined to establish a garrison at St. Peter's. The force designated to accomplish this object consisted of three hundred men of the sixth regiment of infantry under the orders of Colonel Leavenworth, who had distinguished himself as commandant of the ninth

the Sioux to pass and repass, hunt, or make other use of the said districts as they have formerly done without any other exception than those specified in article first.

In testimony whereof we, the undersigned, have hereunto set our hands and seals, at the mouth of the river St. Peter's, on the 23d day of September, 1805.

Z. M. Pike, 1st lieut. (L. S.)
and agent at the above conference.

his
Le Petit Corbeau, ✕ (L. S.)
mark

his
Way Ago Enagee, ✕ (L. S.)
mark.

and twenty-second regiments in the battle of Chippeway.* They left Detroit in the spring of 1819, and proceeding by the way of Green Bay and the Fox and Ousconsing rivers entered the Mississippi at Prairie du Chien, where they left a detachment to erect a garrison, and proceeding up the river reached the mouth of the St. Peter's in season to complete their cantonements before the commencement of winter. They first located themselves on the rich bottom lands which extend along the south bank of the St. Peter's, but not finding it a healthy situation, removed in the spring of 1820, to an eminence on the west bank of the Mississippi, a mile distant from the old cantonement—a situation which is extremely pleasant and salubrious, and where they will remain until the permanent works are completed upon the bluff at the junction of the two rivers.

Since their arrival, the garrison have cleared and put under cultivation about ninety acres of the choicest bottom and prairie lands, which is chiefly planted with Indian corn and potatoes; besides a large hospital—a regmental, and several company, and private gardens, which supply vegetables in great abundance for all the men. Here we were first presented with green corn, pease, beans, cucumbers, beets, radishes, lettuce, &c. The first green pease were eaten here on the 15th of June, and the first green corn on the 20th of July. Much of the corn is already too hard to be boiled for the table, and some ears can be selected which are ripe enough for seed corn. We found the wheat entirely ripe, and melons nearly so. These are the best commentaries that can be offered upon the soil and cli-

* See Fay's Battles, page 215.

mate. To ascertain, however, that the former is of the richest quality, a cursory examination is only required. It presents all the peculiar appearances which characterize the fertile alluvions of the valley of the Ohio. In favour of the climate all the officers of the garrison speak in terms of the highest admiration. The atmosphere is represented as beautifully serene and transparent during the summer season, and free from that humidity which produces haziness and opacity; and although the meteorological registers* of the garrison indicate a high atmospheric temperature, it is observed that the fervour of the heat is greatly mitigated by the almost continual currents of the air, which prevent the weather from becoming sultry or oppressive. It is probable, however, that this effect is in some measure owing to the eligible situation of the garrison, at an elevation of about one hundred and fifty feet above the Mississippi river. The latitude of St. Peter's is 45°. —. —.

LXIX. DAY.—(*July* 31*st.*)—The river St. Peter's flows through the centre of the Sioux territories,

* It is rendered the duty of the Post-Surgeons at the frontier garrisons to keep a meteorological register of the weather, and to transmit abstracts of it, periodically, to the War Department.—With a view of comparing the results with my own observations, and of drawing some general conclusions, with regard to the climate of St. Peter's, I called on Doctor P——ll of the garrison and requested permission to copy his register, but regret that he did not think proper to assent without an injunction that it should not be made public. Is there any thing in the state of the weather at St. Peter's, of so much importance to the government, as to require secrecy? I am satisfied that gentlemen of the medical profession in the United States do not often subject themselves to the imputation of narrow-mindedness or illiberality.

and is both the largest and the least known, of all the tributaries of the upper Mississippi. It has never been explored except by voyageurs and traders, whose whole attention has been directed to the collection of peltries from the aborigines, and remains to this moment, undescribed in American geography. All, however, who have been questioned on the subject, both Indians and traders, agree in saying, that it is a long stream, made up of a great many tributaries, and flowing in its whole extent through a country of the most luxuriant fertility and delightful appearance. Carver ascended it two hundred miles, and found it to preserve in that distance, a uniform width of about one hundred yards, with a great depth of water, and represents its southern fork as originating very near the banks of the Missouri, and its northern, in a district of highlands called the Shining Mountains. "These mountains" he observes, "take their name from an infinite number of crystal stones of an amazing size, with which they are covered; and which when the sun shines full upon them, sparkle so as to be seen at a very great distance." After the most diligent enquiry, I have not been able to procure any information concerning these mountains, or their crystalline productions. To the first tributary of the St. Peter's on the northern bank, falling in forty miles above its mouth, Carver gave his own name, which I have adopted upon the chart of our track. The other tributary most known is the Terre Bleu, or Blue-earth river, which flows in from the south, a hundred miles west of the Mississippi, by a mouth of fifty yards in width. It is chiefly noted for the blue clay which the Indians procure upon its banks, and which is much employed in painting their faces and other parts of their bodies. The locality of this substance, as communicated by the Indians to Governor Cass, is the declivity of a hill one hundred and twenty feet in height, in the rear of the village of Sissitongs, one mile above its confluence with the St. Peter's. It is found at the foot of a sand stone bluff, between two strata of the rock, in a vein about fifteen inches in thickness. They have dug under it, so far as a man can go leaving out his legs. The vein does not extend far up and down the river. It is elevated about twenty feet above the level of the waters of the river, during the highest floods. Three miles below this, on the St. Peter's, there is a vein of green clay, of similar size, and situated between layers of the same kind of rock. About half way up a perpendicular bluff of rock, (they say) there is a break or platform, fifty feet broad, with a spring running over it. The clay is found where this spring issues from the rock, and is abundant. I procured specimens of both these varieties of clay. They appear to present alumine in combination with substances with which it has not heretofore been observed. They are considerably mixed with sand, and dry in the air without a disposition to crack in the manner of common clays. This is probably owing to the admixture of sand, which by rendering the mass porous in a higher degree, allows it to part with its moisture with greater rapidity. The two varieties only differ in the intensity of colour, one being a light green, the other partaking somewhat of blue. The colouring matter appears to be carbonat of copper. These clays possess all the plasticity of common clays when first taken up, and acquire a considerable degree of hardness, on drying. The St. Peter's also, affords a red paint, which is very much employed by the Sioux. This is procured at a spot called the Big Stone, at the extreme head of the river. A large spring rises from a level dry plain, and a few feet beyond it, this paint is found. They take it up with the point of a knife. The stratum is about eight inches thick, but just below the surface is mixed with common earth. It is perfectly dry, and void of all adhesive properties. The opening where the paint is procured, is about ten feet in diameter. It has long been resorted to, and they pretend that the quantity is *annually renewed.* The spring is fifteen or twenty feet in diameter, the water good, and rises in great abundance. The same substance is found at a few other places on an adjoining prairie. This red paint, proves to be the native red oxide of iron, in one of its most pure and beautiful forms. By sifting it, and grinding the powder in oil, it would prove a valuable and durable pigment, and its preparation may hereafter become an object in the commerce of the region.

There is also found upon some parts of this river a white clay, which has been thought proper for the manufacture of fine porcelain, but it appears to be entirely different from the *Petuntz* of the Chinese, or the porcelain earth of Limoges, or Monckton.—The latter proceed from the decomposition of graphic granite which is mostly composed of feldspar, and occur in dry, white, friable masses, without any of that pasticity which distinguishes the classes of common clays. But the white clay of St. Peter's, is very adhesive, and resembles the colourless clays of the Rhine, which are employed in the lining of furnaces where an intense degree of heat is required, and in the fabrication of chemical, and other crucibles. The specimens which I procured, are veined a little with red. It may prove valuable in the manipulations of the glass-maker.

This river has long been noted as the locality of that beautiful red stone of which the Indians manufacture the bowls of their pipes, but after all that has been said on the subject, by Carver, Breckenridge, and others, it does not appear that it is found upon the immediate banks of this stream. The quarry is situated in the prairie country intermediate between the St. Peter's and the Sioux river of the Missouri. It is said that the stratum does not exceed a foot in thickness, and that it is found two or three feet below the soil. The Indians go once a year to procure their supplies, and as it has been resorted to for a very long period, the excavations are said to be extensive, and if the accounts are to be relied on, cover an area of fifty acres. This stone is a red steatite, intermediate in its qualities, between the common soap-stone and serpentine. It yields very readily to the knife when first taken from the quarry, and as it has no grit, may be sawed without injury to a common hand saw, but it acquires a degree of hardness by long exposure to the air. It will not take a polish by the processes pursued in our marble-yards, as I have ascertained by submitting a piece of the stone to the experiment, but the Indian pipes assume a glossy appearance after long use.— A considerable degree of skill is manifested by the Indians in cutting their pipes, and the form and dimensions are regulated by a scrupulous regard to *fashion.* The bowls are invariably an inverted cone with a massy projection from the small end for receiving the stem, as represented by figure 4th in plate 2d. This part of the pipe is generally ornamented with carved work, and surmounted with a kind of comb. The stem consists of wood, and is usually from three to four feet in length by two or three inches in breadth and shaved down thin, so as to resemble a spatula. This stem is highly ornamented with porcupine quills, of various colours, neatly braided in bands and checquer-work with the exception of a small part on each end, which is left to be painted over with green or blue clay. (See fig. 8. plate II.) Pipe stems of this kind are appropriated to the chiefs, and are carefully laid aside for high days of ceremony and feasting, and are presented to the agents of government, as tokens of their sincerity, at all public conferences. There is another kind of stem which is peculiar to the common warriors or soldiers, and consists of a perforated rod profusely ornamented with stained horse hair, eagle's quills, and the beautiful green feathers taken from the head and neck of the wild duck.— (See fig. 9. plate II.)

"A little way," says Carver, "from the mouth of the St. Peter's, on the north side of it, stands a hill one part of which, that towards the Mississippi, is composed entirely of white stone, of the same soft nature as that I have before described, for such indeed is all the stone of this country: but what appears remarkable is, that the colour of it is as white as the driven snow. The outward part of it is crumbled by the weather into heaps of sand, of which a beautiful composition might be made; or, I am of opinion, that when properly treated, the stone itself would grow harder by time, and have a very noble effect in architecture." The rock here alluded to, is a white sand stone, which is first seen on descending the river, at the falls of St. Anthony, and forms the imposing bluffs on each side of the river from that point to the vicinity of the village of La Petit Corbeau, a distance of thirty-five miles. It is overlayed by a stratum of secondary lime stone, containing petrified concholites, and attaining, altogether, an elevation of about two hundred feet above the river. On the top of this bluff, at a spot directly opposite the site of the proposed fortification at St. Peter's, a singular formation of native copper has recently been discovered. It consists of small pieces of this metal, from half an ounce to a pound in weight, scattered over a natural hillock of small water-worn pebbles, or river-gravel. This is covered by a deposit of ash-like earth of a foot in thickness and tapering away very gradually towards the edge of the hillock. Then succeeds a deposit of six feet in thickness, of common alluvial soil, in which large fragments of lime stone, quartz, and hornblende, are plentifully imbedded, and lastly, a stratum of rich black alluvion without any imbedded substances, and apparently composed, in a great measure, of decayed leaves and other vegetable matter. This is eighteen inches in depth, and forms the surface of the country which is a kind of open highland prairie, covered with grass, and scattering oaks. Being told of this discovery by some of the officers of the garrison, by whom it was first noticed in quarrying stone for chimnies, I visited the spot, and made a minute examination of appearances, and in the course of a short time found a number of specimens of the copper at the spot indicated. They were all enveloped with a green oxide.

The river St. Peter's enters the Mississippi behind a large island which is probably three miles in circumference, and is covered with the most luxuriant growth of sugar maple, elm, ash, oak, and walnut.—At the point of embouchure it is one hundred and fifty yards in width, with a depth of ten or fifteen feet. Its waters are transparent, and present a light blue tint on looking upon the stream. Hence the Indian name of Wate-paw-mené-Sauta, or Clear-water-river. Among the forest trees upon its banks we noticed the box-elder *(acer negundo)* or ash-leaved maple. The inner bark of this tree, boiled down with the common nettle into a strong decoction, is said to be used by the Indians as a remedy for lues venerea, and to be a sovereign cure for that disorder.

There is a mineral spring, in a deep ravine, a mile northwest of the new cantonement. It deposits a yellow earthy substance in great abundance upon the stones and sticks of wood over which it passes. The water appears to be impregnated with iron and sulphur. Another similar but less copious spring is found on the banks of the Mississippi very near the cantonement. It is not, however, so highly charged with chalybeate properties.

Among the luxuriant herbage which characterizes the prairies of St. Peter's, is found a species of aromatic grass, upon which a high value is set by the aborigines. It throws off the most fragrant odour, and retains its sweetness, in a considerable degree, in the dried state. It is cut in a particular stage of its growth in the month of June, when it throws off its aroma most profusely, and continues to be gathered until it has run into seed, and is too dry to be plaited. The Indian women braid it up in a very ingenious manner and lay it aside in their cabins, as a kind of nostrum, and I have once seen it in the form of a wreath braided with certain leaves and flowers, decorating the temples of a warrior who had just returned in triumph from battle. Whether this grass is the same with the *heracleum panaces* of Kamschatka, and of which the inhabitants distil an intoxicating liquor, similar in some respects to brandy, I am unable to determine. It appears probable it may possess some properties in common with the holcus fragrans of Pursh.

Sir Francis Drake in his first visit to the Gulf of California, in 1587, found there a small burrowing animal which he describes with "a head like a conie, the feet of a mole, and the tail of a rat, with a pouch under each cheek." It appears to be the same animal which is here known by the name of the *gopher*, and which, so far as my reading extends, remains undescribed in zoological works. I had previously noticed the ravages of this animal in the prairies of Arkansas, ploughing up in some instances entire fields, and mentioned it in my remarks upon the Missourian mines, but owing to its extreme shyness, could never obtain a sight of the animal.—We were here, however, gratified, through the politeness of Col. Leavenworth, who directed a couple of soldiers to exert themselves in procuring one. It is about ten inches long from the nose to the insertion of the tail, with a body shaped very much like that of a large wharf-rat, which it also resembles in the colour of its hair and the length and nudity of its tail. Its legs are short, and each foot furnished with five long and sharp claws. It has two large fore teeth in each jaw, resembling those of the squirrel, but its most remarkable character is a pouch on each side of the jaw formed by a duplicature of the skin of the cheek. These project inwardly, where they are accommodated by an unusual width, and flattening out of the head. As the animal lives wholly under ground, like the mole, these pouches serve the purpose of bags for carrying the earth out of their holes. They are filled with the fore claws, and emptied at the mouth of the hole by a power which it possesses of ejecting the pouches from each cheek, in the manner that a cap or stocking is turned. In this way it works its path under ground, and ploughs up the prairies in many places in such a manner, that the white hunters of Missouri and Arkansas frequently avail themselves of the labours of the gopher by planting corn upon the prairies which have been thus mellowed. It lives entirely upon the roots of plants eating all with indiscriminate voracity, and has been found particularly destructive to beets, carrots, and other tap-rooted plants in the military gardens at St. Peter's.

LXX. Day.—(*August 1st.*)—A treaty of peace was this day concluded between the Sioux and Chippeways in the presence of Governor Cass, Colonel Leavenworth, Mr. Tallifierro, the Indian agent at St. Peter's, and a number of the officers of the garrison. These two nations have been at war from the earliest times, and the original causes of it are entirely forgotten, but still the ancient enmity is carefully transmitted from father to son. It is supposed to have arisen from a dispute respecting the limits of their territories, and favourite hunting grounds, but if so, nothing was agreed upon in the present instance to obviate the original causes of enmity. It was only stipulated that hostilities should immediately cease on both sides. Several of the chiefs delivered their opinions upon the subject, and the Sioux appeared to manifest some indifference to the treaty, but finally consented to drop the hatchet; and the ceremony concluded with smoking the pipe of peace and shaking hands. In this nearly every individual present united. The Sioux who attended the council were numerous, having been gathering in from the different villages from the time of our arrival; on the part of the Chippeways there were only present the deputies who accompanied us for that purpose from the sources of the Mississippi. The conduct of the latter, on our approach to St. Peter's, manifested the anxiety they felt on the subject, at the same time that it reveals a new trait in the character and customs of the Indian tribes. During the first two or three days after our departure from Sandy Lake, they proceeded very much at their ease, sometimes ahead of the expedition, at others in the rear—very seldom with us, and at night they usually encamped by themselves three or four hundred yards off: But the moment we entered the Sioux territories, they made it a point to keep close with the expedition, never venturing ahead, or lagging much in the rear, and at night they formed their encampment in the midst of ours. As we approached the falls of St. Anthony they requested of Governor

Cass, a flag for their canoe, which was granted, and during the whole of that day they kept a peace-pipe hoisted on the bow of their canoe. When we embarked below the falls of St. Anthony, they commenced beating upon their drum, singing, whooping, and frequently firing into the air, increasing the tumult as we came near to the fort, that the Sioux might be advertised of their approach; but the principal object of these ceremonies was to let their enemies know, that they came unto their territories upon a mission of peace—openly and boldly—and expected to be received by them with sentiments of corresponding liberality, frankness, and conciliation. Nor were they disappointed; they were taken by the hand in a friendly manner by those Sioux who had collected on our first landing at the garrison, and the pipe of peace immediately smoked between them, and this ceremony continued as fast as the Sioux arrived, so that the object of the public treaty held at the department of the Indian agent, where these ceremonies were repeated, was more with a view of having it witnessed by the agents of the United States, than to render binding upon their respective tribes, a pacification which had already been privately and individually determined upon. It has, however, been mentioned, that there was some indifference manifested to this treaty on the part of the Sioux, and those chiefs and warriors who discovered this unconquerable spirit of animosity, could not be induced to smoke the pipe of peace, although the cessation of hostilities had their tacit consent. Whether the peace will prove a permanent one, may be doubted. All their ancient prejudices will urge them to a violation of it, while past experience abundantly shews how difficult it has been to preserve a lasting peace between two powerful rival tribes of savages, whose predominant disposition is war, and if a durable peace should result from the laudable exertions of the agents of government in effecting this pacific conference, it will probably be owing in a great measure to a continuance of those exertions, supported as they are, by the influence of the garrisons at St. Peter's, Prairie du Chien, Council Bluffs, Green Bay, and other minor posts along our extensive Indian frontiers. In 1805, a treaty of peace was concluded between the Sioux and Chippeways at the instance of Lieutenant Pike. It continued *as long as he remained among them.* In the fall of 1818, a pacification took place at St. Louis under the auspices of Governor Clark, between the Osages and the Cherokees. The latter renewed hostilities *before they reached their homes.* This only proves, that treaties of peace between Indian tribes, like those between civilized nations, only amount to a momentary cessation of hostilities, unless the limits of their territories, and other subjects of dispute, are accurately defined, and satisfactorily settled.

The numerical strength of the Sioux nation was stated by the late General Pike at 21,675, three thousand eight hundred of whom are warriors. This is the most powerful Indian tribe in North America. It consists of seven bands, namely, the Minokantongs, the Yengetongs, the Sissitongs, the Wahpetongs, the Titongs, the Mendewacantongs, and the Washpecoutongs. These are independent bands, under their own chiefs, but united in a confederacy for the protection of their territories, and send deputies to a general council of the chiefs and warriors whenever the concerns of their nation require it. If one of the tribes is attacked, the others are expected to assist in the repulsion of the enemy. They inhabit all the country between the Mississippi and Missouri rivers, from north latitude about 46° to the junction of these rivers near St. Louis, with trifling exceptions in favour of some scattered bands of Foxes, Sacs, and Kickapoos. Their country also extends south of the Missouri, where the principal part of the Titongs reside, and east of the Mississippi to the territories of the Chippeways—the Winnebagoes, and the Menomonies. The greatest chief of the nation, at present, is Talangamane, or the Red wing.

The Minokantongs, or people of the waters, are located at St. Peter's, and along the banks of the Mississippi towards Prairie du Chien. They reside in four principal villages, distinguished by the names of their respective chiefs; Chatawaconamie, or La Petit Corbeau—Talangamane, or the Red wing—Tatamane, or the wind-that-walks, and Wabashaw.

The Yengetongs and the Sissitongs inhabit the upper parts of the river St. Peter's, and are sometimes called the Sioux of the Plains. Their traffic is principally in Buffalo robes. The first chief is Muckpeanutah, or the Red Cloud. The Wahpetongs, or people of the Leaves, are the most erratic in their dispositions of all the Sioux. They inhabit the St. Peter's between the Prairie De François and the White Rock, during a part of the year, and generally go out to hunt above the falls of St. Anthony towards the sources of the river De Corbeau, and upon the plains which give origin to the Crow, Sac, and Elk rivers. Their principal chief is Wakunska, or the Rolling Thunder.

The Titongs inhabit both banks of the Missouri, and rove in quest of game over an immense extent of country. They are said to be related to the Mahas, and some other bands south of the Missouri.

The Mendewacantongs, or people of the Medicine Lake,—the Washpecoutongs, or people of the Leaves *who have ran away*, and some other scattered bands whose names are unknown, inhabit the country generally, from the St. Peter's south to the mouth of the Missouri, and are chiefly located upon the sources of the rivers Ocano, Iowa, and Desmoines.

The Sioux are generally represented as a brave, spirited, and generous people, with proud notions of their origin as a tribe, and their superiority as hunters and warriors, and with a predominant passion for war. They speak the Narcotah language, which is peculiar to themselves, and appears to have little affinity with any other Indian tongue. It is not so soft and sonorous as the Algonquin which abounds in labials, but more so, than the Winnebago, which is the most harsh and gutteral language in America. The Narcotah sounds to an English ear, like the Chinese, and both in this, and other respects, the Sioux are thought to present many points of coincidence. It is certain that their manners and customs differ essentially from those of any other tribe, and their physiognomy, as well as their language, and opinions, mark them as a distinct race of people.—Their sacrifices and their supplications to the unknown God—their feasts after any signal deliverance from danger—their meat, and their burnt offerings—the preparation of incense, and certain customs of their females, offer too striking a coincidence with the manners of the Asiatic tribes before the commencement of the christian era, to escape observation, while their paintings and hieroglyphics bear so much analogy to those of the Azteeks of Mexico, as to render it probable that the latter are of Naudowessian origin. But these hints are merely thrown out for the investigation of the future enquirer, as my limited opportunities of observation, and the short period of our sojournment among them, forbid any thing like systematic research, which is the more to be regretted as this tribe has recently assumed a more interesting attitude with respect to the United States, and as the time for conducting these enquiries with any probability of success, is rapidly receding under the pressure of an enterprizing European population. It is to be hoped that some spirited traveller, possessed of the necessary qualifications, will select their territories as the theatre of his researches, and I doubt not, that he would find more among them to elucidate the origin and history of the aborigines of our country, than among any other tribe upon the continent.

"From my knowledge of the Sioux nation," observes Lieutenant Pike, "I do not hesitate to pronounce them the most warlike and independent nation of Indians within the boundaries of the United States, their every passion being subservient to that of war; but at the same time their traders feel themselves perfectly secure of any combination being made against them, but it is extremely necessary to be careful not to injure the honour of an individual, which is certainly the cause of the many broils which occur between them. But never was a trader known to suffer in the estimation of the nation by resenting any indignity offered him; even if he went to taking the life of the offender. Their gutteral pronunciation—high cheek bones—their visages, and distinct manners, together with their own traditions, supported by the testimony of neighbouring nations, put it in my mind beyond the shadow of a doubt, that they have emigrated from the northwest point of America, to which they had come across the narrow streights, which in that quarter, divide the two continents; and are absolutely descendants of a Tartarean tribe."*

As an instance of the generosity of this nation, the following anecdote is related. La Petit Corbeau, chief of a small band of Sioux, located upon the banks of the Mississippi, towards the confines of the Chippeway territories, going out one morning to examine his beaver trap, found a Sauteur in the act of stealing it. He had approached without exciting alarm, and while the Sauteur was engaged in taking the trap from the water, he stood maturely surveying him with a loaded rifle in his hands. As the two nations were at war, and the offence was in itself one of the most heinous nature, he would have been justified in killing him upon the spot, and the thief looked for nothing else, on finding himself detected. But the Sioux chief walking up to him discovered a nobleness of disposition which would have done honour to the most enlightened of men. "Take no alarm, said he, at my approach; I only come to present to you the trap of which I see you stand in need. You are entirely welcome to it. Take my gun

* Pike's Expeditions.

also, as I perceive you have none of your own, and depart with it to the land of your countrymen, but linger not here, lest some of my young men who are panting for the blood of their enemies, should discover your foot steps in our country, and fall upon you." So saying, he delivered him his gun and accoutrements, and returned unarmed to the village of which he is so deservedly the chief.

There are several antique mounds and circumvallations upon the banks of the St. Peter's, which are said to indicate an industrious population, and an intimate acquaintance with geometrical solids, which are still to be traced among the full-grown trees of the forest which now overshadows these enigmatical works. The most remarkable of these, are stated to be about forty miles above the mouth of the St. Peter's, near the junction of that branch which is denominated Carver's river. I regret that I can say nothing concerning them from actual inspection.—They are among the number of interesting traits, the examination and description of which, would so richly reward an exploration of this important river.

About six miles west of the new cantonement there are several beautiful little lakes, situated in the prairies. They consist of the purest water and are surrounded with a handsome beach of yellow sand and water-worn pebbles, among which are to be found fragments of the most highly coloured carnelians, and ribband agates. The largest of these lakes is about four miles in circumference, and is called Calhoun lake. It is stored with the most exquisite flavoured black bass and several other varieties of fish, and has become a fashionable resort for the officers of the garrison. The intermediate country is a prairie, and is travelled in all directions on horseback. It is not, however, a level plain, but consists of gentle slopes and ascents, and the clumps of trees which are scattered over it, give a pleasing variety to the scene. In the season of verdure, the waving heath-grass,—the profusion of wild flowers, and the sweet-scented Indian grass, while they fill the air with a refreshing fragrance, delight the eye with the richness and never-ending variety of their colours; and viewed under the influence of a gentle western breeze, which is seldom wanting, leave nothing to complete the picture of the most enchanting rural beauty.

Among the animated productions of nature which serve to enliven and diversify the scene, there is a new species of burrowing squirrel, something larger than the common striped ground squirrel, with an elongated body and short legs, approaching in shape the mustela nivalis, or brown weasel. But the most striking difference is found in its colour, which is a reddish brown with four longitudinal black stripes upon the back, spotted with yellow, and resembling in this respect, the skin of the African leopard. It is a beautiful little animal—burrows in the ground, and feeds upon ground nuts and esculent roots. It has been found destructive to the gardens at St. Peter's.

The temperature of the atmosphere, and the changes of weather during the journey from Sandy lake, are indicated by the following—

Meteorological Table.

1820.	A. M. 5	7	8	P. M. 2	8	9	Mean temp.	Winds.	WEATHER.
July 25			71	85	74		76		Fair. Rain at night.
- 26	61			81	61		67	S. W.	Mor.cloudy,with rain—ev'n clear.
- 27	62			80	75		72		Fair.
- 28	62			76	61		66		Morn. fair—afternoon rain.
- 29	50			74	62		62		Fair. Flying clouds.
- 30		60		76		63	66	N W.	Fair.
- 31		65		81		69	72	W.	- -
Aug. 1		67		83	70		73	W.	- -

8)554

$69\frac{2}{8}$ mean temperature.

CHAPTER XI.

JOURNEY,

FROM ST. PETER'S TO PRAIRIE DU CHIEN.

LXXI. DAY.—(*August 2d.*)

LEAVING the mouth of the St. Peter's at nine o'clock, we proceeded down the Mississippi thirty-eight miles, and encamped at twilight upon the west shore, nine leagues below the village of La Petit Corbeau. About twelve miles below the new garrison at St. Peter's, we stopped to examine a remarkable cavern on the east banks of the Mississippi, called *Wakon-teebe*, by the Narcotah or Sioux Indians, but which, in compliment to the memory of its first European visitor, should be denominated Carver's cave. It is situated in a rock of the most beautiful white sand stone, at the head of a small valley about four hundred yards from the banks of the river. Its mouth is about sixty or seventy feet wide and twenty in height, but the former soon decreases to about twenty feet, and the latter to seven. This width gradually lessens as you advance during the first hundred yards, but the height remains nearly the same, so that a man can walk without stooping.—Then it tapers into a narrow passage, where it is necessary to creep, which suddenly opens into a spacious chamber. From this a narrow crevice continues as far as it has been explored. Some of our party pursued it four hundred yards by the light of wax candles. It is very damp and chilly. There is a handsome stream of pure water running from its mouth. The temperature of the air in the cave was 54°—that of the water 47°. As it is situated in sand stone rock, it affords no stalactites, or spars. Some parts of the rock at the mouth are coloured green, probably by the carbonat of copper. The bed of the brook is composed of a crystalline sand of the most snowy whiteness, originating from the disintegration of the surrounding walls. Scattered over this, are a number of small pebbles of so intensely black a colour as to create a pleasing contrast, when viewed through the medium of a clear stream. These, on examination, proved to be masses of lime stone, granite, and quartz, coloured externally by a thin deposit of earthy matter, and I conclude the colour to proceed from the gallic acid, with which the water, percolating into the cavern, through the beds of oak leaves of the superincumbent forest, may be partially saturated. This cave has been visited by most persons who have passed up the Mississippi, if we may judge from the number of names found upon the walls. Among them we were informed was that of Captain Carver, who visited it in 1768, but we did not observe it. His grant of land from the Indians, is dated in this cave, but the cave itself, appears to have undergone a considerable alteration since that period, for he says that "about twenty feet from the entrance begins a lake, the water of which is transparent, and extends to an unsearchable distance." As the rock is of a very friable nature, and easily acted upon by running water, it is probable that the lake has been discharged, thus enlarging the boundaries of the cave. He also remarks, "At a little distance from this dreary cavern, is the burying place of several bands of the Nawdowessie (Sioux) Indians. Though these people have no fixed residence, living in tents, and abiding but a few months in one spot, yet they always bring the bones of their dead to this place; which they take the opportunity of doing when the chiefs meet to hold their councils, and to settle the public affairs for the ensuing summer." We noticed no bones or traces of interment about the cave, but perhaps a further examination of the adjacent region would have led to a discovery.

Four miles below Carver's cave, we landed at the village of La Petit Corbeau, or the Little Raven. Here is a Sioux band of twelve lodges, and consisting of about two hundred souls, who plant corn upon the adjoining plain, and cultivate the cucumber, and pumpkin. They sallied from their lodges on seeing us approach, and gathering upon the bank of the river fired a kind of *feu-de-joie*, and manifested the utmost satisfaction on our landing. La Petit Corbeau was among the first to greet us. He is a man below the common size, but brawny and well proportioned, and although rising of fifty years of age, retains the looks and vigour of forty. There is a great deal of fire in his eyes which are black and piercing—his nose is prominent and has the aquiline curve, his forehead falling a little from the facial angle, and his whole countenance animated, and expressive of a shrewd mind. We were conducted into his cabin which is spacious, being about sixty feet in length by thirty in width—built in a permanent manner of logs, and covered with bark. Being seated, he addressed Governor Cass in a speech of some length, in which he expressed his satisfaction on seeing him there, and said that in his extensive journey he must have experienced a good many hardships and difficulties, and seen a great deal of the Indian way of living, and of the country—all of which would enable him to see things in their proper light. He said he was glad that the Governor had not, like many other officers and agents of the United States who had lately visited those regions, passed by his village without calling. He particularly alluded to the officers of the establishment at St. Peter's, and said they had generally passed upon the other side of the river. He observed that he had attended several councils at St. Peter's, and given away a number of pipes, but got nothing in return. He acquiesced in the treaty which had lately been concluded with the Chippeways, and was happy that a stop had been put to the effusion of human blood. He then adverted to a recent attack of a party of Fox Indians upon some of their people towards the sources of the river St. Peter's, in which nine men had been killed. He considered it a dastardly act, and said if that *little* tribe, should continue to haunt their territories in a hostile manner, they would at length drive him into anger, and compel him to do a thing he did not wish. These were the principal topics of his speech; some minor points were adverted to, and he several times repeated his obligations for the honour of our visit. He spoke with deliberation, and without that wild gesticulation which is common among savages. Two or three other persons afterwards spoke, but I was not struck with any expressions of much point. They repeated several things that had before been said, and delivered pacific sentiments in the most furious manner.

While these things were going forward, the Indian women were busily engaged in gathering green corn, and each one came into the centre of the chief's cabin and threw a basket full upon a common pile, which made a formidable appearance before the speakers ceased, and it was absolutely necessary to forbid their bringing more. This was intended as a present, and we took away as much as we could conveniently find storage for, in our canoes.

Our attention was now drawn off by the sounds of Indian music which proceeded from another large cabin at no great distance, but we found the doors closed, and were informed that they were celebrating an annual feast, at which only certain persons in the village were allowed to be present, and that it was not customary ever to admit strangers. Our curiosity, however, being excited, we applied to Governor Cass to intercede for us, and were by that means admitted. The first striking object presented was two large kettles full of green corn, cut from the cob and boiled. They hung over a moderate fire in the centre of the cabin, and the Indians, both men and women, were seated in a large circle around them. They were singing a doleful song in the savage manner, accompanied by the Indian drum, and gourd-rattle. The utmost solemnity was depicted upon every countenance not engaged in singing, and when the music ceased, which it frequently did for a few seconds, there was a still and mysterious pause, during which certain pantomimic signs were made, and it appeared as if they pretended to hold communication with invisible spirits. Suddenly the music struck up, and the singing commenced, but as we did not understand their language, it is impossible to say what they uttered, or to whom their supplications or responses were addressed. In the course of these ceremonies a young man and his sister, joining hands, came forward towards the centre of the cabin. We were told they were about to be admitted to the rights of partaking of the feast, but there was nothing striking in the ceremony, and all its interest was lost to us, because we could not understand the questions which were asked and the answers given. The voice of every one appeared to be taken in their admission, which was unanimous. When this ceremony ceased, one of the elder Indians, dished out all the boiled corn into separate dishes for as many heads of families as there were present, putting an equal number of ladles full into each dish. Then, while the music continued, they, one by one, took up their dishes and retiring from the cabin by a backward step, so that they still faced the kettles, separated to their respective lodges, and thus the ceremony ceased. We are told, however, that several important things were omitted on account of our being present. From all that could be learned, it was a feast in honour of the Cereal goddess, or manito, of the Indians, which is annually held when the corn first becomes suitable for boiling in the ear.

LXXII. Day.—(*August 3d.*)—We embarked at five o'clock. On descending the river six miles, we passed the mouth of the river St. Croix, which enters on the east shore by a channel of one hundred yards in width. It is connected by a portage of two pauses, with the Bois Brule river of Lake Superior, and in its whole extent is not interrupted by a single fall or rapid. It is said to be the most practicable, easy, and expeditious water communication between the Mississippi river and Lake Superior.—About five hundred yards above its mouth, it expands into a lake, called Lake St. Croix, which is thirty-six miles long, and from one and a half to three in breadth. Sixty miles above the head of this lake, the southwest company have an establishment. The country around its mouth is claimed by the Sioux; its sources are inhabited by a band of Foille avoine Chippeways, and the Chippeways of the Burnt woods. There is an island in the Mississippi opposite its junction. At this place, the river bluffs assume an increased height, and more imposing aspect, and in the course of the succeeding fifty miles, we are presented with some of the most majestic and pleasing scenery which adorns the banks of the upper Mississippi. In many places the calcareous bluffs terminate in pyramids of naked rocks, which resemble the crumbling ruins of antique towers, and aspire to such a giddy height above the level of the water, that the scattered oaks which cling around their rugged summits seem dwindled to the most diminutive size;—at others, the river is contracted between two perpendicular walls of opposing rock, which appear to have been sundered to allow it an undisturbed passage to the ocean, and not unfrequently, these walls are half buried in their own ruins, and present a striking example of the wasting effects of time upon the calcareous strata of our planet. Sometimes, there is a rock bluff on one bank, and an extensive plain of alluvion on the other, contrasting with the finest effect, the barrenness of the mineral, with the luxuriant herbage, and the rural beauty, of the vegetable kingdom. Again, the hills recede from either shore, and are veiled in the azure tint of the distant landscape, while the river assumes an amazing width, and is beautified with innumerable islands, and we find ourselves at once bewildered between the infinity of its channels, and the attractive imagery of its banks. Nor is the presence of animated nature wanting, to enrich and beautify the scene. The deer is frequently seen standing in the cool current of the stream, gathering the moss from the hidden rocks below, or surveying our approach from the grassy summit of the impending cliff, with an unconcern, which tells us how little it is acquainted with the sight of man. The whole tribe of waterfowl are found upon the river, and by the variety of their plumage, and their shapes—the wildness of their notes—and the flapping of their wings, serve to diversify the scene, while the well known notes of the robin, and other singing birds upon the shores, which are the same that we have listened to in childhood, recall a train of the most pleasing reflections. Nor is the red man, the lord of the forest, wanting. His cottage is disclosed by the curling smoke upon the distant hills, where he surveys with a satisfied eye the varied creation upon the plains below;—the deer—the elk—the water fowl—the river which floats his canoe—the trees which overshadow the grassy hills upon which he reposes during the heats of noon—the thickets, where he arouses the sleeping bear—the prairie, which gives vigour to his constitution, and while he lifts his eye in gratitude to the great spirit of life, for all these various blessings, exclaims with the genuine poet of nature

"Creation's heir—the world—the world is mine."

At twelve o'clock we arrived at the Sioux village of Talangamane, or the Red wing, which is handsomely situated on the west banks of the river, six miles above Lake Pepin. It consists of four large, and several small lodges, built of logs in the manner of the little Raven's village. Talangamane is now considered the first chief of his nation, which honour it is said he enjoys both on account of his superior age and sagacity. He appears to be about sixty, and bears all the marks of that age. Very few of his people were at home, being engaged in hunting or fishing. We observed several fine corn fields near the village, but they subsist chiefly by taking sturgeon in the neighbouring lake, and by hunting the deer. The buffalo is also occasionally killed, but they are obliged to go two days journey west of the Mississippi, before this animal is found in plenty. We observed several buffalo skins which were undergoing the Indian process of tanning.—The hair having been taken off in the manner of dressing deer skins, the hides were stretched out upon the ground and covered with a decoction of oak and other bark, prepared by boiling the bits of bark in water. A black colour was thus communicated to the skin, and it is probable that sufficient of the astringent principle of the bark is thus made to unite with the gluten of the skin, to give it, in some degree, the properties of leather. The idea is probably borrowed from their intercourse with the frontier settlers, although the nearest tan-yard is at St. Louis, eight hundred miles below.

Half a mile east of Red wing's village there is an isolated mountain, standing upon the brink of the river, called the Grange, from the summit of which you enjoy the most charming prospect. The immense valley of the Mississippi, with the numerous channels and islands of the river—the prairies and forests—with the windings of a number of small rivers which flow into the Mississippi, spread like a map below the eye. The calcareous bluffs which bound this valley, and terminate the prospect towards the west, in a line of lofty grey cliffs, throw an air of grandeur upon the scene, which affords a pleasing contrast with the deep green of the level prairies, and the silvery brightness of the winding river. Turning the eye towards the east, Lake Pepin spreads its ample sheet across the entire valley of the river, from bluff to bluff, and the indentures of its shores recede one behind another, until they become too faint to be distinguished, and are terminated on the line of the horizon. The altitude of this mountain cannot fall short of eight hundred feet above the bed of the river. It presents an abrupt mural precipice towards the Mississippi, but slopes off gradually towards the south, and is covered with grass, and a few scattering oaks. Its sides are strewed with beautiful crystals of violet coloured, and radiated quartz, and with masses of iron ore crystallized in cubes and octahedrons. A specimen of lead ore (*galena*) was also shewn to us by one of Talangamane's people, and a mine is reported to exist in the vicinity, but we could procure no information which is to be relied upon, concerning its situation and extent.

In ascending this mountain we first noticed the rattlesnake, (*crotalus horridus*) which is found, however, as far north as the falls of St. Anthony. (north latitude 45°.) One of the most remarkable facts in the natural history of this dreadful animal, is, that its poison may be taken internally without any danger. A spoonful, it is affirmed, may be swallowed at a time, without producing any ill effects upon the constitution. This, is the characteristic difference between animal and vegetable poisons. It is well known that the virus of this animal is secreted in a small cavity at the root of the fangs, which are shaped like the claws of a cat, and are hollow, and that it is ejected through these tubes at the instant it inflicts the wound. It has been stated, on the authority of Mr. Peale, proprietor of the Philadelphia museum, that an animal punctured with the fangs of the rattlesnake, for years after they have been taken out and dried, will produce almost instant death, and that he employed acids and alkalies to deprive them of this poisonous property, without success. The poison of serpents is found to be more virulent, and to operate with greater activity, in warm, than in cold climates, nor is it equally fatal to all animals. The hog, for instance, devours the rattlesnake without danger, and is even said to thrive and fatten upon it. Charlevoix mentions a plant, which is an antidote to the bite of this snake, called the rattle snake plant (*herbe a serpente a sonettes*) which grows abundantly throughout this country. "This plant," he remarks, "is beautiful and easily known. Its stem is round and somewhat thicker than a goose-quill, rising to the height of three or four feet, and terminates in a yellow flower of the figure and size of a yellow daisey. This flower has a very sweet scent. The leaves of the plant are oval, narrow, sustained, five and five, in form of a turkey cock's foot, by a peduncle or foot stalk an inch long." In another place, speaking of the *citron*, he remarks "The root of this tree is a mortal and most subtil poison, and at the same time a most sovereign antidote against the bite of serpents. It must be bruised and applied instantly on the wound: this remedy is immediate and infallible." The plant alluded to in both instances, appears to be the common mandrake, or podophyllum peltatum of modern botany. The poisonous properties of this plant are mentioned by another of the elder travellers of the region, whose work has long since ceased to be quoted, the Baron La Hontan, who says that the expressed juice of this plant, taken internally, produces instant death; and relates an instance of an Iroquois woman, making use of it on the disease of her husband. She soon fell into shivering fits, and expired in his presence.

In our times the common plantain (*plantago major*) has been frequently mentioned as an infallible cure, both for the bite of the rattlesnake, and the tarantula, or great black field spider; but I cannot allude to any particular cases in which it has been successfully applied. There is an old story, which relates that the curative qualities of the plantain, in cases of animal poison, was first discovered in the following manner: An aged black man in one of the southern states, being out in the field, happened to witness a combat between the tarantula and a toad: the latter appeared frequently to be vanquished, but as often retreated to a stem of plantain, growing near, and eating some of the leaves, returned to the combat. Observing this, the plantain was pulled up, when the toad on returning, and finding it taken away, immediately swelled up and died. This gave the hint for applying it in cases of the bite of venomous snakes, and the discoverer alluded to, acquired celebrity for the cures he effected by the use of it. Whether the Virginia snake-root, (*aristolochia serpentaria*) is applied as an antidote to the poison of serpents, I am unable to say. Ergotted rye, is also among the number of simples, which have been lately recommended in cases of the bite of the rattlesnake.

At one o'clock in the afternoon we entered Lake Pepin. This beautiful sheet of water is an expansion of the Mississippi river, six miles below the Sioux village of Talangamane, and one hundred below the falls of St. Anthony. It is twenty-four miles in length, with a width of from two to four miles, and is indented with several bays, and prominent points, which serve to enhance the beauty of the prospect. On the east shore, there is a lofty range of limestone bluffs, which are much broken and crumbled—sometimes run into pyramidal peaks—and often present a character of the utmost sublimity. On the west, there is a high level prairie, covered with the most luxuriant growth of grass, and nearly destitute of forest trees. From this plain several conical hills ascend, which, at a distance, present the appearance of vast artificial mounds or pyramids, and it is difficult to reconcile their appearance with the general order of nature, by any other hypothesis. This lake is beautifully circumscribed by a broad beach of clean washed gravel, which often extends from the foot of the surrounding highlands, three or four hundred yards into the lake, forming gravelly points upon which there is a delightful walk, and scalloping out the margin of the lake, with the most pleasing irregularity. In walking along these, the eye is attracted by the various colours of the mineral gems, which are promiscuously scattered among the water-worn debris of granitic, and other rocks, and the carnelian, agate, and chalcedony, are met with at every step. The size of these gems is often as large as the egg of the partridge, and the transparency, and beauty of colour, is only excelled by the choicest oriental specimens. There is no perceptible current in the lake, during calm weather, and the water partakes so little of the turbid character of the lower Mississippi, that objects can be distinctly seen through it, at the depth of eight or ten feet.—It is plentifully stored with a variety of fish, the most remarkable of which is the *shovel-nosed sturgeon*, which is so called from a protuberance which extends from the end of the nose about fourteen inches—is four in width, and quite thin, in which respect, as well as in the shape of this process, it bears a striking resemblance to a physician's *spatula*. In other respects its size and general appearance corresponds with the small sturgeon of lakes Huron and Superior. This extension of the nose, appears designed to enable the animal to agitate the mud along the shores, and on the bottom of the Mississippi, in quest of certain animalcula, which are supposed to be its favourite food. The shores of this lake, also, appear favourable to the growth of crustaceous fish, and an examination of the different varieties which are presented, would probably result in the discovery of one or two new species. In no place have I ever noticed the fresh water muscle, attain so large a size. One of these, which I procured, measures seven inches in length, by five and a half in width, and the thickness, taken at right angles with the most convex part of the shell, is a little less than four inches.

Lake Pepin receives two of the tributary streams of the Mississippi, called the river *au Canoe*, and Porcupine-quill river. The former has, by a general mistake, (which I did not myself detect until my map was engraved) been called Cannon river; and I have elsewhere spoken of it, under the name of Ocano, being the popular pronunciation of the French term. It flows into Lake Pepin from the west, near its head; and is one of the principal hunting grounds of the Red wing's band. Porcupine-quill river, enters in a large bend on the east shore, about midway of the length of the lake, and is noted as the ancient site of a French fort and trading factory. We did not stop to examine the remains of this establishment, which it is said, are still visible.

In passing through Lake Pepin, our interpreter pointed out to us a high precipice, on the east shore of the lake, from which an Indian girl, of the Sioux nation, had many years ago, precipitated herself in a fit of disappointed love. She had given her heart,

42

it appears, to a young chief of her own tribe, who was very much attached to her, but the alliance was opposed by her parents, who wished her to marry an old chief, renowned for his wisdom and his influence in the nation. As the union was insisted upon, and no other way appearing to avoid it, she determined to sacrifice her life in preference to a violation of a former vow, and while the preparations for the marriage feast were going forward, left her father's cabin, without exciting suspicion, and before she could be overtaken, threw herself from an awful precipice, and was instantly dashed to a thousand pieces. Such an instance of sentiment is rarely to be met with among barbarians, and should redeem the name of this noble-minded girl from oblivion. It was Oola-Ita. (*Oo-la-i-ta*)

Having descended the river sixty-seven miles, we encamped on a gravelly beach on the east shore of Lake Pepin, at six o'clock in the evening, the weather threatening a storm. In the vicinity of our encampment, we observed the asparagus growing along the shore. The seeds had probably been dropped by some former traveller. At eight o'clock, it commenced raining, and continued, at short intervals, during a great part of the night, attended with severe thunder, and the most vivid flashes of lightning.

LXXIII. Day.—(*August 4th.*)—We proceeded on our descent at five o'clock. The rain had ceased before day light, but the morning remained cloudy. The lake is two miles and a half wide, opposite the spot of our encampment, but narrows gradually towards its outlet, which is ten miles below. The scenery during this distance is highly picturesque and beautiful. The precipices on the east are high, and shoot up into spiral points, yet are covered partially with grass and shrubbery. On the west we observe nothing but an elevated level prairie. The contrast produces the finest effect. At the precise point of exit of the Mississippi river, from Lake Pepin, the Chippeway, or Sauteaux river, comes in from the east. It is half a mile wide at its mouth, and its sources are connected with the Montreal river of Lake Superior. Below the junction of this stream, the Mississippi has an increased width, and contains a great number of small willow and cotton-wood islands, and the navigation is rendered more difficult, on account of the innumerable sand bars which here first make their appearance. They are attributable, in a great measure, to the immense quantity of sand brought down by the Chippeway river.

A few miles below Lake Pepin on the west bank of the Mississippi, are the remains of one of the most interesting and extensive of those ancient circumvallations, which are so frequently found throughout the valley of the Mississippi, and its confluent streams, and whose origin, notwithstanding the lapse of half a century since they first began to attract the notice of philosophic enquirers, still remains veiled in the impenetrable mist of obscurity. The work in question was in fact one of the earliest that excited notice, but the hints which were thrown out by Carver in 1768, with respect to this work, appear to have escaped the attention of succeeding travellers and enquirers, and as yet no plan of it, has been taken. As our opportunities did not allow us to supply this deficiency, by actual observation, I shall here present the remarks of the enterprising traveller alluded to, in order to excite the attention of those who may hereafter visit the region.

"One day having landed on the shore of the Mississippi, some miles below Lake Pepin, whilst my attendants were preparing my dinner, I walked out to take a view of the adjacent country. I had not proceeded far before I came to a fine, level, open plain, on which I perceived, at a little distance, a partial elevation that had the appearance of an intrenchment. On a nearer inspection, I had greater reason to suppose that it had really been intended for this many centuries ago. Notwithstanding it was now covered with grass, I could plainly discern that it had once been a breast-work of about four feet in height, extending the best part of a mile, and sufficiently capacious to cover five thousand men. Its form was somewhat circular, and its flanks reached to the river. Though much defaced by time, every angle was still distinguishable, and appeared as regular, and fashioned with as much military skill, as if planned by Vauban himself. The ditch was not visible, but I thought on examining more curiously, that I could perceive there certainly had been one. From its situation also, I am convinced that it must have been designed for this purpose. It fronted the country (the west) and the rear was covered by the river; nor was there any rising ground for a considerable distance that commanded it; a few straggling oaks were alone to be seen near it. In many places small tracks (paths) were worn across it by the feet of the elks and deer, and from the depth of the bed of the earth by which it was covered, I was able to draw certain conclusions of its great antiquity. I examined all the angles and every part with great attention, and have often blamed myself since, for not encamping on the spot, and drawing an exact plan of it. To shew that this description is not the offspring of a heated imagination, or the chimerical tale of a mistaken traveller. I find, on enquiry since my return, that Monsieur St. Pierre and several other traders have, at different times, taken notice of similar appearances, on which they have formed the same conjectures, but without examining them so minutely as I did. How a work of this kind could exist in a country that has hitherto (according to the generally received opinion) been the seat of war to untutored Indians alone, whose whole stock of military knowledge has only, till within two centuries, amounted to drawing the bow, and whose only breast-work even at present, is the thicket, I know not. I have given as exact an account as possible of this singular appearance, and leave to future explorers of these distant regions, to discover whether it is a production of nature or art. Perhaps the hints I have here given might lead to a more perfect investigation of it, and give us very different ideas of the ancient state of realms that we at present believe to have been from the earliest period only the habitations of savages."*

This is the first notice, to the best of my recollection, ever taken by a transatlantic writer of those antique works, which are now daily discovered, in every part of the western country, and after all that has been poured out upon this subject, the conclud-

* Carver's Travels, p. 30.

ing observation of Carver, made in the American wilderness sixty years ago, embraces half the sum of our knowledge upon the subject at the present day. The fact of the existence of a very extensive work at the place above mentioned, is corroborated by a conversation I have had on that subject with Mr. Harman V. Hart, of the city of Albany, who has spent five years as a trader in the Sioux countries, and frequently visited the works in question, as well as those upon the river St. Peter's, which are noticed in another part of this journal.

At four o'clock in the afternoon, we made a short halt at the Sioux village of Wabashaw, which is eligibly situated on the west bank of the Mississippi, sixty miles below Lake Pepin. It consists of four large lodges, with a population of, probably, sixty souls. A present of tobacco and whiskey was given, and we again embarked at twenty minutes before five o'clock.

A few miles below Wabashaw's village, an isolated mountain, of singular appearance, rises out of the centre of the river, to a height of four or five hundred feet, where it terminates in crumbling peaks of naked rock, whose lines of stratification and massy walls, impress forcibly upon the mind the image of some gigantic battlement of former generations. Around its lower extremity, the alluvion of the river has collected, forming a large island, covered with a heavy forest, whose deep green foliage forms a pleasing contrast with the barren grandeur of the impending rocks, which project their gothic pinnacles into the clouds, and cast a sombre shadow over the broad and glittering bosom of the Mississippi. This singular feature in the topography of the country, has long attracted the admiration, and the wonder, of the voyageurs of the Mississippi, who have bestowed upon it the appellation of The Mountain that sinks in the Water, (*La Montaigne qui Trompe dans l'Eau,*) an opinion being prevalent among them, that it annually sinks a few feet. This island-mountain is four or five miles in circumference, with a mean width of half a mile, and by dividing the channel of the river into two equal halves, gives an immense width to the river, and thus increases the grandeur of the prospect. It is further remarkable as being the only fast, or rocky island, in the whole course of this river, from the Falls of Peckagama, to the Mexican Gulf. The west channel of the Mississippi, opposite this mountain, receives a small tributary, called The River of the Mountain that Sinks in the Water, and the east channel, another of similar size, called Buffalo river, (*La riviere au Bœuf.*) Both may be considered in the fourth class, as respects size and importance, of the tributaries of the Mississippi. About five miles below the Sinking Mountain, we encamped on the west shore of the river, at seven in the evening, having been twelve hours upon the river, and descended the current seventy miles. Immediately in the rear of our camp, there was a lofty range of river bluffs. I hastened to take a glimpse of their geological character before the daylight disappeared, and on gaining the summit, had a commanding view of the extensive tract of bottom land on the opposite side of the river, which consists, in part, of a heavy wooded forest, interspersed with patches of prairie, and bounded at the distance of four or five miles, by a range of calcareous bluffs, corresponding, in general appearance, to that upon which I stood. The scene is checquered by the devious course of Black River, which joins the Mississippi in front,—by the mountain that sinks in the water above, and the broad Mississippi, with its numerous islands and channels, at a depression of four or five hundred feet below. Turning the eye towards the west, the country has the general elevation of the river bluffs. It is wooded with oak—with tracts of prairie—and lies in ridges, some of which are entirely covered with grass, and destitute of forest trees. At the rapids of Black River, one day's journey in a canoe from its mouth, there is a saw-mill recently erected, by a gentleman at Prairie du Chien, where boards and scantling are already sawed for the purposes of building at the latter place. Thus is the empire of the arts, and the march of European population, gradually extending into regions which have, heretofore, only resounded to the savage war whoop, or if they have ever before witnessed a civilized population, (as our tumuli, and antiquities would lead us to infer,) the light of history, and the voice of tradition, cast not a solitary beam to illumine our researches, or direct us in elucidating the mysterious history of the aboriginal tribes, and the ancient state of society, arts, and religion, upon our continent.

A short time previous to our encampment, we observed a large grey wolf in the river before us, making its way for the opposite bank. In a moment every canoe was pointed towards it,—every muscle was strained to intercept its landing; and we shot down the stream with the rapidity of an eagle who pounces upon his prey. The whooping of the Indians,—the shots that were fired,—and the tumult of so many paddles dashing in the water, gave great spirit to this scene, but it was only of momentary duration, as the wolf soon gained the sandy shore of the river, and shaking the water from his meagre flanks, sprang into an adjoining thicket, and in a moment disappeared.

LXXIV. DAY.—(*August 5th.*)—It is ninety miles from the spot of our encampment to Prairie du Chien. We embarked a few moments after three in the morning, and reached the Prairie, at six in the afternoon. As we descend, the Mississippi has a gradual increase of size, and its valley a corresponding width.—The calcareous bluffs continue on either shore. In the course of this day, the river has been swelled by the rivers Embarras, La Claire, and Badaxe, the two former uniting at the point of their entrance into the Mississippi.

The village of Prairie du Chien is pleasantly situated on the east bank of the river, on the verge of one of those beautiful and extensive natural meadows, which characterize the valley of the Mississippi. It consists of about eighty buildings, including the garrison, the principal part of which are of logs, arranged in two streets parallel with the river, and is estimated to have an aggregate population of five hundred. This, is exclusive of the garrison, now consisting of a company of infantry, ninety-six strong, under the command of Capt. Fowle.

The village of Prairie du Chien takes its name from a family of Fox Indians who formerly resided there, and were distinguished by the appellation of *Dogs.* The present settlement was first begun in

1783, by Mr. Giard, Mr. Antaya, and Mr. Dubuque. There had formerly been an old settlement about a mile below the site of the present village, which existed during the time that the French held possession of the Canadas, but it was abandoned, chiefly on account of its unhealthy situation, being near the borders of an extensive tract of overflowed grounds. The early settlers, according to the principles adopted by the French colonists in the Canadas, intermarried with Indian women, and the present population is the result of this connexion. In it, we behold the only instance which our country presents, of the complete and permanent civilization of the aborigines; and it may be doubted, after all that has been said upon the subject, whether this race can ever be reclaimed from the savage state, by any other method. The result, in the present instance, is such as to equal the most sanguine expectations of the philanthropist, in regard to a mixed species. They are said to exhibit evidences of enterprise, industry, and a regard to order and the laws, at the same time, that we perceive the natural taciturnity of the savage, happily counterpoised by the vivacity and suavity of the French character, producing manners which are sprightly without frivolity, and serious without becoming morose.

Prairie Du Chien is the seat of justice for Crawford county, which has recently been erected in this part of the Michigan Territory,* and a court of

* The Northwestern Territory does not at present exist in law. On the admission of the state of Illinois into the Union, the regions northwest of it, and *east* of the Mississippi river, extending to its source, were incorporated with the government of Michigan.

justice has already been established. There is also a company of militia formed out of the Gallico-savage population, who perform the usual services with promptitude. There is a school, however, wanting, for the rising generation, and a suitable opening appears to be presented for a person who could unite the characters of a moral and religious instructor.

The fortification at this place consists of four lines of log barracks facing a square parade ground, and defended by bastions at the northwest and south-east angles. The logs are squared and whitewashed, and the works occupy a considerable extent of ground, and have a very neat, and imposing appearance. There is a large and fertile island in the Mississippi, opposite the village, and a high calcareous bluff on the opposite bank.—The Ousconsing joins the Mississippi one league below.—There is a Bayou, or marsh, at the point of confluence, which extends into the prairie to within a mile of the village, and is thought to render it unhealthy at particular seasons. The lead mines are situated on the west bank of the river twenty-five leagues below.

CHAPTER XII.

VISIT,

TO THE LEAD MINES OF DUBUQUE, ON THE UPPER MISSISSIPPI.

LXXV. Day.—(*August 6th.*)

As a delay of several days was anticipated at Prairie du Chien, I solicited Governor Cass for permission to employ the time in visiting the lead mines of the upper Mississippi, which had acquired some celebrity from their reputed extent, and the novel circumstance of their being worked by the Indian tribes. I left the prairie at half past eleven in the morning, in a canoe manned by eight voyageurs, including a guide. Three miles below, we passed the mouth of the Ousconsing, which is a large and majestic stream, and communicates by a short portage with the Fox river of Green Bay—a route which we are to pursue on our return to Detroit. Nine leagues below the Ousconsing, Turkey river enters the Mississippi on the west bank, by a mouth of sixty yards in width. This stream is one of the principal hunting grounds of the Fox Indians, and communicates, by its main northwestern fork, with the Terre Bleu of St. Peter's. There is a Fox village (now deserted) of twelve lodges, a mile below, on the east bank of the Mississippi. Here I encamped at seven o'clock in the evening, having descended the river thirty-one miles against a strong head wind. I found the lodges to be large, and built of logs, in the same substantial manner practised among the Narcotah bands. The cause of their being now deserted, is the fear entertained of an attack from the Sioux, in retaliation for the massacre lately perpetrated upon the banks of the St. Peter's. The desertion appears to have taken place after they had planted their corn, and from the order in which the village is left, it may be concluded that its re-occupation is kept in view. I found several small gardens and corn fields adjoining the village, in which squashes, beans, and pumpkins were abundant, but the corn had been nearly all destroyed, probably by wild animals. Walking back from the river half a mile, to examine the geological character of an adjoining bluff, I was surprised to find an extensive field of water and musk-melons, situated in the midst of a grove of small, scattering trees, but without any inclosure. Some of the fruit had been destroyed by animals, but a great abundance still remained, although I found none perfectly ripe. This must have been owing to the shaded situation of the vines, and not to a defect of climate, as we found the water-melon in full maturity at Prairie du Chien, which is thirty miles north.

LXXVI. Day.—(*August 7th.*)—We had frequent peals of thunder during the night, and the atmosphere threatened a rain-storm, as daylight approached. I embarked at half past three in the morning. It commenced raining in twenty minutes afterwards, and continued incessantly until my arrival at the Fox village of the Kettle chief, where I landed at ten o'clock, having descended the river forty-five miles.

The Kettle chief's village is situated on the west bank of the river, and consists of nineteen lodges, built in two rows—pretty compact—with a population of two hundred and fifty souls. In the Mississippi river, directly opposite this village, there is a large island, where a number of traders are constantly stationed for the purpose of supplying the Indians with merchandize, and purchasing their lead. Concluding I should there find an interpreter of the Fox language, I first landed upon the island, and met with the most friendly reception from the traders, who readily communicated to me the information I sought, respecting the location, number, and value of the mines, and the method of working them, together with specimens of the ores, and accompanying minerals. The rain ceased an hour after my arrival, when I proceeded across an arm of the Mississippi to the Kettle chief's village, to solicit his permission, and procure Indian guides, to explore the mines which are situated in the interior. I was accompanied on this visit by Mr. Gates, as interpreter, and by Dr. S. Muir, a trader of the island, who politely offered to go out with me. On entering the Kettle chief's lodge, I found him suffering under a severe attack of bilious fever. As I approached him, he sat up on his pallet, being unable to stand, and bid me welcome, but soon became exhausted by the labour of conversation, and was obliged to resume his former position. He appeared to be a man of eighty years of age—with a venerable look, but reduced to the last stage of physical debility, yet retaining, unimpaired, his faculties of sight and hearing, and his mental powers; and he spoke to me of his death with calm resignation, and as a thing to be desired. On stating the object of my visit, some objections were made by the chiefs who surrounded him, and they required further time to consider the proposition. In the mean time, I learned from another source, that since the death of Dubuque, to whom they had formerly granted the privilege of working the mines, they had manifested a great jealousy of the whites—were afraid they would encroach upon their rights—denied all former grants, and did not make it a practice even to allow strangers to view their diggings, &c. Apprehending some difficulties of this kind, I had provided myself with some Indian presents, and concluding this to be the true cause of the reluctance manifested, directed one of my voyageurs to bring in a present of whiskey and tobacco; and in a few moments afterwards received their assent, and two guides were furnished to conduct us out. One of these, was a soldier-chief of the Fox tribe, called *Sca-bass*, or the yelling wolf; the other, *Wa-ba-say-ah*, or the white Fox skin.

The district of country generally called *Dubuque's Lead mines*, embraces an area of about twenty-one square leagues, commencing at the mouth of the little Maquanquitons river, sixty miles below Prairie du Chien, and extending along the west bank of the Mississippi, seven leagues in front by three in depth. The principal mines are situated upon a tract of one square league, commencing immediately at the Fox village of the Kettle chief, and extending westward. This is the seat of the mining operations formerly carried on by Dubuque, and of what are called the *Indian diggings.* The ore found is the common sulphuret of lead, with a broad foliated structure, and high metallic lustre. It occurs massive, and disseminated, in a reddish loam, resting upon lime stone rock, and sometimes is seen in small veins pervading the rock, but it has been chiefly explored in alluvial soil. It generally occurs in beds or veins, which have no great width, and run in a certain direction three or four hundred yards,—then cease, or are traced into some crevice in the rock, having the appearance of a regular vein. At this stage of the pursuit most of the diggings have been abandoned, and frequently, with small veins of ore in view. No matrix is found with the ore which is dug out of the alluvial soil, but it is inveloped by the naked earth, and the lumps of ore are incrusted by an ochreous earth. Occasionally, however, some pieces of calcareous spar, are thrown out of the earth in digging after lead, and I picked up a solitary specimen of the transparent sulphat of barytes, but these substances appear to be very rare. There is none of the radiated quartz, or white opake heavy spar, which is so common at the Missouri mines. The calcareous rock upon which this alluvial formation, containing lead ore, rests, appears to be referable to the transition class. I have not ascertained its particular extent about the mines. The same formation is seen, overlayed by a distinct stratum of compact lime stone, containing numerous petrifactions, at several places, between the mines and Prairie du Chien. The lead ore at these mines is now exclusively dug by the Fox Indians, and, as is usual among savage tribes, the chief labour devolves upon the women. The old and superannuated men also partake in these labours, but the warriors and young men, hold themselves above it. They employ the hoe, shovel, pick-axe, and crow-bar, in taking up the ore. These things are supplied by the traders, but no shafts are sunk, not even of the simplest kind, and the windlass and bucket are unknown among them.—They run drifts into the hills so far as they can conveniently go, without the use of gun-powder, and if a trench caves in, it is abandoned. They always dig down at such an angle that they can walk in and out of the pits, and I descended into one of these, which had probably been carried down forty feet. All this, is the work of the Indian women and old men, who discover a degree of perseverance and industry, which is deserving of the highest commendation. When a quantity of ore has been got out, it is carried in baskets, by the women, to the banks of the Mississippi, and there ferried over in canoes to the island, where it is purchased by the traders at the rate of two dollars for a hundred and twenty pounds, payable in goods at Indian prices. At the profits at which these goods are usually sold, it may be presumed to cost the traders from seventy-five cents to a dollar, cash value, per hundred weight. The traders smelt the ore upon the island, in furnaces of the same construction used at the lead mines of Missouri, and observe, that it yields the same per centum of metallic lead. Formerly, the Indians were in the habit of smelting their ore themselves, upon log-heaps, by which a great portion was converted into what are called *lead-ashes*, and thus lost. Now, the traders induce them to search about the sites of those ancient fires, and carefully collect the lead ashes, for which they receive a dollar per bushel, delivered at the island, payable in merchandize.

There are three lead mines, in addition to those above mentioned, situated upon the upper Mississippi, which are worked by the Indian tribes, namely, the Sissinaway mines,—mine au Fevre,—and the mines of the little Maquanquitons.

I. *The Sissinaway Mines.*—These are situated fifteen miles below the Kettle chief's village, on the east shore of the Mississippi, and at the junction of the Sissinaway river.

II. *Mine au Fevre.*—Situated on the river au Fevre, which enters the Mississippi on the east shore, twenty-one miles below Dubuque's mines. The lead ore is found ten miles above its mouth. At this place, there is a considerable quantity of sulphat of barytes, and the ore is often found crystalized in regular cubes, octahedrons, &c.

III. *Mine of Maquanquitons.*—This is a short distance up the little Maquanquiton's river, which flows into the Mississippi fifteen miles above Dubuque's mines. It has been the least explored of any.

The Fox, or Outagami Indians, upon whose territories these mines are situated, are settled upon both banks of the Mississippi, between Prairie du Chien and Rock rivers, and claim the lands thus occupied, and extending a certain distance east and west of the river. They are bounded by the lands of the Sioux of the Missouri, on the west,—by the Winnebagoes, and Pottawattamies, on the east, and by the Sacs and Kickapoos on the south. Their principal village is that called the Kettle Chief's, at

Dubuque's mines, seventy-five miles below Prairie du Chien. They have another village at the Rock river rapids, a hundred and sixty miles below. It consists of fourteen lodges, and a hundred and fifty souls. On the east bank of the Mississippi, near the foot of Rock island, there is a large village of Foxes and Sacs, living promiscuously together.—It consists of sixty lodges, being one of the largest and most populous Indian villages on the continent. They have also a small village at the mouth of Turkey river, thirty miles below Prairie du Chien, but it is at present temporarily deserted. These villages comprise the strength of the Fox tribe, which is estimated at four hundred souls. They are nearly related to the Sacs, from whom they have seceded within the last century. They also claim relationship with the Chippeways. Of their own origin they know very little. As far as their traditions extend, they came from the neighbourhood of Kingston, in Upper Canada. From thence they were driven into the vicinity of Michilimackinac, and afterwards to Green Bay, and along the river which falls into its head, and bears their name. At Fox river, they suffered a signal defeat, from a body of combined French and Indians, at a place since called *La Butte de mort*, or the Hill of the dead; and were driven to the banks of the Ousconsing, from which they subsequently emigrated, to the country they now occupy. They speak the Algonquin language, with a great many peculiarities, and corruptions, and are supposed to be one of the numerous bands into which that once powerful nation, has been scattered. The name of Reynards or Foxes, appears first to have been bestowed on them, during their sojournment at Green Bay. The history of their migrations and wars, shews them to have been a restless and spirited people—erratic in their dispositions, having a great contempt for agriculture, and a predominant passion for war. By this means, they have been continually changing—suffering—and diminishing, until they are reduced to a hundred fighting men. Still, they retain their ancient character, and are constantly embroiled in wars and disputes with their neighbours, the results of which shew, that they have more courage in battle, than wisdom in council. In their dealings with the traders, they are cunning and deceitful. In their engagements, they lack punctuality, and in their friendships, constancy; yet they profess a fawning friendship for all. Hence the French traders early applied to them, in derision, the term of *dogs*, and *foxes*. They are at present waring with the Sioux, and lately surprised and killed nine of that nation, on a branch of the St. Peter's, called Terre Bleu, where they both resort to procure the blue clay, with which they are fond of painting themselves.—There is now a war party of twenty men, in the same direction, under a half-breed, by the name of Morgan. This party went out by Turkey river, and are supposed to have marched against the Sissitongs of the St. Peter's. They are also on bad terms with the Pawnees, and Osages, south of the Missouri, and with the Winnebagoes, in their own neighbourhood, from whom they occasionally steal horses, and are plundered in return.

In 1780, a discovery of lead ore was made upon their lands by the wife of Peosta, a warrior of the Kettle chief's village, and extensive mines have since been discovered. These, were granted by the Indians to Julien Dubuque at a council held at Prairie du Chien in 1788, by virtue of which he settled upon the lands—erected buildings and furnaces, and continued to work the mines, until the year 1810. In the meantime (1796) he received a confirmation of the Indian grant from the Baron de Carondelet, Governor of Louisiana, in which they were designated the "Mines of Spain."

"Julien Dubuque," by a stone monument which stands on a hill near the mines, "died on the 24th of March, 1810, aged 45 years, 6 months." After his death, the Indians burnt down his house and fences, and erased every vestige of civilized life, and they have since revoked, or at least, denied the grant, and appear to set a very high value upon the mines. Dubuque dying in debt, his claims were assigned to his creditors, by whom they were presented for confirmation, to the board of Commissioners appointed by the United States Government in 1806, to determine upon the land titles and grants of the newly acquired Territory of Louisiana. By this Board, the claim of the assignees was determined to be valid, and a memorial of their proceedings transmitted to the Treasury Department, at Washington, for the final decision of Congress. In this stage of the investigation, Mr. Gallatin, transmits, by way of report, to the President of the United States, the following facts, and remarks, which may be considered as embracing the views of the government, in relation to one of the most important of the western land claims, which still remain undecided.

FACTS.

" In 1788, Dubuque purchased from the Indians, an extent of seven leagues front on the Mississippi, by three leagues in depth, containing upwards of one hundred and forty thousand acres, and the most valuable lead mines of Louisiana, situated about five hundred miles above St. Louis. The sale is very vague; they permit Dubuque to work the mine as long as he pleases, and till he thinks proper to abandon it, without confining him to any time; and they also sell him the hill and contents of the land (or mine) found by Peosta's wife, and if he finds nothing in it, he may work where he pleases, and work quietly. In 1796, he presents his *requete*, to Governor Carondelet at New-Orleans, stating that he has made a settlement (habitation) or settled a plantation amongst the Indians, that he has purchased from them a portion of land with all the mines therein contained; that the *habitation* is but a *point*, and inasmuch as the mines he works, are three leagues from each other, he requests the governor to grant him the *peaceable possession* of the mines and lands, contained within certain natural boundaries, and which he states as being above six leagues in front, and three in depth.

" The governor refers the application for information to A. Todd, who had the monopoly of the Indian trade on the Mississippi.

" A. Todd reports, that no objection occurs to him, if the governor thinks it convenient to grant the application, provided that Dubuque shall not trade with the Indians without his permission.

" Governor Carondelet, writes at the foot of the request, " granted as is asked (concedido como se solicita) under the restrictions mentioned by Todd, in his information, 10th November, 1796."

"Governor Harrison in his treaty with the Sacs and Foxes, of the 3d November, 1804, introduces an article, by which it is agreed, that nothing in the treaty shall affect the claim of individuals who might have obtained grants of land from the Spanish government, known to, and recognised by the Indians, though such grants be not included within the boundary line fixed by the treaty with said Indians. And the same governor certifies that the article was inserted with the intention of particularly embracing Dubuque's claim. The claim having been laid before the commissioners, they made on the 20th September, 1806, the following decision:

"A majority of the board, John B. C. Lucas dissenting, ascertain this claim to be a complete Spanish grant, made and completed prior to the 1st day of October, 1800.

"A copy of that decision, tested by the assistant clerk of the board, has been delivered to Aug: Chouteau, who had purchased from Dubuque, one undivided half of the claim."

REMARKS.

"I. Governor Harrison's treaty adds no sanction to the claim: It is only a saving clause in favour of a claim, without deciding on its merits, a question which indeed he had no authority to decide.

"II. The form of the concession, if it shall be so called, is not that of a patent, or final grant, and that it was not considered as such the commissioners knew, as they had previously received a list procured from the records at New-Orleans, and transmitted by the Secretary of the Treasury, of all the patents issued under the French and Spanish governments, in which this was not included, and which also showed the distinction between concession, and patent, or complete title.

"III. The form of the concession is not even that used, when it was intended ultimately to grant the land; for it is then uniformly accompanied with an order to the proper officer to survey the land, on which survey being returned, the patent issues.

"IV. The Governor only grants as is asked; and nothing is asked but the peaceable possession of a tract of land on which the Indians had given a *personal* permission to work the lead mines as long as *he* should remain.

"Upon the whole, this appears to have been a mere permission to work certain distant mines, without any alienation of, or intention to alienate, the domain.—Such permission might be revoked at will; how it came to be considered as transferring the fee simple, or even as an incipient and incomplete title to the fee simple, cannot be understood.

"It seems, also, that the commissioners, ought not to have given to any person certificates of their proceeding, tending to give a colour of title to claimants. They were by law directed to transmit to the treasury a transcript of their decisions, in order that the same might be laid before Congress for approbation or rejection."*

The mines of Dubuque were among the objects to which the attention of Lieutenant Pike was di-

* Collection of Land Laws of the United States, printed at Washington, 1817.

rected, in his voyage up the Mississippi in 1805, but a number of circumstances prevented him from visiting the mines, or from procuring much information upon the subject. It did not suit the views of Mr. Dubuque, to encourage his visit—the mines were represented at a great distance—he pretended to have no horses at command, &c. Under these circumstances, Lieutenant Pike contented himself, by proposing to Mr. Dubuque, a number of queries in writing, but the answers given, do not appear to be entitled to full confidence, and are somewhat equivocal.*

* Queries proposed by Lieutenant Pike, to Mr. Dubuque—with his Answers.

1. What is the date of your grant of the mines from the savages?

Ans. The copy of the grant is in Mr. Soulard's Office, at St. Louis.

2. What is the date of the confirmation by the Spaniards?

Ans. The same as to query first.

3. What is the extent of your grant?

Ans. The same as above.

4. What is the extent of the mines?

Ans. Twenty-eight or twenty-seven leagues long, and from one to three broad.

5. Lead made per annum?

Ans. From 20 to 40,000 pounds.

6. Quantity of lead per cwt. of mineral?

Ans. Seventy-five per cent.

7. Quantity of lead in pigs?

Ans. All he makes, as he neither manufactures bar, sheet-lead, or shot.

8. If mixed with any other mineral?

Ans. We have seen some copper, but having no person sufficiently acquainted with chemistry, to make the experiment, properly, I cannot say as to the proportion it bears to the lead.

J. DUBUQUE,
Z. M. PIKE.

Lead Mines, 1st Sept. 1805.

Having examined the mines with as much minuteness, as the time allotted to me, would permit, I returned to the Mississippi in the evening, and proceeding two leagues up the river, encamped upon an island, at eight o'clock.

LXXVII. Day.—(*August* 8*th.*)—I embarked at four o'clock in the morning—passed the mouth of Turkey river at two o'clock—and encamped upon a small island, one league below the mouth of the Ousconsing, at eight in the evening, having been sixteen hours in my canoe, and ascended the river sixty-three miles.

LXXVIII. Day.—(*August* 9*th.*)—I passed the mouth of the Ousconsing before day-break, and reached Prairie du Chien, at six in the morning, after an absence of three days, during which, I have travelled a hundred and fifty miles, forty-five of which were made under an exposure to a rain storm.

The valley of the Mississippi between Prairie du Chien, and the lead mines of Dubuque, is about two miles in width, and consists of a rich deposit of alluvial soil, a part of which, is prairie; and the remainder, covered with a heavy forest of elm, sugar tree, black walnut, ash, and cotton wood. It is bounded on each side by corresponding bluffs of calcareous rocks, which attain a general elevation of four hundred feet, and throw an interest over the scene—which prairies and forests—woody islands, and winding channels, beautiful and picturesque, as they certainly are, must fail to create. It is to these bluffs,—now shooting into spiral columns, naked and crumbling—now sloping into grassy hills or intersected by lateral vallies—here, grouped in the fantastic forms of some antiquated battlement, mocking the ingenuity of man—there, stretching as far as the eye can reach in a perpendicular wall—but ever varying—pleasing—and new—it is to these bluffs, that the valley of the upper Mississippi, owes all its grandeur and magnificence. Its broad and glittering channel—its woodless prairies and aspiring forests–its flowering shrubs and animated productions—only serve to fill up, and give effect to the imposing outline, so boldly sketched by the pencil of nature, in these sublime and pleasing bluffs.—Yet, there is much in the detail of the scene, to admire—in the beauty of its tints—the fancy of the grouping—and the mellowness of the shades.

Among the humbler growth, which adorns the borders of the forest, the cornus florida, the sarsaparilla, and the sumach, are frequently to be seen, still beautiful in the unbleached verdure of spring, and bathing their impending branches in the rushing stream, where the splendid foliage of the autumnal forest, is already visible in the rich hues of the fading maple, the heart-leaved aspen, and the populus angulata.

The tall grass of the prairies, although it has also assumed the yellow hue of autumn, and rustles in the northern breeze, is yet occasionally chequered with green copses of shrubby oaks, and beautified with the peculiar tribe of heath-flowers, which linger unblown, through the sultry heats of July, to scatter their fragrance over the fading fields of August. The channel of the river, is often expanded to an amazing width, and spotted with innumerable islands, some of which, are nothing more than a bank of yellow sand just looming above the water, and crowned with a brushy growth, of young willows and slender cotton woods: others, present copses of the tallest trees, which are not unfrequently precipitated bodily into the stream, by the undermining currents of the river, or hang from the new fallen alluvial banks, with their branches dipping into the stream. Perched upon these, we invariably find the heron, and king-fisher, who, with motionless anxiety, watch for their finny prey. The eagle, and the hawk, choose a more elevated seat to watch for their food, while the buzzard, with an easy wing, is continually sailing through the air, eagerly scanning the lower plains, for its favourite carrion. The white pelican, is also, very frequent, along this part of the river, but is always found upon the point of some naked sand bar, which I conclude to be the most favourable spot for taking its food. The duck, and the goose, appear to be the only species of water-fowl, which are always in motion, and it is rare to see them seated upon the shore, but, this may be less the result of their superior activity, and natural sprightliness, than the strong necessity of continually searching for those aquatic plants, which constitute their favourite food. The pigeon, the snipe, the wild turkey, the raven, and the jay, are also common along this part of the Mississippi, and contribute, by their appearance, to enliven and diversify the scene. Nor, is it uncommon, during the heats of noon, to behold the savage, reclining beneath the grateful shade of the oak, upon some breezy knoll of the contiguous bluff.—

"Nor feels for aught, nor has a wish that goes
Beyond his present succour and repose.—
To-day's support employs to-day his thought,
To-morrow's meal must be to-morrow sought."

Satisfied with present competence, he thinks not of the long, and dreary winter, which shall soon deform his native sky—of the pinching hunger, which shall await his improvidence—of the precariousness, of the chace—of the rapid diminution of his tribes, before the resistless march of European population—of the evils, they have introduced into it; and of its slow, certain, and total annihilation: but, dreaming of the beauty of his native mountains, envies not eastern monarchs their possessions, while all his bliss—all his hopes—and all his ambition, are centered in the unrestrained enjoyment of liberty, and the land of his forefathers.

"Dear is that shed to which their souls conform,
"And dear the hill that lifts them to the storm;
"And as a babe, when scaring sounds molest,
"Clings close, and closer, to the mother's breast—
"So the loud torrent, and the whirlwind's roar,
"But binds them to their native mountains more."

GOLDSMITH.

CHAPTER XIII.

JOURNEY,

FROM PRAIRIE DU CHIEN, BY THE OUSCONSING AND FOX RIVERS, TO GREEN BAY.

LXXVIII. Day.—(*August 9th.*)

DURING our stay at Prairie du Chien, we observed a remarkable instance of natural deformity, in the person of an Indian, who had just come in from the interior. This singular being, was provided by nature, with double the usual number of joints in each arm, and leg, by which means, he was rendered, in some measure, helpless, and unable either to stand, or walk. By an effort of savage ingenuity, however, this redundancy of joints, was made the means of procuring locomotion, by coiling his legs in a large wooden bowl, in which he rolled himself along, over a smooth surface, with considerable facility. The powers of his mind, were not, however, in the least affected, by this corporeal degradation, but appeared, on the contrary, vigorous, and superior to the generality of his tribe. He spoke several Indian tongues, and conversed fluently in the French language, as it is generally spoken by the Canadian voyageurs, and northwest traders ; and his whole countenance bespoke intelligence, and mental activity.

We left Prairie du Chien at half past ten in the morning, and entering the Ousconsing three miles below, ascended that river eighteen miles. It is a wide, and shallow stream, running over a bed of sand—with transparent waters—and chequered with numerous small islands, and sand bars. It has an alluvial valley, of a mile in width, bounded on each side by calcareous hills—which frequently, present naked precipices towards the river.—The predominating trees, are oak, elm, and maple.

LXXIX. Day.—(*August* 10*th.*)—Quitting our encampment at five o'clock, A. M. we ascended the river thirty-six miles. During this distance, it is joined by a small tributary from the right bank, called Blue river. It is a stream of small size—with clear water—and originates in highlands, near the banks of Rock river. No change is observed in the appearance of the Ousconsing—there is no perceptible diminution, either in the width of the river, or its valley. The bluffs, continue to bound the river on both sides. The weather was fair and warm during the fore part of the day, but suddenly clouded up, in the afternoon, when we had a shower of rain, attended with thunder and lightning.

LXXX. Day.—(*August* 11*th.*)—On ascending the river sixteen miles, we passed the mouth of Pine river, a stream of thirty yards wide, entering on the left, at the junction of which, there is a village of Winnebagoes, of four lodges. Here we stopped a few moments. The Indians appeared friendly, and presented us some dried venison:—we engaged two of them to pilot us up the river, to the portage, and make some mineral discoveries. The navigation of the river above, is considerably impeded by sand bars, and small islands, and some time is lost, in searching for the proper channel. The water is shallow—clear—and very warm.—The current is strong, although without any falls or rapids. Numerous muscle, and other shells, are strewed along the sandy shores, some of which are very large, others, exceedingly small, with transparent shells, and colours beautifully variegated.—The plover, wild goose, king-fisher, and small yellow bird, are seen along this part of the river. The river bluffs continue, sometimes receding a mile or two from the river, and giving place to bottom lands, and patches of prairie, then shutting in close upon the water's edge. In the course of the day, we overtook a barge and Indian canoe, which had been despatched in advance, from the Prairie, on the eighth, under the charge of Mr. Chase. We encamped at twilight, at the head of the *Spruce Channel*, having ascended the river thirty-four miles.

LXXXI. Day.—(*August* 12*th.*)—Proceeded up the river at twenty minutes before five—weather fair.—Ascended forty miles, and encamped on a sand bar, on the left shore. Highlands continue.—Trees, oak, elm, and maple. Alluvial bottom lands: and prairies, occasionally, on either shore. Rock strata, compact lime stone, reposing upon white sandstone. A shower of rain, at six in the evening.

LXXXII. Day.—(*August* 13*th*.)—Ascended thirty-eight miles.

LXXXIII. Day.—(*August* 14*th*.)—A rain storm after twelve o'clock at night—cleared off at seven in the morning, when we embarked, and reached the portage between the Ousconsing and Fox rivers, at one o'clock P. M.—distance sixteen miles. Crossed over the portage, and encamped on the head of Fox river.

The entire distance from the Prairie du Chien to the portage of the Ousconsing, is one hundred and eighty-two miles, in which distance the navigation is not impeded with a fall or rapid, but the water runs with great velocity, and may be estimated to have a mean descent of two feet per mile. This is equal to the Mississippi, below the junction of the Missouri. We were five days engaged in the ascent, without, however, devoting much time to the examination of the contiguous country. The width of the river is eight hundred yards at its mouth, and decreases to about four hundred at the portage.—A chain of limestone hills extends from the Mississippi, on each shore, to within twenty miles of the portage, where it ceases on the south shore, but continues on the north, receding, however, a considerable distance from the river. This tract is called the Highlands of the Ousconsing. In passing through it, the river presents a number of interesting and picturesque views, the most striking of which is that of the Sugar Loaf mountain, and La Petit Gris. The geological character of this tract of country, presents little variety. A dark grey compact limestone, forms the surface rock, and is bedded on white sandstone. The former, is, however, so far as observed, destitute of organic remains, and perhaps, the latter, might be considered as a variety of grauwacke. There are some scattered lumps of iron ore upon the hills, and a lead mine is reported to exist upon the south shore, about eighty miles east of the Mississippi. The Indians also report that they have frequently found copper and silver upon this river, but the guides who accompanied us, with a promise to discover the localities of these minerals, either amused us with idle tales, or avoided conducting us to the places, where these metals may, in reality, exist; by stating a great many difficulties and excuses. A Winnebago Indian, who had promised to bring in a specimen of silver ore, presented, with great ceremony, to Governor Cass, some small detached folia of mica, and the same substance, in its natural association in granitic rock. This shows, what little reliance can be placed upon Indian information, with respect to mineralogy, even when their veracity is not called in question. It would be well, however, if, in regard to the mineral kingdom, only, this people had not yet adopted the maxim, that "all is not gold that glitters."

The Ousconsing is ascended in canoes ninety miles above the portage, and is connected by short portages, with the Ontonagon, and Montreal rivers of Lake Superior. The largest wild animals now found along its banks, are the deer, the bear, and the fox. The elk, and buffalo, have been driven off many years ago. Neither is it a favourite resort of water fowl, which is probably owing to the fact, that it does not afford the wild rice, at least, in any considerable quantity. Geese and ducks occasionally alight in it, on their migratory journies, but do not tarry long. We observed the snipe, plover, grouse, king-fisher, wild turkey, and some smaller birds. Two kinds of rattlesnake are also found along its banks. The first, which inhabits the hills, is the crotalus horridus, and attains a large size. I killed one, in coming up the river, measuring four feet in length, and furnished with nine rattles. The Indians, on opening it, took out eleven young. The other variety is small, seldom exceeding eighteen inches in length, and is confined to the lowlands and prairies. This is called the prairie rattlesnake, and is common about the portage.

This river was formerly inhabited by the Sacs and Foxes, who raised large quantities of corn and beans upon its fertile shores, but they were driven off by the Chippeways, instigated by the French.—It is now possessed by the Winnebagoes, a savage, and blood-thirsty tribe, who came, many years ago, from the south, and are related to some of the Mexican tribes. Their largest village, upon this stream, is three or four miles above the portage, and consists of forty lodges.

The length of the portage, from the Ousconsing, to the Fox river, is a mile and a half, across a level prairie. There is a good waggon road, and a Frenchman lives on the spot, who keeps a number of horses and cattle, for the transportation of baggage, for which twenty-five cents per hundred weight, is demanded. Such is the little difference in the level of the two streams, that during high water, canoes frequently pass, loaded, across the lowest parts of the prairie, from one river to the other. The portage is very muddy in the spring and fall, being over a rich alluvial soil, but we found it dry, and pleasant.

LXXXIV. Day.—(*August* 15*th.*)—We embarked at the head of Fox river, at half past three in the afternoon, and descended fifteen miles to the *Forks.* The river in this distance, is about twenty yards wide, but often expands into little lakes, or ponds, and is extremely devious in its course. It is filled with wild rice, which so chokes up the channel, that it is difficult to find a passage through it. The shores slope up gently from the water's edge, and are covered with scattering oaks, and prairie grass, but they do not attain much elevation, and disclose no rock strata.

LXXXV Day.—(*August* 16*th.*)—Thirty miles below its forks, the Fox river expands into a lake, called Lac du Bœuf, which is nine miles in length, by one and a half in width, and abounds in wild rice. Twelve miles lower, the river expands into another lake, called Puckaway, which is twelve miles long, by two in width. This is also filled with wild rice, and rushes, and with abundance of water fowl in the season. There is a village of Puants or Winnebagoes, of seven or eight lodges, on the west shore. We encamped at the foot of this lake, having descended the river sixty-three miles. The course of the river is less serpentine than about its source, but the channel continues to be filled with wild rice, reeds, and bulrushes. The adjoining country lies in gentle slopes, and is finely diversified with woods and prairies. It appears to be well adapted to the raising of stock, and any quantity of grass might be cut on the prairies. The soil is of the richest kind, and is capable of supporting a dense agricultural population.

LXXXVI. Day.—(*August* 17*th.*)—Fox river, which has scarcely a perceptible current above Lake Puckaway, has a visible one, below it, where its mean velocity may be reckoned at one mile per hour. A few miles below our encampment, we passed three Winnebago lodges on the right bank, and a short distance lower down, five more on the left. The forest here becomes heavier, and approaches nearer the margin of the river, and among its trees, we here first noticed the poplar and the birch. The river De Loup joins the Fox river, twenty-eight miles below Puckaway lake, and there is a grass-covered hill near the point of junction, called *La Butte de Mort*, or the hillock of the dead, where the Fox nation were nearly exterminated many years ago, by the French and Chippeways. It is now the site of a small Winnebago village, and affords a picturesque view from the river. We encamped seventeen leagues below this spot, on the left shore, having descended the river seventy miles.

LXXXVII. Day.—(*August* 18*th.*)—The night was remarkably cold, with a dense fog in the morning, and we now first enjoyed an exemption from the attacks of the musquitoes. We embarked at half past five, A. M.—wild rice continues along the shores—the stream increases in width—no rocks in situ—some pebbles and detached blocks of hornblende granite, and limestone along the shore—also, an abundance of muscle and cockle shells.—Trees, oak, maple, and hickory.—Soil, a rich alluvion.

On descending fifteen miles, we passed the mouth of the Menomonie or Wolf river, which is nearly of equal size with the Fox, and is noted for its abundant production of wild rice, and the myriads of wild fowl, that resort to it, at certain seasons. Five miles below the junction of these streams, we entered Winnebago lake, at ten o'clock in the morning.—This is a handsome sheet of clear water, twenty-four miles long, by ten in width. It receives a considerable tributary on the south, called Crocodile or Rice river, which is connected by means of a short portage, with the Rock river of the Mississippi.—Near the upper end of this lake, there is a village of Winnebagoes, of ten lodges, and another, of a like number of lodges, at its outlet. There is also a village of Menomonies, of sixty souls, on the southern shore, about half way between the lower Puant village, and the mouth of Crocodile river. The Fox river, where it issues from Winnebago lake, has a rapid, extending a mile and a half, over which the canoes pass, with half loads. We here entrusted our canoes to Indian pilots, and proceeded on foot, to the termination of the rapids. Nine miles below, is the fall of the grand Konomee, where the river has a perpendicular descent of five feet. Here is a portage of one mile. The canoes are lifted over the falls, and conducted to the place of embarkation below. The fall is over a ledge of limestone rock, apparently of the transition class. Some calcareous spar is found imbedded. The entire descent of the river at this portage, is probably fifteen feet. We encamped at the foot of the grand Konomee, some time after dark, having progressed altogether sixty miles.

LXXXVIII. Day.—(*August* 19*th.*)—It is twelve miles from the Grand Konomee to the falls of Kakalin, during which distance, the bed of the river is full of fragments of rock, with shallow water ; and may be considered at this season, as one continued rapid. The river is skirted by alluvial ridges, covered with white and black oak, and prairie grass. This deposition rests upon calcareous rock, which appears in horizontal strata at the water's edge, and in the bed of the river. It contains no imbedded remains, but, on breaking it, discloses minute cavities, filled with calcareous spar in a variety of crystalline forms, and often connected with iron pyrites. Disseminated through the rock, are also found, small particles of sulphuret of zinc, or black blende. These appearances are particularly apparent, in the flat rocks at the Kakalin, and for two or three miles above, on the north shore. In descending this part of the river, we cannot avoid remarking, the immense quantity of muscle shells scattered along the shore, and sometimes piled up in the bed of the stream. On enquiring of the Indians the cause of this singular appearance, they observed, that the muscle is the common food of the muskrat, which fishes for these crustacea, in the bed of the stream, and carrying them to the mouth of its habitation, upon the banks of the river, there opens them upon one spot. We reached the Kakalin at noon, and found it the site of a Winnebago village of eleven or twelve lodges, and two hundred souls. There is a portage of one mile, across a level prairie, and the river has an aggregate descent of twenty feet. We proceeded eight miles below, and encamped on the north shore, having descended but twenty miles during the day. This is owing to the low stage of the water, and the difficulties of the rapids, which have been such, that we were compelled to leave our barge upon the rocks, between the rapids of the Konomee and the Kakalin.

LXXXIX. Day.—(*August, 20th.*)—A heavy fog in the morning, prevented us from quitting our encampment until seven o'clock.—Six miles below, we passed the rapids of the little Kakalin, which, however, oppose no serious obstacle to the navigation of the river, on the descent. Here, we found a small party of United States soldiers, who were engaged in preparing the foundation for a saw mill, which is to be erected at that spot for the accommodation of the garrison, and settlement at Green Bay. There is another small rapid, seven miles below, called Rock rapid, from which it is five more to the garrison, where we arrived at one o'clock P. M. The settlement of Green Bay commences at the little Kakalin, twelve miles above the fort; and is very compact, from the Rock rapid. Here, we are first presented with a view of the fort; and nothing can exceed the beauty of the intermediate country—chequered as it is, with farm houses, fences, cultivated fields, the broad expanse of the river—the bannered masts of the vessels in the distant bay, and the warlike array of military barracks, camps, and parades. This scene burst suddenly into view, and no combination of objects in the physiognomy of a country, could be more happily arranged, after so long a sojournment in the wilderness, to recall at once to the imagination, the most pleasing recollections of civilized life; and indeed, the circumstances of our return, would have produced a high degree of exhilaration; without the additional excitements of military music, which now saluted our ears, and the peals of artillery which bid us welcome to the fort.

The settlement of Green Bay is one of ancient standing, having been first begun by the French about the year 1670. It now consists of sixty dwelling houses, and five hundred inhabitants, exclusive of the garrison. There are seventy of the inhabitants enrolled as militia men, and it is said fifty more will be added during the ensuing year, who are now subject to military duty. The inhabitants are, with few exceptions, French, who have intermarried with Indian women, and are said generally, to be indolent, gay, intemperate, and illiterate; but I cannot speak from personal observation. They are represented to have been subservient to the interests of the British, during the late war. This settlement is now the seat of justice for Brown county, in the territory of Michigan, and the ordinary courts of law are established.

The fort is situated on a handsome grassy plain, on the north bank of Fox river, near the point of its entrance into Green Bay. It consists of a range of log barracks, facing three sides of a square parade, and surrounded by a stockade of timber, thirty feet high, with block houses at the angles. The whole is white washed, and presents a neat military appearance. It is at present garrisoned by three hundred men, under Captain Whistler, who has the temporary command of the post, during the absence of Colonel J. L. Smith. There are also about three hundred infantry, in cantonments, at Camp Smith, three miles above fort Brown, on the south side of the river, where preparations are making to erect a permanent fortification of stone, during the ensuing year. The site chosen for the work is extremely beautiful, airy, and commanding. A party of men have been employed during the summer, in quarrying the building stone, near the Rock rapid. On visiting this quarry, I found it to consist of a bluish-grey limestone, semicrystalline in its structure, and containing small disseminated masses of blende, sometimes in cavities along with calcareous spar, and iron pyrites.

XC. Day.—(*August 21st.*)—Fox river has been characterized by one of the oldest writers on American topography,* as "a muddy stream, abounding equally in rocks and savannahs, and inclosed with a steep coast, and frightful rocks," but these traits, although generally characteristic of the river, are not all applicable to any individual sections of it; for wherever its banks are muddy or marshy, there are no rock strata, and in passing over those shallows, where the latter crop out, particularly in a birch-bark canoe, and during the summer season, when the water is lowest, the term "frightful" will convey a just idea of the dangers and difficulties of the navigation.

The entire length of this river is two hundred and sixty miles, fifty of which consist of lakes. Its most

* La Hontan, p. 111, vol. 1.

extreme northwestern tributary is the outlet of *Lac Vaseux*, which unites with the portage branch, after running thirty miles in a southeasterly direction. This point is called the Forks of the river, and is fifteen miles distant from the portage of the Ousconsing. It is a hundred and ninety miles from thence to the outlet of Winnebago lake, in which distance it is swelled by the Menomonie, Deloup, and several smaller streams, and expands into a number of little lakes, the largest of which are Puckaway and Du Bœuf. This is the favourite region of wild rice, and water fowl, and during all this distance, the river has neither a fall or a rapid, but runs with so still a current, that it has scarcely a perceptible motion. Neither are the rock strata upon which the soil is based, at any spot visible; but as far as the eye can reach, the country presents a beautiful variety of woods and prairies—long sloping hills, which are crowned with copses of oak, and extensive vallies, covered with a luxuriant growth of the wild rice, the scirpus lucustris, and other aquatic plants. Through such a valley, the Fox river pursues its broad, still, and devious course, and is so prolific in the various species of water plants, that often, where it is a mile in width, there is scarce open space enough in its centre, to allow the passage of a canoe; but it has every where a fine depth of water, and is free from stagnation. Here, as the rice begins to ripen, the various tribes of water fowl instinctively repair, to dispute, with the savages, their claims to the harvest, and are killed in such numbers, that the Indians, while the season lasts, are not put to the trouble of hunting for any other description of animal food. The region is also highly favourable to the innumerable tribes of fresh water crustacæ, reptiles, and amphibious quadrupeds. Among the latter, the otter, mink, and muskrat are still common; but the beaver and martin, once so numerous, are becoming very rare. The soil is every where of the most fertile kind.

On approaching the foot of Winnebago lake, we perceive a ridge of highlands running parallel with its eastern shore, and apparently barricading the passage of the river in that direction, which, as if conscious of the obstruction, first turns to the north, but gradually winds about to the east, and south east, and passing through this ridge is bordered with elevated, and, in some places, rocky banks, and the channel is broken by the Konomee falls, and by the Winnebago, the little, and grand Kakalin, and the Rock rapids. The distance occupied by these obstructions, (from the outlet of Winnebago lake to the Rock rapids,) is forty miles, and the navigation of this part of it, during the summer season, is attended with difficulty and fatigue.

This is the section of the river "inclosed with a steep coast and frightful rocks," but the latter present no formidable obstacle to the navigation, during the spring and fall; and the coast, although elevated two or three hundred feet, is far from being sterile, or mountainous. The soil is a red loam, supporting a heavy forest of oak, pine, hickory, and maple, and interspersed with occasional patches of highland prairie. This part of the river has very little wild rice, but is abundantly stored with white and black bass, carp, pike, suckers, and other fish; and is resorted to by the Indians with a certain prospect of sustenance, during a part of the year.

From the Rock rapid to Green Bay, a distance of six miles, the river flows with a smooth current—is more than a mile wide, and is joined, in the intermediate distance, by two considerable streams, called Devil and Duck rivers, the former of which enters on the south shore, directly opposite the site of old fort Le Bay.

There is perhaps no stream, of secondary magnitude, in the northwestern parts of America, which affords so many facilities to savage life, or which actually supports so great a savage population, as Fox river; and taking into consideration the great fertility and extent of its tillable soil—the rural beauty of the country—its advantageous position for commerce, either with the north or south, and its salubrious and delightful climate, it will probably hereafter, when the Indian tribes yield before an industrious emigration, support one of the most compact, extensive, and valuable agricultural settlements in the Michigan territory.

The junction of this river with Green Bay, affords one of the most favourable positions for witnessing a phenomenon, which has attracted the attention of travellers from the earliest times, without, however, having, as yet, elicited any very satisfactory explication of an apparently reversed order of nature. I allude to the appearances of a regular tide at this place, but in so doing, it is more with a view of presenting an outline of those facts which have been observed by others, than of entering into any disquisition on the subject myself.

In the year 1689, the Baron La Hontan, on reaching Green Bay, remarks, that where the Fox river is discharged into the bay, he observed the water of the lake swell three feet high, in the space of twenty-four hours, and decrease as much in the same length of time. He also noticed a contrariety, and confliction of currents in the narrow strait which connects lakes Huron and Michigan, which he says, "are so strong, that they sometimes suck in the fishing nets, although they are two or three leagues off. In some seasons, it so falls out, that the currents run three days eastward—two days to the west—one, to the south—and four to the northward; sometimes more, and sometimes less. The cause of this diversity of currents could never be fathomed, for in a calm, they will run in the space of one day, to all points of the compass, without any limitation of time, so that the decision of this matter must be left to the disciples of Copernicus."*

In 1721, Charlevoix remarks similar appearances, but treats the subject with unusual brevity, evidently, from the difficulties which occurred to him, in giving any satisfactory explanation. He supposes lakes Huron and Michigan to be alternately discharged into each other through the strait of Michilimackinac, and mentions the fact, that in passing that strait, his canoe was carried with the current *against a head wind.* In another place, in speaking of an apparent flux and reflux of the lakes, he supposes that it was "owing to the springs at the bottom of the lakes, and to the shock of their currents, with those of the rivers, which fall into them from all sides, and thus produce those intermitting motions.†

In 1819, Captain Henry Whiting, of the United

*La Hontan's voyages to Canada.

†Charlevoix's Journal, vol. 1, p. 314.

States army, made a series of observations during seven or eight days, upon these oceanic appearances, which serve to shew, that the water at Green Bay, has a rise and fall daily, but that it is irregular as to the precise period of flux and reflux, and also as to the height it attains.

On reaching Green Bay, during the present expedition, Governor Cass directed one of the men, to drive a stake at the water's edge, upon the banks of Fox river, at the spot of our encampment, which was a mile above its discharge into the bay, and to mark the height of the water. It appeared, from frequently inspecting this gauge, during the period of our stay, which was, however, but two days, that there was a considerable rise and fall of the water—that there was a difference as to the time consumed in passing from its minimum to its maximum height, and that although it arose against a strong wind blowing out of the river, the rise, under these circumstances was *less*, than in ordinary cases.

From all these circumstances, there is reason to conclude, that a well conducted series of experiments, will prove, that there are no regular tides in the lakes, at least, that they do not ebb and flow twice in twenty-four hours, like those of the ocean—that the oscillating motion of the waters is not attributable to planetary attraction—that it is very variable as to the periods of its flux and reflux, depending upon the levels of the several lakes, their length, depth, direction, and conformation—upon the prevalent winds and temperatures, and upon other extraneous causes, which are in some measure variable in their nature, and unsteady in their operation.

Lake Michigan, from its great depth of water—

its bleak and unguarded shores—and its singular length and direction, which is about four hundred miles from north to south, appears to be peculiarly exposed to the influence of the currents of the atmosphere, to whose agency we may attribute, at least in part, the appearances of a tide, which are more striking upon the shores of this, than of any of the other great lakes. The meteorological observations which have been made, in the *Transalleghanian states*, indicate the winds to prevail, either north or south, through the valley of the Mississippi; but seldom across it, so that the surface of this lake, would be constantly exposed to agitation, from the atmosphere. These winds would almost incessantly operate, to drive the waters through the narrow strait of Michilimackinac, either into lake Huron or lake Michigan, until, by their natural tendency to an equilibrium, the waters thus pent, would re-act, after attaining a certain height, against the current of the most powerful winds, and thus keep up an alternate flux and reflux, which would always appear more sensibly in the extremities and bays of the two lakes; and with something like regularity, as to the periods of oscillation; the velocity of the water, however, being governed by the varying degrees of the force of the winds.

Something analogous to this, is perceived in the Baltic, which has no regular tides, and therefore experiences no difference of height, except when the wind blows violently. "At such times," says Pennant, "there is a current in, and out of the Baltic, according to the points they blow from, which forces the water through the *sound*, with the velocity of two or three Danish miles in the hour. When the wind blows violently, from the German sea, the water rises in several Baltic harbours, and gives those in the western part, a temporary saltness; otherwise, the Baltic looses that other property of a sea, by reason of the want of tide, and the quantity of vast rivers it receives, which sweeten it so much, as to render it, in many places, fit for domestic use."

48

CHAPTER XIV.

JOURNEY,

FROM GREEN BAY TO CHICAGO.

XCI. Day.—(*August* 22*d.*)

ON reaching Green Bay, the escort of soldiers, which had thus far accompanied us, and the Indians, who were taken along as hunters, were no longer deemed necessary, either to our sustenance or safety; and the former were ordered to join their respective companies, in the garrison, while the latter were furnished with a canoe and provisions, to proceed, at their own convenience, to their homes, on the eastern shores of Lake Michigan. We here, also, embraced the opportunity of shipping to Detroit, our collections, in the different departments of natural history, and a part of our personal baggage, &c. by the schooner Decatur, which sailed from the bay the morning after our arrival. Thus reduced in numbers, and lightened of baggage, the expedition was still further diminished by detaching a canoe with eight men, under the orders of Mr. Trowbridge, accompanied by Mr. Doty, and Mr. Chase, to proceed around the western shores of Green Bay, to Michilimackinac; while the remainder of the party, still numbering two canoes, and sixteen men, coasted southerly to Chicago, and thence around the eastern shores of Lake Michigan, to Michilimackinac.

We parted from Mr. Trowbridge, at the mouth of Fox river, at half past two in the afternoon, and proceeding along the eastern shore of Green Bay twenty five miles. encamped on the beach at twilight. The shore is a fertile alluvion, covered with sugar maple, elm, oak, hemlock, and poplar. The bay has a sandy beach, and transparent waters. In a short time we were overtaken by the Indians, who had recently constituted a part of the expedition, and they encamped with us. In the course of the evening, they endeavoured to point out to us by moonlight, a rocky island, at three or four miles distance, in which there is a large cavern, which has been employed, by their tribes, from the remotest times, as a repository for the dead. They appeared to regard the spot, as the monument of a long race of heroes, sages, and warriors, whose deeds were deservedly embalmed in the memories of a grateful posterity; and spoke of it in a manner, evincing a high spirit of ancestry; and, as if, like the castle of Fredolfo, it borrowed all its lustre from the heroes whom it enshrined.

"It hath a charm the stranger knoweth not—
"It is the dwelling of mine ancestry!
"There is an inspiration in its shade;
"The echoes of its walls are eloquent,
"The words they speak, are of the glorious dead;
"Its tenants are not human—*they are more!*
"The stones have voices, and the walls do live,
"It is the house of memories dearly honoured,
"By many a long trace of departed glory."

MATURIN.

XCII. Day.—(*August* 23*d.*)—It is twenty miles from the spot of our encampment, to Sturgeon bay, which is six miles wide and fifteen in length, narrowing gradually towards its head, where it receives a small stream. From this spot, there is a portage of three pauses, across the peninsula, to Lake Michigan, where we arrived at an early hour in the afternoon, but were prevented from embarking, by a strong head wind. The shore of the lake is alluvial, with a sandy beach, strewed with fragments and pebbles of primitive and secondary rocks, among which are found water worn masses of greasy, and translucent quartz, chalcedony, petrified madrepores, &c. The forest trees are maple, beech, hemlock, &c.

XCIII. Day.—(*August* 24*th.*)—Following around the numerous indentations of the shore, we progressed, in a general direction south, forty six miles. In the course of the day, we passed the mouth of a small river, flowing from the west, called La Fourche. Among the forest trees, the beech (*fagus ferruginea*) has been conspicuous: oak, pine, poplar, birch, hemlock, and maple, have also been abundant. The banks of the lake are a sandy alluvion, reposing upon transition limestone, which is occasionally seen in ledges, elevated two or three feet above the water, upon the prominent points of the shore. Petrifactions, continue to be found, lying promiscuously among fragments of granite, hornblende, sienite, quartz, limestone, &c.

XIV. Day.—(*August* 25*th.*)—In coasting forty miles along the shore, we came to the mouth of a large stream, called Manitowacky, where there is a village of Menomonie Indians, of six lodges. Five miles beyond, we encamped upon the beach, having progressed fifteen leagues, as indicated by a lunar observation. The country consists of a succession of sand hills, covered with pine. The banks of the lake are elevated from twenty to sixty feet, with a broad sand beach, strewed with granitic and calcareous pebbles, &c. In walking along some parts of the shore, I observed a great number of the skeletons and half consumed bodies of the pigeon, which, in crossing the lake, is often overtaken by severe tempests, and compelled to alight upon the water, and thus drowned, in entire flocks, which are soon thrown up along the shores. This causes the shores of Lake Michigan to be visited by vast numbers of buzzards, eagles, and other birds of prey. The Indians also make use of these pigeons, as food, when they are first driven ashore, preserving such in smoke, as they have not immediate occasion for. Vast broods of young gulls, are also destroyed during the violent storms, which frequently agitate this lake.

XCV. Day.—(*August* 26*th*)—Progressed forty-three miles, and encamped, some time after dark, at the mouth of Milwacky river. This is a stream of sixty yards wide at its mouth, and is ascended a hundred miles in canoes, being connected by a short portage, with the Rock river of the Mississippi :—a route frequently travelled in canoes, by the Pottowatomies and Menomonies. There are two American families, and a village of Pottowatomies, at its mouth. It is the division line between the lands of the Menomonies and Pottowatomies; the latter claim all south of it.

XCVI. Day.—(*August 27th.*)—A head wind detained us a considerable part of the day, but we advanced thirty-five miles, passing, in that distance, the Sac and Skeboigon rivers. Five miles south of the Milwacky, there is found a bed of white clay upon the shore of the lake; and a short distance back, in a prairie, a vein of red oxide of iron, both of which substances, are much employed by the Indians, as paints. Fifteen miles further south, commences a range of high clay bluffs, covered with sand, on the verge of the lake, which extend, with occasional depressions, fifteen or twenty miles. At the foot of this, at the water's edge, there is a large body of pyrites, of a brass yellow colour—great weight, and crystallized in a variety of regular forms, the most common of which is a cube, truncated at the angles. Some of these crystals are six or eight pounds in weight, with an imposing metallic lustre. They occur in beds in a tenacious blue clay, from which they are washed by the waves, and left in promiscuous piles along the shore, where, being exposed to attrition, their crystalline forms are gradually obliterated, and they assume, at last, the shape of spheroidal and globular pebbles, parting, also, in the course of this process, with their natural external lustre. It is only those masses, which are newly exposed, that present, under the deceptive glare of polished brass, those beautiful geometrical solids, which sulphur, in its various associations and combinations, in the mineral kingdom, so frequently assumes. At the spot of our encampment, thirty-five miles south of Milwacky, I found a singular liquid mineral, resembling asphaltum, contained in cavities in a calcareous rock. Where it had suffered a natural exposure to the weather, it had the colour and consistence of dried tar, but on obtaining a fresh fracture, it was so liquid as to flow from the cavities, and presented an olive brown colour, inclining to black.

XCVII. Day.—(*August* 28*th.*)—Proceeded forty miles. The shore, during this distance, is principally prairie, upon which the oak tree predominates. In some instances, there are hillocks of sand, either wholly destitute of vegetation, or capped with scattering pines. Among the detached rocks of the shore, are found, calcareous spar, crystallized quartz, cacholong, jasper, toadstone, &c.

XCVIII. Day.—(*August* 29*th*).—We reached Chicago at five o'clock in the morning, after proceeding ten miles. The village consists of ten or twelve dwelling houses, with an aggregate population, of probably, sixty souls. The garrison stands on the south shore of Chicago creek, four or five hundred yards from its entrance into the lake, and, like the majority of our frontier posts, consists of a square stockade, inclosing barracks, quarters for the officers, a magazine, provision store, &c. and defended by bastions at the northwest, and southeast angles. It is at present occupied by a hundred and sixty men, under the command of Captain Bradley.

The village of Chicago is situated in the state of Illinois, the northern boundary line of which, commences, on the lake shore, about twenty miles north of the fort, and running due west, strikes the Mississippi between Dubuque's lead mines, and Prairie du Chien. It is two hundred and seventy-five miles, from Chicago to Green Bay, by the way of the lakes, and the portage of Sturgeon bay—and four hundred to the island of Michilimackinac.

Chicago creek is eighty yards wide, at the garrison, and has a bar at its mouth, which prevents shipping from entering, but is deep within. It is ascended eleven miles in boats, and barges, where there is a portage of seven miles across a prairie, to the river Plein, the main northwestern fork of the Illinois.

The intervening country consists of different strata of marl and clay, presenting great facilities for canal excavation, and the difference in the level of the two streams is so little, that loaded boats of a small class, may pass over the lowest parts of the prairie, during the spring, and autumnal freshets.—But at mid-summer, it is necessary to transport them over land, to mount Juliet, a distance of thirty miles. From thence the navigation is good, at all seasons, to St. Louis, a distance of four hundred miles.

XCIX. Day.—(*August* 30*th.*)—The country around Chicago is the most fertile and beautiful that can be imagined. It consists of an intermixture of woods and prairies, diversified with gentle slopes, sometimes attaining the elevation of hills, and irrigated with a number of clear streams and rivers, which throw their waters partly into lake Michigan, and partly into the Mississippi river. As a farming country, it unites the fertile soil, of the finest low-land prairies, with an elevation, which exempts it from the influence of stagnant waters, and a summer climate of delightful serenity; while its natural meadows present all the advantages for raising stock, of the most favoured part of the valley of the Mississippi. It is already the seat of several flourishing plantations, and only requires the extinguishment of the Indian title to the lands, to become one of the most attractive fields for the emigrant. To the ordinary advantages of an agricultural market town, it must, hereafter, add that of a depot, for the inland commerce, between the northern and southern sections of the union, and a great thoroughfare for strangers, merchants, and travellers.

There is a valuable and extensive bed of mineral coal, about forty miles southwest of Chicago, on the Fox river of the Illinois, near the point of its embouchure. The stratum of coal, which appears on the banks of the river, is said to have an extensive range towards the northwest, and is only covered by a light deposit of alluvial soil, of a few feet in thickness. There is also, about twenty miles north of Chicago, a bed of red oxide of iron, in a state of great purity, and its preparation as a pigment, may be expected to result from the influx of emigrants. Pyrites, are also very common in this vicinity, yet, it is a singular fact, that the bricks at Chicago, which are manufactured from the earth, taken up on the banks of the creek, *burn white*, like the Stourbridge fire-bricks, indicating, as I am led to conclude, an absence of iron, in any of its numerous forms of combination, at least, in the usual degree. All our common clays burn with some tint, however light, of red, which has been referred, by chemical writers, with much precision, to the presence of oxid of iron.

There is said to be a petrified hickory tree in the bed of the river Kankakee, near its junction with the Illinois, forty-five miles by land, and sixty by the course of the river, from Chicago. It is entire, and partly imbedded in the calcareous rock, forming the bed of the Kankakee.

The open nature of the country around Chicago, exposes it to piercing winds during the winter months, although the same cause, contributes to render it a delightful residence during the summer season. The following is an abstract of a meteorological register, kept by Doctor Wolcott, at Chicago, during the first quarter of the present year.

Atmospheric Heat.

1820.	Average Temperature. at 9 a. m.	Av. Temp. at 2 p. m.	Av. Temp. at 9 p. m.
Jan.	14°	18°	14°
Feb.	29°	36°	30°
M'r. (to 15)	27°	32°	25°

Winds.

Jan.	W. 8 days, W. N. W. 5, W. S. W. 10, N. N. E. 6, E. N. E. 2.
Feb.	E. 7, —— S. W. 7, W. 5, S. 2, S. E. 2, W. S. W. 3, E. N. E. 2.
Mar. (to 15)	N. N. W. 3, E. N. E. 4, N. N. E. 2, N. E. 2, S. W. 2. N. W. 2.

Weather.

Jan.	cloudy 6,—	snow storms 6,—	clear 19.
Feb.	cloudy 8,—	rain 4,—	clear 17.
M'r. (to 15)	cloudy 10,—		clear 4.

The ice in the lake was fourteen inches in thickness, on the 1st of January, and eighteen and three-fourths, (its greatest thickness, during the winter;) on the second of February. The greatest depth of snow was twenty-two inches, on the thirty-first of January. The thermometer stood at 0 on the first and nineteenth of January. The highest degree of heat during that month was 39°.—In February, the highest heat was 59°—in March, 42°.

CHAPTER XV.

JOURNEY,

FROM CHICAGO, THROUGH LAKE MICHIGAN, TO MICHILIMACKINAC.

C. DAY.—(*August* 31*st.*)

GOVERNOR CASS here determined to proceed on horseback, across the peninsula of Michigan, following the Indian trail, to Detroit; and accompanied by Mr. Kinsey, of Chicago, Major Forsyth, and Lieutenant Mackay of the expedition, and one or two attendants, left Chicago at one o'clock in the afternoon, taking the beach road to the river Du Schmein, where the path leaves the lake. In the mean time, Captain Douglass and myself, were left to complete the topographical and geological survey of Lake Michigan, and joining our companions, who were detached from Green Bay on the twenty-second of August, at Michilimackinac, to proceed to Detroit with all practicable despatch.—We were ready to embark at half past two in the afternoon, and bidding adieu to Doctor Wolcott, who, being a resident of Chicago, here left the expedition; we proceeded, with a fair wind, twenty miles south-southeast, and encamped on the shore of the lake. At the distance of eleven miles from Chicago, we passed the mouth of the river Little Konomick, which is a stream of about forty miles in length, flowing in, by a deep and narrow channel, from the south. The shore of the lake, during this distance, is the sandy margin of a prairie, without hills. In one instance only, do any rock strata appear, and then merely at a point, not elevated more than four or five inches above the water. They are calcareous.

CI. Day.—(*September 1st.*)—Detained by head winds. In passing along the shore of the lake, (yesterday) at the distance of a mile and a half from Chicago, the scene of the massacre of the garrison, stationed at that place, during the late war, was pointed out to us. This took place on the fifteenth of August, 1812, the day after the surrender of General Hull, at Detroit. At this eventful period of the war, gloom hung upon every part of our extensive northwestern frontiers. The town of Michilimackinac had already been carried by surprise; and the retrograde movements of the American army, served to flatter the most sanguine hopes of Indian animosity—while the recollection of their recent defeat at Tippacanoe—their ancient prejudices—and above all, their British allies, were every day adding to their infuriated bands—which, rising from the north, the east, and the south, now hung like a gathering tempest over the land, every moment increasing in its gloom, and threatening rapine and destruction, to our unfortified frontiers. In this exigency of the times, while it appeared yet practicable to escape, Capt. Heald, commanding the garrison at Chicago, received orders from Gov. Hull to evacuate the fort, which it would be impossible to succour, in case of an Indian attack; and to proceed with his command, by land, to Detroit. This order was received on the ninth of August, and had it been promptly obeyed, it is probable that the fate of the garrison would have been averted, as the Indians had not yet appeared in force; but owing to an infatuation, which it is difficult to explain, eight days were allowed to elapse, before the order was executed, during which time, the Indians had collected around the garrison to the number of four or five hundred, and by killing the cattle, and other outrageous acts, shewed a determined hostility, although they had not yet menaced the garrison. On the thirteenth, Captain Wells arrived from fort Wayne, with thirty friendly Miamies, to escort the garrison to Detroit, by the request of General Hull. Still, two days were suffered to pass, before the garrison was evacuated, owing to a fatal security in which the commandant indulged, in regard to the dispositions of the Indians—but in which his subalterns, and the inhabitants, did not coincide. At length, on the fifteenth, having distributed among the Indians all the goods remaining in the factory store, with a quantity of provisions; and destroyed the arms and ammunition, which could not be taken away, Captain Heald marched out of the garrison, at nine o'clock in the morning, following along the sandy beach of the lake, which is the usual route to fort Wayne and Detroit. The garrison now consisted of fifty-four regulars, and twelve militia, exclusive of the officers, and the friendly Miamies, under Captain Wells. They were accompanied by several baggage waggons, containing provisions and ammunition, and eighteen women and children; the whole force comprising the entire population, both civil and military of Chicago. The face of the country is such, that it is necessary to travel along the sandy shore of the lake, with sand banks on the right, at the distance of from one to two hundred yards, and elevated to such a height, that the country back of it, is completely hid from the view. They had not proceeded more than a mile and a half, when it was perceived that a large body of Indians were lying in ambush behind these sand hills, and they soon encompassed them,—the broad lake extending on the left. This discovery was scarcely made, when the Indians set up their horrid yell, and poured down a warm fire in all directions. Several men fell at the first shot, but Captain Heald formed his men with deliberation, and after firing one round, ordered a charge, and ascended the bank, after sustaining a severe loss.—The Indians in front, fled to the right and left, joining a deadly fire which was kept up from the flanks, and which it was in vain to resist. In a few moments, out of sixty-six soldiers, only sixteen were alive.—Captain Heald succeeded, however, in drawing off these, to an eminence in the open prairie, out of reach of their shot. They did not follow him out, but gathering upon the bank, began a consultation, and made signs for him to approach. He was met by a Pottowatomie chief, called the Black Bird, to whom he surrendered himself, with his Lieut. (Helm) and sixteen men, under a promise that their lives should be spared; but they were afterwards butchered, from time to time, with the exception of

Captain Heald, and three or four men. Among the killed, were Ensign Ronan, Doctor Voorhis, and Captain Wells. The latter had his heart cut out, and other shocking barbarities committed upon his body, having rendered himself particularly obnoxious to the Indians, by his influence among those savage tribes, who remained friendly to the United States. In the course of the action, a party of Indians, raising their furious yells, rushed upon the baggage waggons, where the women and children had taken shelter, and commenced a scene of plunder and massacre, which it would be impossible to describe. Of eighteen women and children, twelve were killed upon the spot. Several of the women, (soldiers' wives) fought with swords.

During the action, a sergeant of infantry, who had already manifested the greatest bravery, was opposed in personal combat with an Indian. Both had already discharged their pieces, when the sergeant saw the Indian running up to him with a lifted tomahawk, but before the blow fell, ran his bayonet in the Indian's breast up to the socket, so that he could not pull it out; yet, in this situation, the Indian tomahawked him, and they both fell dead together.*—The Miamies took no part in this massacre. It was executed by the Pottowatomie tribe. These facts are taken from the description given by an eye-wit-

* A similar instance of courage is mentioned to have occurred in the battle of Oriskany, during the revolutionary war. "There was found an Indian and a white man, both born on the banks of the Mohawk, their left hands clenched in each other's hair, the right grasping in a gripe of death, the knife plunged in each other's bosom. Thus they lay frowning."—*Governeur Morris' Discourse before the New-York Historical Society*, 1812.

ness, Mr. Kinsey of Chicago, and from Captain Heald's official report.*

CII. DAY.—(*September 2d.*)—The wind ceased in the course of the night, and we embarked at early day light. On proceeding twelve miles, we passed the grand Konomick, the mouth of which is choaked up with sand, and the appearance of the country, in the vicinity, is very barren, and uninviting. Twenty miles beyond, we passed the mouth of the river du Chemin, (river of the Road.) Here the path from Chicago to Detroit, by land, leads out into the prairies. The distance to Detroit, is computed to be three hundred miles. There is a plain horse path, which is considerably travelled by traders, hunters, and others. It is, however, intersected by innumerable cross paths, leading to different Indian villages and settlements, so that it could not be pursued by a stranger, without a guide. The country is said to be handsomely diversified with prairies, woods, hills, and streams, and furnishes every facility for waggon roads, settlements, water-mills, &c.—In the spring and fall, some danger is to be apprehended in crossing several of the streams, but there are none which may not be safely forded at midsummer.

At a point intermediate, between the grand Konomick, and the river du Chemin, we passed the spot, on the beach of the lake, where the schooner Hercules, was wrecked in the fall of 1816, and all on board perished. The mast, pump, and some fragments of spars, scattered along the shore, still serve

* See Fay's Battles, p. 65

to mark the spot, and to convey some idea of the dreadful storms which at certain seasons agitate this lake. The voyageurs also pointed out to us, the graves of those who perished, who appear to have been buried at different places, along the shore, where they happened to be washed up. Among these, was Lieutenant William S. Evileth, an intelligent and promising young officer of engineers, whose death has been much lamented. He had been employed in the re-building of the military works at Chicago, which were burnt down by the Pottowatomies, during the late war, after the massacre of the garrison; and had embarked the day previous to the shipwreck, at Chicago, to return to his friends, after a summer spent in arduous and useful service. It was late in November, when the navigation is attended with so much peril; and the first intelligence of the fatal catastrophe, was communicated by finding the wreck of the vessel, and the bodies of the passengers, strewed along the shore. Several days had however elapsed before this discovery was made, and the bodies were so beat and bruised by the spars of the wreck, that the deceased could not be recognised by their features. The wolves had gnawed the face of Lieutenant Evileth in so shocking a manner, that he could not have been recognised had it not been for the military buttons of his clothes. His grave is situated beneath a cluster of small pines, on the declivity of a sand bank, and is marked by a blazed sapling. His memory would appear to deserve some tribute of respect, more grateful to the feelings of humanity, from those with whom he was formerly associated; and perhaps this suggestion has not occurred to the officers, stationed at the neighbouring garrison.

The little river du Galien, enters the lake ten miles beyond the river du Chemin, by a mouth nearly closed with drifting sands. We encamped on the beach twelve miles beyond it, having progressed altogether a distance of fifty-four miles.

CIII. DAY.—(*September 3d.*)—We reached the river St. Joseph, in travelling fourteen miles. This is one of the largest and most important streams which flows into the lake on its eastern shore. It is ascended one hundred and twenty miles in canoes, and is connected by a short portage, with *a river of the same name*, which runs into the Miami of the Lake, near fort Wayne—a route which is frequently travelled by the Indians. This stream was formerly the seat of a French fort, and missionary family, and continued for many years to be one of the most important places in the region. It is particularly described by Charlevoix, Hennepin, and other early French travellers and missionaries. The lands upon its banks are represented to be rich and beautiful, and heavily timbered with black walnut, oak, maple, and elm; but its mouth is skirted by sand hills, of the most sterile appearance, and supporting nothing but pines and poplars. There is found, towards the sources of this river, a variety of singular petrifactions, which may be referred to the genus of *Phytolites*. They consist chiefly, of the leaves, branches, and roots of trees, mineralized by the calcareous earth, which appears to be held in solution by one of the higher tributaries of the St. Joseph, in the bed of which these organic reliqua are found.*

It is twenty-four miles from the St. Joseph, to the Blackwater river, which is a stream of sixty miles in length, and is ascended in canoes nearly to its source. Like all the streams which enter on this side of the lake, its mouth is almost closed with yellow sands. In the intermediate distance between St. Joseph's and the Blackwater, I found along the shore, a number of specimens of chalcedony, common jasper, quartz, and some madrepores, and other organic relics. We encamped twelve miles beyond the latter, upon the sandy shore, having proceeded fifty miles.

CIV. Day.—(*September 4th.*)—On travelling ten miles, we passed the river Kikalemazo, which appears from its mouth, to be a stream of considerable size. Along the shore of the lake, between this stream and the Blackwater, the ludus helmontii,† is very abundant.

* These vegetable petrifactions were discovered by Governor Cass, in his tour across the peninsula of Michigan, from Chicago to Detroit; and I am indebted to the zeal, which he uniformly manifested during the expedition, to promote the cause of science, for the very interesting specimens I possess from this locality; and which were conveyed nearly two hundred miles on horseback, through the woods.

† "This name is given to orbicular masses of calcareous marl, usually from one to eighteen inches diameter, whose interior presents numerous fissures or seams, which divide the mass into irregular prisms. These fissures are usually lined or filled by some crystallized substance, as calcareous spar or quartz, which have undoubtedly entered by filtration. These masses are usually found in beds of marl."

Cleaveland's Mineralogy.

Eight miles beyond the Kikalemazo, there is a river of secondary size, called Black river or Iroquois chiefly noted for the ginseng, which is abundantly found upon its banks. Thence, it is seven leagues to Grand river, which is next in point of size, and importance, to the St. Joseph. This stream is said to afford one of the finest tracts of farming land in the Michigan territory. It forms the boundary line between the territories of the Pottowatomie and Ottoway tribes; and is at present the residence of a numerous savage population. A bed of gypsum, of a fine quality for agricultural purposes, has recently been discovered upon the navigable waters of this stream.

The next stream of considerable size is the Maskagon, which enters the lake twelve miles from Grand river, at the mouth of which we encamped, at eight o'clock, having advanced, during the day, a distance of fifty-four miles. The margin of the lake presents a dreary prospect of sand banks, covered with pine and poplar. The shore is sandy, with occasional banks of pebbles; but no rock strata appear in situ. The only birds, seen along this part of the coast, are the gull, and the crow.—We passed, at a short distance from Grand river, a number of spars, and pieces of timber, belonging to the wreck of an English vessel, cast away several years ago on this part of the coast.

We encamped at the mouth of the Maskagon at twilight, and had a few moments to examine the singular appearances of this part of the coast, which consists of conical hills of loose sand, that are changing their forms and position during every gale of wind; and in some places, present a few poplars, pines, or hemlocks. In a few moments after landing, one of the men, who had been sent out to procure wood, returned, bringing with him two singular productions, which he denominated *sand horns.*—They were found attached to the lower part of a dead poplar (*populus tremuloides*) standing upon the summit of one of those conical hills of naked sand, which characterize the mouth of the Muskagon; and in cutting down the tree, fell off. On examining the tree, I found several smaller productions of the same kind, attached to the bark, in the manner, and in the form of common fungi. The sand horns are a foot in length, branching out in various forms, like the corals of the ocean, having the granular structure, of grey sand stone rock, with the organic external form of the club-fungus. (See the plate.) There is no appearance, however, of a stipe or stem in breaking off one of the branches, nor are there any indications of a nucleus at the point of attachment to the tree. In hardness, it is intermediate between a porous sand stone, and certain steatites; and I have observed during wet weather, that it acquires a certain degree of flexibility. Muriatic acid has no action upon it, either in the concentrated or diluted form, but there is an effervescence in diluted sulphuric acid, and a part of the powder is held in solution, forming a kind of jelly, while the pure grains of silicious sand, are precipitated to the bottom of the glass, in the common form. These circumstances indicate a combination of vegetable and mineral matter, not exactly in the form of a common petrifaction, but somewhat analogous; and will authorize us in classing them among those organic remains, whose prototype is

PLATE VIII.

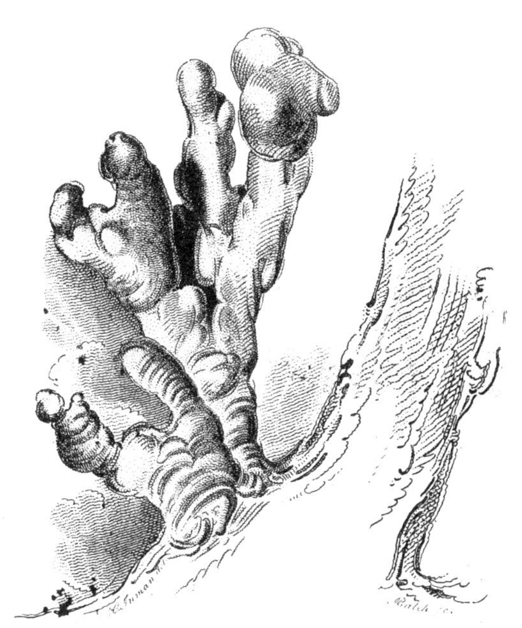

FUNGITE.

(Silicated Club-fungus)

ALBANY. PUBLISHED BY E. & E. HOSFORD [illegible]

taken from the vegetable kingdom. These constitute the genus Phytolite, in Martin's Systema Reliquiorum, under which, the present discovery will furnish the occasion of erecting a new species, that shall embrace petrifactions, of the various species of the botanical order Fungi.

CV. Day.—(*September 5th.*)—It is twelve miles from the Maskagon to White river—then thirty-one to the Pentwater, or Black river, with an Indian village in the intermediate space; and nine more to the river Marquette, which takes its name from one of the most enterprising of the Catholic missionaries, who, during the early settlement of Canada, devoted themselves, in so extraordinary a manner, to the reformation of the savage tribes. He was one of the first discoverers of the Mississippi, and the founder of Michilimackinac.

"Father Joseph Marquette," says Charlevoix, "a native of Laon in Picardy, where his family still maintains a distinguished rank, was one of the most illustrious missionaries of New France. This person travelled over all the countries in it, and made several important discoveries, the last of which was that of the Mississippi, which he entered with the Sieur Joliet, in 1673. Two years after this discovery, an account of which he has published, as he was going from Chicago, which is at the bottom of Lake Michigan, to Michilimackinac, he entered on the eighth day of May, 1675, the river in question, the mouth of which was then at the extremity of the lower ground, which, as I have already taken notice, you leave on the right hand as you enter. Here he erected his altar, and said mass. He went afterwards to a small distance, in order to return thanks, and begged the two men who conducted his canoe to leave him alone for half an hour. This time having passed, they went to seek him, and were surprised to find him dead; they called to mind, however, that on entering the river, he had let drop an expression, that he should end his days at that place. However, as it was too far to carry his body to Michilimackinac, they buried him near the bank of the river, which from that time has retired by degrees, as out of respect for his remains, as far as the cape, the foot of which it now washes; and where it has opened itself a new passage."

Fourteen miles north of the river Marquette, Sandy river throws itself into the lake, by a mouth of only ten yards wide, being choaked up, in some measure, by the sands, which are beat up by the lake. We encamped four miles beyond the latter, at a late hour, having progressed, with a favourable wind, seventy miles.

CVI. Day.—(*September 6th.*)—The distance from Sandy, to Manistic river, is seventeen miles—thence thirty, to the river Au Betsie, and two to Gravelly Point, where we encamped, after proceeding forty-five miles. We were detained a couple of hours in the morning, by rain, which continued, with short intermissions, during the day. There is a great uniformity in the appearance of the coast, which is characterized by sand banks, and pines. In some instances, a stratum of loam, is seen beneath the sand, and the beech and maple are occasionally intermixed with the predominating pines of the forest: but our impressions in passing along the coast, are only those produced by barren scenery or uncultivated woods.

> " No hamlet smoking through the mists of dawn,
> No garden blushing with its fostering dew,
> No herds wild browsing on the dasied lawn—
> No busy village charms the admiring view."

CVII. Day.—(*September 7th.*)—The weather still remained cloudy.—We embarked at early daylight. In going thirteen miles, we passed a small stream called Plate river; and nine miles beyond reached a noted point, on the east shore of the lake, called the Sleeping Bear. The shore of the lake here, consists of a bank of sand, probably two hundred feet high, and extending eight or nine miles, without any vegetation, except a small hillock, about the centre, which is covered with pines and poplars, and has served to give name to the place, from a rude resemblance it has, when viewed at a distance, to a couchant bear. There are two islands off this part of the coast, in plain view from the shore, which are called the Sleeping Bear islands.

Fifteen miles beyond the Sleeping Bear, we passed Carp river, a small stream; and a like distance beyond it, encamped on the southern cape of Grande Traverse Bay, which is the most considerable indentation in the eastern shore of Lake Michigan, being nine miles wide, and about twenty or twenty-five in length, narrowing towards its head, where it receives the Ottoway river. At this place, the rock strata first appear in situ, in travelling from Chicago to Michilimackinac, with the exception of a point near the little Konomick, formerly mentioned. It is calcareous, stratified, and with shells sparingly imbedded. It scarcely appears above the water in the ledge, but large detached masses of it, with enormous boulders of hornblende, and granite, are lying in the water near the shore, and render it dangerous to turn this cape in canoes, during the night, or in cases of a strong wind.

A visible eclipse of the sun had been calculated for this day, to commence at seven o'clock, twenty minutes; but we could perceive no obscuration, notwithstanding that the sun shone out, a great part of the time between six and eight o'clock, and we were prepared to observe the commencement and duration of the eclipse, by the telescope, and the darkened glasses of a common sextant. The atmosphere was cloudy and obscure at daylight, but lightened towards six o'clock, and between that and eight, a succession of fleecy clouds passed rapidly before the sun, sometimes veiling it entirely for a number of minutes, but during the intervals, it shone forth with its usual effulgence, and we could observe no diminution in the light, the transparency, or the temperature of the air. This eclipse was observed according to the predictions at Philadelphia, &c.

CVIII. Day.—(*September 8th.*)—We were favoured with a calm, in crossing the Grand Traverse, which is nine miles. It is then six miles to La Petit Traverse, which is two leagues across; and nine more, to the Indian village of L'Arbre Croche. This consists of about forty families of Ottoways, who are settled upon a very fertile tract of land, and raise corn, potatoes, pease, beans, cucumbers, and pumpkins, not only in sufficient quantity for their own subsistence, but they annually take a quantity of corn to the Michilimackinac market.—They reside in permanent, and comfortable houses, and number altogether, about three hundred souls. There was formerly a Jesuit Mission established at this place, but it declined with the fall of the French power in the Canadas. The site of the chapel, and the clerical mansion, was designated by our Canadian conductors, as we passed a point of land at the northern extremity of the village, which still continues to be called *Point a'la Mission.* A cluster of islands in the lake, called the Beaver islands, are visible in passing along the coast, between the Sleeping Bear and L'Arbre Croche; and are noted as affording safe anchorage ground to vessels navigating the lakes. It is twenty-four miles from *Point a'la Mission* to Wagashonz or Fox Point, in the straits of Michilimackinac, and nine from thence to the site of old 'Mackinac; in the vicinity of which, we encamped after dark, having progressed fifty-seven miles.

CIX. Day.—(*September 9th.*)—The approach of day light, which disclosed to our view, the island of Michilimackinac, brought with it, a gale of wind which created such a swell on the lake, that we could not venture to embark. At eleven o'clock, the swells broke with less fury along the shore, although still too boisterous to attempt the traverse in loaded canoes; but counselled rather by our impatience than our judgment, we determined to hazard the attempt, in a light canoe, strongly manned by our best voyaguers, who volunteered on the occasion, and had the good fortune, after being tossed upon the billows for several hours, to reach the harbour of Michilimackinac in safety.

CX. Day.—(*September* 10*th.*)—Our friends, from whom we parted at Green Bay on the 22nd of August, had arrived there several days before us, having experienced favourable winds, and completed the passage in eight days. On separating from us at the mouth of Fox river, they coursed around the western shores of Green Bay to Detour, which is the point of the northern peninsula separating Green Bay from Lake Michigan; and thence along the northwestern margin of the lake to Point St. Ignace, and Michilimackinac. The entire distance by that route, is computed at two hundred and eighty miles. Green Bay has two considerable indentations, called Little Bay de Noquet, and Great Bay de Noquet. Between Fox river and Little Bay de Noquet, a large stream throws itself into the bay, called Menomonie river, which is connected with some of the tributary waters of Lake Superior. Between Detour and Point St. Ignace, the Mino Cockien, Manistique, and some smaller rivers, enter the lake. This part of the country is generally barren, consisting mainly of sandy pine ridges, or naked calcareous rocks. The western shores of Green Bay, afford some fine lands, mixed, however, with a portion that is either low and swampy, or rocky and sterile. In passing these coasts, Mr. Trowbridge and Mr. Doty, procured a number of specimens illustrative of the mineralogy and geology of the region. "The most interesting of these," says the former in a note to me on the subject, "will probably be the organic remains, which you will find in the lower part of the collection; they were procured in Little Noquet Bay, on the northeast side, where ridges of limestone show themselves frequently. In another part of our collections, you will find a specimen of the limestone weighing about two pounds, of which the upper stratum is composed, (*secondary limestone,*) and likewise, two pieces of the lower stratum, resembling blue pipe-stone, which were quite soft when first taken up. (*Earthy compact limestone*) The middle stratum was composed of these remains. (*Pectinites.*)

" About ten miles northeast of the Great Bay de Noquet, we found flint, or hornstone, of which specimens are sent. It was found in small quantities attached to the limestone rocks. (*This is the common hornstone in nodules.*)

" There is also a specimen of marble, (*transition limestone*) which, however, we saw little of; but since our arrival, are informed that a large bluff composed of the same, is seen from thirty to forty miles from this place, on the lake shore. That which we procured, was sixty miles from this."

The canoe, with our baggage, which we left on the peninsula, on the morning of the ninth, traversed the strait of Michilimackinac to Point St. Ignace, in the evening of that day, and rejoined us this morning in the harbour of Michilimackinac.

CXI. Day.—(*September 11th.*)—Several years ago, a brilliant specimen of native copper, weighing ten or twelve pounds, of an irregular shape, was brought to this place by one of the traders, who had procured it from an Indian on the banks of Winnebago lake. Differing little in its external character from other masses of the same substance, which have been so frequently found throughout this region, I should not bring the circumstance into notice, were it not to illustrate by the following fanciful story, the fertility of invention and the powers of ima gination, possessed by some of the savage tribes. The Indian related, that passing in his canoe during the afternoon of a beautiful summer's day, across Winnebago lake, when the sun was just visible above the tops of the trees, and a delightful calm prevailed over the face of the waters, he espied at a distance in the lake before him, a beautiful female form standing in the water. Her eyes shone with a brilliancy that could not be endured, and she held in her hand a lump of glittering gold. He immediately paddled towards the attractive object, but as he came near, he could perceive that it was gradually altering as to its shape and complexion; her eyes no longer shone with brilliancy—her face lost the hectic glow of life—her arms imperceptibly disappeared; and when he came to the spot where she stood, it was a monument of stone, having a human face, with the fins and tail of a fish. He sat a long while in amazement, fearful either to touch the super-human object, or to go away and leave it; at length, having made an offering of the incense of tobacco, and addressed it as the guardian angel of his country, he ventured to lay his hand upon the statue, and finally lifted it into his canoe. Then sitting in the other end of the canoe, with his back towards the miraculous statue, he paddled gently towards the shore, but was astonished, on turning round, to find nothing in his canoe, but the large lump of copper, "which," he concluded, taking it carefully from a roll of skins, "I now present to you."

CXII. Day.—(*September 12th.*)—At Michilimackinac.

CHAPTER XVI.

RETURN TO DETROIT.

CXII. Day.—(*September* 13*th.*)

WE left Michilimackinac at three o'clock in the afternoon, and proceeding ten miles, encamped at Point aux Pins on the lower extremity of the island of Bois Blanc. This island is from ten to twelve miles in length, by three in width at the widest part, stretching in the form of a crescent between the island of Michilimackinac and the peninsula of Michigan. The lower part of it, consists of a sandy plain covered with pitch pines (*pinus resinosa*) but by far the greatest portion of the island is a fertile soil, well adapted for tillage, and bearing a forest of elm, maple, oak, ash, and white wood, the latter being the predominating tree. In the summer season, it has a luxuriant under-growth of grass, vines, and succulent plants, and serves as pasturage ground for the cattle and horses of the inhabitants of Michilimackinac, and also as a repository of fire-wood and building timber; and is, in every respect, a most valuable appendage to that settlement.

CXIV. Day.—(*September* 14*th.*)—Detained by unfavourable winds during the morning.—In the meantime, Capt. Douglass revisits 'Mackinac, and returns in the evening, when the wind abating, we proceeded across the Traverse to the main shore—a distance of four miles. While detained on Bois Blanc, a vessel bound for Michilimackinac, passed up through the narrow strait, which separates the island from the main shore. It is interesting to contemplate the progress of commerce through regions, which at no remote period, were only traversed in bark canoes; and which, perhaps, in a still shorter period, may smile under the hand of agriculture, civilization, and the arts. Every fact, connected with the early settlement of a country, acquires, in process of time, a moral importance of which we are scarcely aware; and the historian siezes with avidity upon the insolated records of the introduction of any improvement in agriculture, inventions in the arts, and other changes which affect the condition and comfort of men, however unimportant in themselves, to characterize the early stages of society, in every country. Only a hundred and forty-one years have now elapsed, since the first vessel of European construction, was launched upon the northern lakes. The date, and the facts connected with its construction, are well authenticated by the concurrent testimony of all the early travellers of the region; and have been already mentioned, in a former part of this Journal; but it is added by Father Hennipen, that this vessel, called "the Griffin," was wrecked during the same year in Lake Michigan, with a cargo of furs and skins, valued at sixty thousand livres. It is now two years since a steam boat was introduced upon the lakes. This vessel, called the "Walk-in-the-Water," in allusion to a

Wyandot chief, made its first trip to the island of Michilimackinac during the summer of 1819; and produced as great a degree of astonishment among the Indians, who had assembled to witness its arrival, as it would have done, had such a vessel entered the mouth of the Tiber during the meridian splendour of the arts and arms of emperial Rome. The latter must have been equally surprised to see a ship ploughing rapidly through the water, without the aid of sails or oars; but with this difference—that the ancient Roman could readily have been made to comprehend the nature of the power by which it was propelled, whereas to the savage mind, it remained wholly incomprehensible and mysterious.—Like all appearances, however, which are not understood, whether of natural or artificial creation; it was conjectured to be the work of super-human agency, and they were not slow in accounting for it, by a reference to the sublime system of Indian mythology. According to this, *Miccabo*, who is the spirit of water, and answers to the Neptune of the heathens, exerts an influence over all those various tribes of the creation, who are compelled to inhabit the streams, rivers, and lakes; and they supposed that he had summoned from the great salt lake, (meaning the ocean) a number of large fishes, or *Missi-kikons*, who were employed to draw this vessel through the water in so extraordinary a manner, in return for some signal favour received from the white men. Such is the facility with which the northern Indians account for the most extraordinary phenomena.

CXV. Day.—(*September 15th.*)—A violent rain

storm during the night;—we embarked at day break, and descended to Presque Isle, a distance of forty-four miles.

CXVI. Day.—(*September* 16*th.*)—Rainy—embarked at five in the morning, and proceeded to Thunder Bay, on the north cape of which we encamped, at an early hour in the afternoon, the lake threatening a violent storm;—distance thirty miles.

At the spot of our encampment, and around the shores of Thunder Bay, petrifactions of the encrinite, pectinite, celleporite, &c. are abundant. They occur imbedded in compact limestone, which appears in horizontal strata along this part of the coast, although it does not attain a great elevation above the surface of the water. The application of these relics, in determining the geological ages of the different mineral strata, composing the crust of the globe, was certainly one of the happiest and the most important of the discoveries for which the sciences of mineralogy and geology stand indebted to the celebrated Werner. No sooner was this fact advanced, than men of science in all parts of the world, began to perceive that certain limestones, slates, schists, &c. were characterized by containing the imbedded remains of plants, shells, polypi, and fishes; while other rocks, and different species of the same genus of rocks, were entirely free from these remains, thus furnishing evidence, which appears incontrovertible in the present state of the science, that the former are of the most recent formation. A minute examination of the different species of imbedded relics found in similar rocks, in countries the most distant and remote, served also to shew a coincidence in the composition, relative position, and petrifactions of rocks, which has laid the foundation of the theory of universal stratification, and of the formation of all mineral strata, through the agency of watery menstruæ either by subsidence, or by crystallization; and perhaps there is nothing which the combined lights of geology and philosophy at the present period, tend more conclusively to prove, than that the different continents of the earth, were simultaneously created, however since disrupted by earthquakes, washed away by seas, or dilapidated by time.

"Neither an attentive examination of the geological constitution of America," says the Baron de Humboldt, "nor reflections on the equilibrium of the fluids, that are diffused over the surface of the globe, lead us to admit, that the new continent emerged from the waters at a later period than the old: we discern in the former the same succession of stony strata, that we find in our own hemisphere; and it is probable, that, in the mountains of Peru, the granites, the micaceous schists, or the different formations of gypsum and gritstone, existed originally at the same periods, as the rocks of the same denominations in the Alps of Switzerland. The whole globe appears to have undergone the same catastrophes. At a height superior to that of Mount Blanc, on the summit of the Andes, we find petrified sea-shells; fossil-bones are spread over the equinoctial regions; and what is very remarkable, they are not discovered at the feet of the palm trees in the burning plains of Oronoco, but on the coldest and most elevated regions of the Cordilleras. In the new world, as well as in the old, generations of species long extinct, have preceded those, which now people the earth, the waters, and the air."*

CXVII. Day.—(*September 17th.*)—We proceeded across Thunder Bay, at five o'clock in the morning, landing a few moments upon the island near its centre, and passing successively, the spot of our former encampment, at the mouth of the river au Sables, and the northwest cape of Saganaw Bay, encamped on the western shore of the latter, at Sandy Point; having made a journey of fifty-five miles. Here we found a family of Saganaw Indians, who had taken up a temporary residence at that place, attracted by the abundance of water fowl, found in a contiguous inlet. These people lead a wandering life, abiding but a short time at a place, changing their habitations whenever the deer, the fish, or the wild fowl, promise an easier subsistence at another place. They live in tents formed of rush-mats, supported by a few slender poles; and all their moveable effects and household goods, together with the family, are readily transported in a birch bark canoe. On entering the tent, we found no person in, but the squaw and children, who manifested none of that timidity, and apparent fear, which it is common to find among unfrequented tribes. The woman was engaged at the moment, in picking the feathers from a number of wild ducks, apparently just killed, which lay at her side, and our entrance appeared to have no more effect upon her than it probably would, had one of her own family entered. She continued her work. This may be considered as the result of the confi-

* Humboldt's Researches, vol. i. p. 11.

dence they repose in the whites,—the frequency of their interviews with traders and travellers, and the uniform justice which they have received from our citizens and our government. We observed a number of smoked squirrels, fish, and ducks, hanging in the upper part of the tent; indicating a degree of care, for the subsistence of their children, and forecast as to the uncertainties of the chase, which is highly honourable to the judgment and the paternal feelings of these people. They have a method of taking fish through the ice in the winter season, which is equally novel and ingenious. After a hole has been cut through the ice, they encompass it with a slender circular frame of rods, or a kind of open basket, over which a blanket is thrown to exclude the light. The savage now lays himself down upon the ice, with his head under this hood, and playing a decoy or artificial fish upon the surface of the water with one hand, holds a drawn spear in the other, and when the large trout suddenly dart up to seize their fancied prey, pierces the body of his victim with unerring certainty. The spear is short, and loosens itself from the handle the moment it is struck, but is attached to a strong line, with which he plays the fish a while in the water below, and draws it out as soon as it becomes sufficiently enfeebled with the wound. This method of fishing was first noticed by Mr. Hudson, a missionary among the Saganaws, to whose manuscript journal I am permitted to refer for the facts.

CXVIII. Day.—(*September* 18*th.*)—Crossed Saganaw Bay, stopping an hour upon the island of Shawangunk, and encamped in the eastern cove of Point aux Barques;—distance forty-two miles. The island of Shawangunk is an alluvial plain of four or five miles in circumference, based upon a calcareous rock which is compact, stratified, without organic remains, and containing very large imbedded masses of chalcedony, and calcareous spar. These, have been broken out by the violence of the waves around the margin of the island, and lie promiscuously among the fragments of limestone torn up by the storms, and among large boulders of granite, hornblende, trap, greenstone porphyry, quartz, argillite, and sienite. The island is covered with a beautiful growth of oak, and its numerous little bays and inlets appear to be a favourite resort of aquatic birds.

CXIX. Day.—(*September* 19*th.*)—Detained at Point aux Barques, by head winds. An opinion is prevalent among the inhabitants of the region, that the northwestern lakes are gradually running out, or in other words, that the level of the waters is constantly lowering: some suppose this diminution to take place periodically, others, by a constant and imperceptible exhaustion. I have been informed by an intelligent person at Michilimackinac, who has been in the habit of making observations upon the rocks which project above the water, that the level of Lake Huron has fallen a foot within the last eight years. It has also been advanced, that this decrease continues for a definite period of years, as seven, or fourteen, and that at the expiration of a like period, after sinking to its minimum level, it attains its former height in the same gradual and imperceptible manner, and that thus a ceaseless ebbing and flowing of the lakes, is produced. A moment's reflection, however, will render it manifest that in a country so extensive and thinly populated, a number of circumstances may operate to produce a deception with respect to the permanent diminution of water, as the prevalence of certain winds, the quantity of rain and snow that falls around their shores, &c. There can be no doubt that the extra quantum of water discharged during the spring and fall, by the numerous streams and rivers flowing into these lakes, produces a corresponding rise in the lakes themselves, which suffer a gradual diminution as midsummer approaches. It is also obvious, that the evaporation of water, must vary greatly during the different seasons, in our fluctuating climate; and produce a sensible departure from the standard levels of the different lakes. Conclusions, therefore, drawn from the appearances of any particular point along this great chain, should be received with great caution; and they must always be exposed to error in the precise ratio that the temperature of the air, the quantity of rain which has fallen, and the prevalent winds, during the times which shall be selected for experiment, shall have been correctly registered and compared.

Philosophers and geologists have not been wanting, who have attributed similar appearances to the ocean itself, and the names of Celsius, Playfair, and Jameson, may be quoted in support of the theory that the level of the seas is gradually diminishing.—It will be sufficient in this place to cite the opinion of the admirable Cuvier on this subject.

"It has been asserted," he observes in his Theory of the Earth, "that the sea is subject to a continual diminution of its level, and proofs of this are said to have been discovered in some parts of the shores of the Baltic. Whatever may have been the cause of these appearances, we certainly know that nothing of the kind has been observed upon our coasts; and, consequently, that there has been no general lowering of the waters of the ocean. The most ancient sea-ports still have their quays and other erections at the same height above the level of the sea as at their first construction. Certain general movements have been supposed in the sea from east to west, or in other directions; but no where has any person been able to ascertain their effects with the least degree of precision."

CXX. Day.—(*September 20th.*)—The winds had abated, but did not cease to oppose our progress at daylight. We embarked at six o'clock in the morning—were driven ashore by the waves at seven—re-embarked at nine, and proceeding against a light head wind until eight in the evening, encamped on the beach of the lake, at the distance of fifty miles from Point aux Barques.

CXXI. Day.—(*September 21st.*)—We quit our encampment at four in the morning, but were driven ashore by the winds on going six miles; and detained during the remainder of the day. At the spot of our encampment, organic remains are abundant, in the detached masses of secondary limestone, which are strewed along the lake. The shore is sandy from the woods to the water, where there is a bed of pebbles and large blocks of granite, hornblende, quartz, micaslate, and greenstone; but no rock strata appear in situ. Among the loose masses of rock, I noticed one of a ton weight, consisting of granite made up of the usual constituents of feldspar, quartz, and mica; and also imbedding globular pebbles of hornblende porphyry, the latter being composed of pure black hornblende, diversified with fragments and crystals of feldspar, quartz, and mixed granite. This fact I had previously noticed along other parts of the shore of Lake Huron, and at Grosse Point, on Lake St. Clair.

CXXII. Day.—(*September* 22*d.*)—Embarking at early daylight, we reached fort Gratiot at five o'clock in the afternoon, after rowing twelve hours against an unfavourable wind. Here we halted half an hour—found the garrison under the command of Lieut. Webb, by whom we were received with cordiality—and descending the river seven miles, encamped at twilight upon Elk island, having progressed fifty-seven miles.

CXXIII. Day.—(*September* 23*d.*)—On reaching Elk island, we concluded to avail ourselves of a calm night to descend the river, and after taking supper and repairing our canoes, again embarked at nine o'clock, and reached Lake St. Clair at half past three in the morning. Here we were compelled to await the dawning of day, as the fog and darkness rendered it impracticable to effect the traverse during the night. Daylight brought with it a strong head wind, and the lake became so much agitated, that the voyageurs considered it unsafe to cross.—Urged by our impatience, however, to terminate the voyage, the experiment was hazarded; and notwithstanding the rain, which shortly commenced, and the increased violence of the wind, we effected the crossing with perfect safety—passed Grosse Point at noon, and landed at Detroit at half past three.

GENERAL INDEX.

GENERAL INDEX.

GENERAL INDEX.

GENERAL INDEX.

ERRATA.

Page 83, in the note, for "Professor Eaton of Burlington College," read, Professor Eaton of the Medical Institution of Middlebury College.

Page 131, line 20th, for "contrast," read *diversity*.

Page 177, line 24th, for "appear," read *appears*.

" line 29th, for the article "a," read *one*.

Page 196, line 10th, for the article "a," read *an*.

Page 248, line 22d. for "these," read *three*.